Nasser in the Egyptian Imaginary

Edinburgh Studies in Modern Arabic Literature
Series Editor: Rasheed El-Enany

Writing Beirut: Mappings of the City in the Modern Arabic Novel
Samira Aghacy

Autobiographical Identities in Contemporary Arab Literature
Valerie Anishchenkova

The Iraqi Novel: Key Writers, Key Texts
Fabio Caiani and Catherine Cobham

Sufism in the Contemporary Arabic Novel
Ziad Elmarsafy

Gender, Nation, and the Arabic Novel: Egypt 1892–2008
Hoda Elsadda

Post-War Anglophone Lebanese Fiction: Home Matters in the Diaspora
Syrine Hout

Nasser in the Egyptian Imaginary
Omar Khalifah

War and Occupation in Iraqi Fiction
Ikram Masmoudi

The Arab Nahḍah: *The Making of the Intellectual and Humanist Movement*
Abdulrazzak Patel

Sonallah Ibrahim: Rebel with a Pen
Paul Starkey

www.edinburghuniversitypress.com/series/smal

Nasser in the Egyptian Imaginary

Omar Khalifah

EDINBURGH
University Press

For my parents, Khalid Khalifah and Iman Afani,
my unassailable certainty

Edinburgh University Press is one of the leading university presses in the UK. We publish academic books and journals in our selected subject areas across the humanities and social sciences, combining cutting-edge scholarship with high editorial and production values to produce academic works of lasting importance. For more information visit our website: edinburghuniversitypress.com

© Omar Khalifah, 2017

Edinburgh University Press Ltd
The Tun – Holyrood Road
12 (2f) Jackson's Entry
Edinburgh EH8 8PJ

Typeset in 11/15 Adobe Garamond by
Servis Filmsetting Ltd, Stockport, Cheshire

A CIP record for this book is available from the British Library

ISBN 978 1 4744 1019 9 (hardback)
ISBN 978 1 4744 1020 5 (webready PDF)
ISBN 978 1 4744 1021 2 (epub)

The right of Omar Khalifah to be identified as author of this work has been asserted in accordance with the Copyright, Designs and Patents Act 1988 and the Copyright and Related Rights Regulations 2003 (SI No. 2498).

Contents

Series Editor's Foreword		vi
Acknowledgements		ix
Note on Transliteration		xi
	Introduction	1
1	Writing to Nasser	19
2	Nasser as Fiction	68
3	Nasser in Fiction	117
4	Nasser on the Screen	162
	Epilogue: Prospects of a Post-2011 Nasser	209
	Bibliography	222
	Index	239

Series Editor's Foreword

The Edinburgh Studies in Modern Arabic Literature is a new and unique series which will, it is hoped, fill in a glaring gap in scholarship in the field of modern Arabic literature. Its dedication to Arabic literature in the modern period, that is, from the nineteenth century onwards, is what makes it unique among series undertaken by academic publishers in the English-speaking world. Individual books on modern Arabic literature in general or aspects of it have been and continue to be published sporadically. Series on Islamic studies and Arab/Islamic thought and civilisation are not in short supply either in the academic world, but these are far removed from the study of Arabic literature qua literature, that is, imaginative, creative literature as we understand the term when, for instance, we speak of English literature or French literature, etc. Even series labelled 'Arabic/Middle Eastern Literature' make no period distinction, extending their purview from the sixth century to the present, and often including non-Arabic literatures of the region. This series aims to redress the situation by focusing on the Arabic literature and criticism of today, stretching its interest to the earliest beginnings of Arab modernity in the nineteenth century.

The need for such a dedicated series, and generally for the redoubling of scholarly endeavour in researching and introducing modern Arabic literature to the Western reader has never been stronger. The significant growth in the last decades of the translation of contemporary Arab authors from all genres, especially fiction, into English; the higher profile of Arabic literature internationally since the award of the Nobel Prize for Literature to Naguib Mahfouz in 1988; the growing number of Arab authors living in the Western diaspora and writing both in English and Arabic; the adoption of such authors and others by mainstream, high-circulation publishers, as opposed to the academic publishers of the past; the establishment of prestigious prizes, such as the International Prize for Arabic Fiction (the Arabic Booker), run by the Man Booker Foundation, which brings huge publicity to the shortlist and winner every year, as well as translation contracts into English and other languages – all this and very recently the events of the Arab Spring have heightened public, let alone academic, interest in all things Arab, and not least Arabic literature. It is therefore part of the ambition of this series that it will increasingly address a wider reading public beyond its natural territory of students and researchers in Arabic and world literature. Nor indeed is the academic readership of the series expected to be confined to specialists in literature in the light of the growing trend for interdisciplinarity, which increasingly sees scholars crossing field boundaries in their research tools and coming up with findings that equally cross discipline borders in their appeal.

After Nasser's (1918–52) seizure of power in the early 1950s in Egypt, ending 150 years of the rule of the dynasty of Muhammad Ali, he was soon, particularly after the Suez Crisis of 1956, to emerge as a charismatic pan-Arab leader whose appeal reached the masses of Arab nations, often over the heads of their own leaders, from Morocco in the west to Iraq in the east. He fired the imagination of the people and became a legendary hero from early on in his political career. Despite his dictatorial rule, his mistakes and final defeat by Israel in 1967, people never lost faith in him until his premature death in 1970, mourned in every corner of the Arab world. Nasser's political legacy in Egypt and the Middle East at large is one whose ripple effect, nearly half a century after his death, can still be seen. In Egypt alone, he has changed once and for all not only its political and economic structures but the very fabric of society. Like all historic leaders, he was, and continues to be, a controversial figure. While reviled in the west as a dictator, he was adored by his people as a liberator and a national hero who stood up to imperialism.

Many hundreds of books must have been written on Nasser in measure to his importance as a major political leader of the second half of the twentieth century. But these will be books by historians, and political and social scientists. But, during his lifetime and, even more so since his death, Nasser has made his way into literature and the arts. As he reshaped Egyptian society, his achievements (and failures, depending on perspective) made their way into the literature produced by the intellectuals of that society. (Naguib Mahfouz, for instance, was one of his harshest critics both during his lifetime and after his death.) But, while intellectuals may have more balanced views of things, the popular psyche or 'imaginary' works in its own ways. And, while Nasser has been, since his death, assessed and reassessed endlessly by different categories of analysts with different conclusions, many of which are unfavourable, his assets with the person in the street and, so to speak, with the person writing in the study or shooting behind the camera, have only risen to mythical levels in the four-odd decades since his death.

This is the phenomenon that the current monograph tries to chronicle and analyse through an examination of the representation of Nasser in a multiplicity of media: fiction, film and television series, and people's letters to the leader. This is work that has not been done before in a dedicated monograph and, while it adopts an approach different from that of historians and political and social scientists, it is bound to be as interesting to them and to their students as it will be to students of literature and culture.

March 2016

Professor Rasheed El-Enany, Series Editor,
Emeritus Professor, University of Exeter;
Professor of Arabic & Comparative Literature,
Dean of Social Sciences and Humanities,
Doha Institute for Graduate Studies

Acknowledgements

I should like first to extend my sincere and heartfelt gratitude to my friend and mentor Noha Radwan for encouraging and supporting me throughout the writing of this book. I am truly indebted to her for believing in my project, for leading me towards various helpful sources and materials, and for providing me with insightful and constructive commentary. I am also grateful to those who have read drafts of this book and shared with me their thoughts, feedback, and edits: Roger Allen, Hamid Dabashi, Gil Anidjar, and Hala Halim. Special thanks go to Professor Rasheed El-Enany, the editor of Edinburgh Studies in Modern Arabic literature, for his remarks, help, and advice. My experience as a graduate student at Columbia University offered me the wonderful opportunity of meeting and learning from great mentors, colleagues, and friends. I am also indebted to my current institution, Georgetown School of Foreign Service in Qatar, for offering me a sabbatical leave in the autumn semester of 2015 which gave me adequate time to conclude this typescript. I am deeply thankful for the support and encouragement of numerous colleagues and friends throughout the years of writing and editing this book; I would like particularly to mention Samia Mehrez, Timothy Mitchell, Stathis Gourgouris, Amira Sonbol, Abbas al-Tonsi, Suzanne Stetkevych, and Elliott Colla.

This project necessitated a trip to Egypt to collect primary sources and conduct some interviews. The visit came a few months after the outbreak of the 2011 revolution and proved to be one of the most memorable experiences I have ever had. I am truly thankful for the wonderful writers, filmmakers, and intellectuals who, despite the turbulent time they were passing through, were generous enough to spare some moments for fruitful discussions: Sonallah Ibrahim, Gamal al-Ghitani, Salwa Bakr, Ibrahim Abdel

Meguid, Amin Haddad, Sharif Yunus, 'Isam Zakariyya, Shirin Abu al-Naga, and Khalid Yusuf. The friendships I made throughout this journey, especially with *shabab al-thawra,* were extremely inspirational. I shall always remember May Sa'd, Ahmad Shukr, Shirin Ghayth, 'Amr 'Awad, Hisham Aslan, and Nagla' Bidir for helping me to navigate my way in Cairo. My room-mate and friend Iyad Ibrahim was a real comrade. Our roaming in Tahrir Square and Muhammad Mahmud Street during the tumultuous November of 2011 will be unforgettable.

The unqualified love, care, and support that I received from my family in Jordan was indescribably blissful. Though physically distant, my parents' tireless words of encouragement alleviated the stress that at times accompanied me while writing this book, and our conversations via Skype were moments of extreme joy. My father, in particular, told me a lot of stories about Gamal Abdel Nasser that constituted my early understanding of the complexity of the president's character. My parents' appreciation for my literary interests was instrumental in leading me to embark on this project, and my words can never capture the amount of gratitude I feel towards them. This book is dedicated to them.

Writing this book would not have been possible without the unconditional love and support of my wife, Yusra Shajrawi. Her gracious attention throughout the long hours of writing was always animating, and her patience with my busy schedule and unpredictable sleeping and waking habits was utterly phenomenal. I cannot thank her enough for everything she did to assist me during the process of writing this book.

The part on Nasser and Children in Chapter 3 has previously appeared in an article that I wrote for *Middle East Critique* [24 (4), 2015]. For permission to republish, I should like to thank the publisher Taylor & Francis (www. tandfonline.com).

Note on Transliteration

I have followed a simplified version of the *IJMES* system for transliterating Arabic names and titles. While *ayn* (') and *hamza* (') were shown throughout the book, diacritical marks were not used. Popular and widespread names, however, were spelled in accordance with their most common English rendition, such as King Farouk, Gamal Abdel Nasser, and Hosni Mubarak. Also, names of authors whose works are available in English translation appeared as they did in the extant English spelling, such as Naguib Mahfouz, Ibrahim Abdel Meguid, and Radwa Ashour. A similar approach was followed with well-known Egyptian film-makers such as Youssef Chahine, Salah Abu Seif, and Kamal El Sheikh. The letter *jim* was spelled (g) with Egyptian proper names. Finally, in line with the common English appearance, *ayn* was dropped from 'Ali' and 'Abdel'.

Introduction

Historical truth . . . is not what took place; it is what we think took place.
(Jorge Luis Borges, *Ficciones*).[1]

He did great things, and failed at many others.
If he has wounded our hearts, all the wounds have healed.
(Ahmed Fouad Negm (1929–2013), *A Visit to the Grave of Nasser*).[2]

On 18 September 2011, almost eight months after the outbreak of the Egyptian revolution and the ousting of President Hosni Mubarak, thousands of Egyptians gathered for the funeral of Khalid Abdel Nasser, the eldest son of late President Gamal Abdel Nasser (1918–70). SCAF, Egypt's Supreme Council of Armed Forces, was ruling the country. While carrying pictures of Nasser and expressing nostalgia for him, the mourners were also chanting, *yasqut yasqut hukm al-'askar* (down, down with military rule!). The irony of the incident did not elude several Egyptian journalists. Many noted how the funeral became an occasion for protesting the rule of the military while celebrating the person who reinstitutionalised it in Egypt in 1952. Indeed, jokes about this irony abounded in newspapers the next day, one of which sarcastically asked whether those protestors had taken Nasser to be an obstetrician![3]

Besides Nasser's continued presence in Egyptian everyday life and discourse, the story above also reveals how many Egyptians separate Nasser as a person from the regime that he had created. For them, Nasser functions as a site of memory, a space of associations at times disconnected from the real figure that he once was. As French historian Pierre Nora argues, sites of memory are 'moments of history torn away from the movement of history, then returned; no longer quite life, not yet death, like shells on the shore when the sea of living memory has receded'.[4] As such, they are the embodiment of memory, the residue of that long process of remembering and forgetting that takes place in living societies before it enters the realm of history. History, on the other hand, is 'the reconstruction, always problematic and incomplete, of what is no longer'.[5] Constituting a counterdiscourse, of which history 'is perpetually suspicious',[6] these sites of memory take the form of films, songs, novels, and paintings, among other media. Once perpetuated, repeated, and systematically propagated, these sites, like Nasser's name and image, emerge as self-explanatory signs whose mere presence is individually deciphered and interpreted by viewers.

This study is about a past that is oriented towards the present, or, as Andreas Huyssen succinctly puts it, a 'present past'.[7] It goes without saying that Nasser has never vanished from Egypt. He has always been there, occupying an unshakable space in the quotidian lives of Egyptians. He is a past that possesses the power of informing, inspiring, alleviating, encouraging; but he is also a contested past, one that could invoke for many Egyptians feelings of fear, defeat, and despair. Whether during Sadat's tenure (1970–81), Mubarak's three decades of rule (1981–2011), or even the 2011 revolution and its (still ongoing) aftermath, Nasser has been an indispensable reference through which Egyptians discuss, gauge, and evaluate the events unfolding before them. Nasser is a charged reference, however, constantly capable of inviting heated debates and discussion. For Nasser, along with his Egyptian nationals, had experienced some of the most volatile, tumultuous events in twentieth-century Egypt. Unsurprisingly, Egyptians clash over the interpretation of these events and, consequently, over how they remember them. It is as though Nasser's life has created for Egyptians what Susan Suleiman calls 'crises of memory', denoting 'moments that highlight the relations between individual memory and group memory, concerning a past event that is stipulated as important by the group at a given time'.[8]

This book is a journey into the location of Nasser in the Egyptian social imaginary. It seeks to understand how Nasser has become an essential component of that imaginary, a set of figures, a metaphor whose specific meanings for Egyptians are constantly debated and contested. 'Every society up to now has attempted to give an answer to a few fundamental questions',[9] remarks Cornelius Castoriadis in his magisterial study of the imaginary. Seen as an attempt to define the society in relation to itself, the world, and the latter's objects, these questions are answer-driven; they are not merely hypothetical or rhetorical for, without answering these questions, 'there can be no human world'. Herein lies the role of the imaginary. It is 'to provide an answer to these questions, an answer that, obviously, neither "reality" nor "rationality" can provide'.[10] Castoriadis's insistence on the subordination of reality to the imaginary stems from his conviction that the latter does not merely reflect things that exist a priori. The imaginary is not an 'image' of some objects that are already found. Rather, it is the unceasing process of creating these objects, and 'what we call "reality" and "rationality" are its works'.[11]

But what is a society's social imaginary? Here it is useful to turn to Charles Taylor's lucid contributions. In his pursuit of the emergence of European modernity, with its three essential elements – the economy, the public sphere, and the sovereign people – Taylor speaks of the birth of a certain European social imaginary. By this social imaginary

> I mean something much broader and deeper than the intellectual schemes people may entertain when they think about social reality in a disengaged mode. I am thinking, rather, of the ways people imagine their social existence, how they fit together with others, how things go on between them and their fellows, the expectations that are normally met, and the deeper normative notions and images that underlie these expectations.[12]

This definition warrants two additional comments. First, language, be it verbal or visible, is the 'medium par excellence in which these social imaginary significations become manifest and do their constitutive work'.[13] Second, Taylor's emphasis on the social imaginary as a precondition for 'common practices' is of a great importance to my discussion of Nasser and the Egyptian imaginary. For Egyptians' imaginary conceptions of Nasser have been tremendously empowering. They were among the driving forces behind certain actions, initiatives, and movements in Egypt which this book aspires to describe. It is as though the image of Nasser has informed a 'direct action' among Egyptians, to use Shahid Amin's apt characterisation of the 'location of the Mahatma [Gandhi's] image within existing patterns of popular beliefs'.[14]

This is not to suggest that the relationship between the Egyptian imaginary and Nasser is one-sided. It is not that the Egyptian imaginary, complete and definite, has offered contesting versions of 'Nasser'. Rather, I argue that Nasser has both produced and been produced by the Egyptian imaginary. It is a reciprocal process, a constant negotiation between Egyptians and their leader over the definitions of both. As this book will demonstrate, Nasser's ideals, dreams, and hopes have often been reclaimed and appropriated by Egyptians who, compelled by a belief in Nasser, have interrogated him based on these very same ideals. In lieu of following the conventional presentation of Egyptians as docile, submissive, and easily manipulated by Nasser's character, this book invites a different look at how the Egyptian imaginary and Nasser have been jointly linked, connected, and coupled. The imagination is not fantasy; it is not an illusion of which reality is always suspicious. On the contrary, it is part and parcel of the 'quotidian mental work of ordinary people'.[15] Unlike fantasy, which 'carries with it the inescapable connotation of thought divorced from projects and actions', the imagination has 'the sense of being a prelude to some sort of *expression*, whether aesthetic or otherwise . . . It can become a *fuel for action*.'[16]

One interesting outcome of this relationship between Nasser and the Egyptian imaginary is how the Egyptian public sphere has transformed Nasser himself into a public. Chapter 1 will dwell on the emergence of an epistolary tradition between Egyptians and Nasser whereby the former transform their president into an audience. Pertinent to this discussion is Michael Warner's useful distinction of several senses of the word 'public'. Upon first hearing it, people usually think of 'the public' as a 'kind of social totality. Its most common sense is that of the people in general. It might be the people organised as the nation, the commonwealth, the city, the state, or some other community.'[17] But there is also another kind of public, one that is essentially formed 'in relation to texts and their circulation'.[18] By situating Nasser as a recipient of their letters, Egyptians have created a case where *the* public speaks to *a* public. Informed by Habermas's well-known treatise on the role of letter-writing in forming the European public sphere,[19] it will be demonstrated how Nasser can be seen at once as part of a general Egyptian public and, equally, as a specific public to whom the general public addresses its letters.

Nasser as a public inevitably invites serious attention to his iconicity, visibility or, that which in a different context, Aziz al-Azmeh terms as the 'pictorial enunciation of power'.[20] As will be discussed in Chapter 4, Nasser challenges facile, unsubstantiated conclusions concerning his stance vis-à-vis the spectacular manifestation of his power. While Nasser's photographs and portraits were ubiquitous throughout Egypt, if not the Arab world, during his tenure, conforming to what Michael Warner notes regarding how public figures 'increasingly take on the function of concretizing that phantasmic body image, or, in other words, of actualizing the otherwise indeterminate image of the people',[21] his visible presence in other public mediums in Egypt is largely ambiguous. For instance, during his lifetime, Nasser hardly appeared in Egyptian film, a conclusion that may seem surprising for a leader often seen as ruling over a totalitarian regime, given that Egyptian cinema was, and still is, the most visible artistic medium in Egypt and the Arab world. In addition, no statue of Nasser has ever been erected in Egypt. If 'power is by nature enunciative', it is still necessary to examine the form(s) of enunciation that Nasser's power took.

No less fascinating is to conceive of Nasser as a resurrection of the notion of the virtuous leader among ordinary Egyptians. In his recent study on nationality and social ideals in modern Egypt, Yaseen Noorani argues that a significant shift has occurred in the Arabic political sphere as of the late nineteenth century. Whereas in pre-modern Arabic discourse virtue resided with the just ruler, 'whose function is to restrain and control the desires of individuals',[22] modernity has witnessed a transformation of virtue from the ruler into the nation itself. This shift was a product of a new conception of nationality that 'alters the relationship between desire and order by transferring the locus of communal order from virtuous figures of authority to the national body as a whole'.[23] The reason why the concept of the just ruler had enjoyed such a salient position in classical Arabic thought stemmed partly from a particular view of the individual, virtue, and social order. Can individuals integrate into society in an ordered manner of their own accord? 'Premodern discourses of virtue', Noorani maintains, 'tend to view this capacity as the by-product of an internal state of self-rule, the control and containment of one's desires, that can be attained by very few people.'[24] Modern discourse, on the other hand, has abolished this need of 'exceptional' people of virtue and instead centred 'on the immanence of moral order within individuals,'[25] that is, *all* people.

The following chapters on Nasser in the Egyptian imaginary, I propose, serve to unsettle this assumed 'modern' view of virtue and the nation. For, with Nasser, the notion of the just ruler was decisively revived. Nasser was a comeback of the virtuous figure of classical Arabic imagination, a continuity with a model of kings, caliphs, and sultans well popularised in bygone eras by poets, storytellers, and prose writers. Fictional and non-fictional accounts of Nasser abound with attributes that easily resonate with those offered about early Arab and Muslim rulers. In addition, one can see shadows of Nasser in the depictions of early rulers who were seen to '[their] subjects as a soul is to a body'.[26] Noorani's otherwise compelling study falls short of locating the Nasser phenomenon within the modern view of virtue and the nation. In fact, one can argue that these depictions of Nasser echo more the values of the classical Arabic *qaṣīda*, particularly that which was composed in praise of caliphs and emirs, than any modern notions of the nation to which Noorani refers. The excellent study of Suzanne Stetkevych on *The Poetics of Islamic Legitimacy* shows how 'the classical Arabic panegyric ode (that is, the celebratory poem dedicated to a patron or ruler, the *qaṣīdat al-madḥ*) created, encoded, and promulgated a myth and ideology of legitimate Arabo-Islamic rule'.[27] In other words, this *qaṣīda*, while addressing a specific ruler, 'does not attempt to portray the character of individual monarchs. Instead, it extolls the role of Kingship which an individual assumes.'[28] Aziz al-Azmeh sums this idealisation eloquently:

> Power in these works is enunciated episodically and ideally, as ideal episodes, as *example* of particular salience or even impeccability which, by being tirelessly repeated, take on some of the characteristics of the ritual enactment and re-enactment of power which is displayed in ceremonial.[29]

But while the celebration in classical Arabic imagination was devoted to the position itself, no matter who occupied it, it is Nasser himself that possessed this unprecedented position in the Egyptian imaginary. I argue that the relationship between Nasser and people in modern Egypt was personalised, and his status was at times elevated above the nation itself. Nasser was mostly codified into certain ideal values that became a repository on which writers draw. Muhammad Jabir al-Ansari (b.1939) reminds us that the notion of the exceptional hero, the saviour of the nation, in its pharaonic,

Islamic, and European manifestations, had a tremendous impact on the ways in which Egyptians viewed Nasser.[30] He mostly became a common reference, a ready metaphor for virtue, honesty, and loyalty even for those who were not fully aware of these associations. Chapter 3 will examine representations of the relationship between Nasser and children in Egyptian fiction, where the latter were being introduced to the worlds of Nasser precisely when their fathers were suffering at the hands of Nasser's regime.

This book studies and analyses the representations of Nasser in Egyptian literature and film. As such, it does not seek to engage in historical arguments and judgements about the deeds and legacy of Nasser, still less to offer another biography of him. Rather, it focuses on how the historical character of Nasser has emerged in the Egyptian imaginary – novels, short stories, autobiographies, and films. Despite the significant position that he occupies in these works, no previous study has been exclusively devoted to illuminate the location of an imagined/narrativised Nasser outside the conventional historical archive; a vacuum that this book aspires to fill. Among the questions that this study aims to raise and discuss are: What are the recurrent images of Nasser in literature and film? Was Nasser ever reimagined in fiction? In other words, were there any alternative fictional accounts of Nasser? Did Nasser emerge *as* fiction, or *through* fiction? How did the image of Nasser develop over the course of time? What is the significance of writing personal letters to Nasser? Did Nasser's gender ever become a significant constituent of his conceived image? Why was the first 'Nasser film' made only in 1996? How was the otherwise overlooked aspect of Nasser's domestic life portrayed in that film?

A foundational premise of this book makes a case for literature and art as alternative archive that questions, erases, distorts, and adds to official history. I argue that the meaning(s) of Nasser for Egyptians must be sought less in recorded history than in fictional narratives. Aristotle famously declared that 'where the historian really differs from the poet is in his describing what has happened while the other describes the thing that might happen'.[31] This book is devoted to the realms of 'as if', the imaginary productions of which history is often negligent – the dreams and nightmares, successes and failures, hopes and anxieties that Nasser evokes in ordinary Egyptians. Unlike history, literature and film give voice to marginalised, voiceless witnesses of society. By creating fictional characters that interact with Nasser, these works constitute a space of knowledge, an invaluable window on to the ways people see, personalise, and negotiate their relationships with the president. Thus, while history 'is the story of the happenings that are, or might be, otherwise knowable', Warner Berthoff reminds us, fiction 'gives us stories – a particular author telling us in his own fashion about made-up events – which are otherwise unknowable and which cannot otherwise exist'.[32]

Offering an answer as to why humans need fiction, German literary critic Wolfgang Iser similarly argues that literature 'reflects something special that neither philosophies of history nor sociological theories are able to capture'.[33] The particularity that is attributed to literature lies precisely in its ability to create other worlds, to enact 'what is not there'.[34] As such, it unmasks alternative realities, perfects the imperfections of nature, and sheds light on clandestine aspirations and desires. It is a mode of thinking of the world that has accompanied humanity throughout history in order to

> gain access to what we otherwise cannot have. We have no access, for example, to the beginning, the end, or the 'ground' out of which we are. The beginning and the end are paradigms of realities that we can neither experience nor know. But there are also experiences, such as identity and love, whose reality is just as incontestable as the fact that we can never know precisely what they are. Evidently, however, we are not prepared to accept the limits of cognition, and so we need images to mirror forth the unknowable.[35]

Salman Rushdie expresses a similar view when he discusses the role that literature can play vis-à-vis politics. He argues that, as the state seeks to impose its own version of the truth, including the truth of what had happened in the past, literary production becomes necessarily politicised. As such, politicians and writers are naturally 'rivals', for 'both groups try to make the world in their own images; they fight for the same territory'.[36]

This book is indebted to the seminal contributions of historian Hayden White, particularly on the relationship between history and fiction. White seeks to break the boundaries between history and fiction, realising that the former is, in fact, 'verbal fictions, the contents of which are as much *invented* as *found* and the forms of which have more in common with their counterparts in literature than they have with those in the sciences'.[37] As such, White argues that 'there are many histories that could pass for novels, and many novels that could pass for histories'.[38] But what is it that both history and fiction share? While White acknowledges that historians and writers are dealing with different kinds of events, he argues that the process of *narrating* these events, translating them discursively, and bestowing meaning on them is one and the same:

> Novelists might be dealing only with imaginary events whereas historians are dealing with real ones, but the process of fusing events, whether imaginary or real, into a comprehensible totality capable of serving as the *object* of a representation is a poetic process. Here the historians must utilise precisely the same tropological strategies, the same modalities in representing relationships in words, that the poet or novelist uses.[39]

History and fiction are interpretive acts, investing as much in relaying events as in *inventing* the causality that holds them together. They are mediating discourses, forms of written language where, as Edward Said reminds us, 'there is no such a thing as a delivered presence, but a *re-presence,* or a representation'.[40]

As this book aspires to show, Nasser constitutes a perfect site for literary and cinematic approaches. Popularly seen as Arabs' 'most charismatic leader since the Prophet Muhammad',[41] Nasser was a larger-than-life character, a legend whose image, voice, ideals, accomplishments, deeds, misdeeds, and defeats have been shaping Egyptian and Arabic life to date. Historians, however, often recognise the complexity of Nasser's character, his contradictory traits, and his sometime inexplicable decisions. Recognising the impenetrable aspects of his life, one of Nasser's biographers declares that 'the precise role of Nasser in Egyptian and Arab ideological development is not easy to assess empirically; still more difficult to uncover is his real motivational base, the internalised set of beliefs that determined his attitudes and behaviour'.[42] Particularly ambiguous is how the relationship between Nasser and Egyptians was personalised and often romanticised, transforming a political leader into an attentive audience, a heart-throb lover, and an enigmatic father. Herein lies a major contribution of this book. I argue that history falls short of capturing the centrality of Nasser in Egyptian life. Commenting on the meaning of Nasser for his fellow citizens, Egyptian intellectual Ghali Shukri (1935–98) believes that the documents of the 'assiduous academic historian' are insufficient to explain the exceptional position of Nasser. It is as though the relationship between Egyptians and Nasser was so charged that it left little room for detached academic investigations:

> Nasser descended upon us like a resurrected Osiris who returned after tens of centuries as a "dream" seeking to realise a miracle. Many non-Egyptians will say that this is mere "poetry" that bears no connection to reason. Unfortunately, there is no response to that. Feeling [Nasser] inevitably necessitates being Egyptian. Only then can you sense the reality of this quasi-metaphysical fiction.[43]

Interestingly, this personalised relationship with Nasser extended to other Arabs as well. Many Palestinian parents and grandparents, for instance, still circulate popular tales about their love and glorification of Nasser, of which two in particular have stuck in my mind. My grandmother used to relay how she and other old women in Burin, a village near Nablus in the West Bank, had spontaneously congregated in the village's main square following the news of Nasser's death in 1970. There, they performed *nuwah*, lamentation that included singing sorrowful songs, tearing their clothes, and slapping their faces. One of the songs ran as follows:

> *ya banat al-quds harrimn al-libs*
> *mat Abdel Nasser u ma harrar al-quds*
> (O daughters of Jerusalem, wear no clothes;
> for Nasser died; Jerusalem was not liberated).

Still more remarkable is a tale about a distant relative who lived in Jordan, Saudi Arabia, and Syria after the *nakba*. No matter where he lived, he would constantly follow Egypt's announcement of the first day of Ramadan, an announcement that is contingent upon the sighting of the new moon and often varies from one country to another. The reason for his decision was that he wanted to begin his fast on the same day as Nasser. Constituting a much larger repertoire that begs for an academic study, these tales are transmitted orally across generations, with a chance potential of disappearing over the course of the years.

This is not to suggest that all of the Egyptian literary and cinematic representations of Nasser were favourable – nothing is further from the truth. As the following chapters will make clear, Nasser emerges as a site for plural interpretations, an instance where narratives compete over the meaning of the past. In other words, there is no monolithic discourse on Nasser but rather various, at times contradictory, views that fragment him into multiple 'Nassers'. Following American historian John Bodnar, I argue that the shaping of the past 'is contested and involves a struggle for supremacy between advocates of various political ideas and sentiments'.[44] Of particular significance, Bodnar explains, is the emergence of official and vernacular cultures, each providing its own narrative on, and interpretation of, historical figures and events. It is from the intersection between these two camps that 'public memory emerges'.[45] My study is about memory and 'dissident memory, counter-memory';[46] it traces the historical developments of Nasser's image among the warring narratives, paying particular attention to the location that Egyptian literature and cinema occupy vis-à-vis the official archive. It will show that these imaginary productions do not constitute one single entity of 'vernacular' culture that seeks to oppose the official narrative on Nasser but rather several cultures that can 'even clash with one another'.[47]

The historical paths and developments which the literary and cinematic Nasser has traversed bespeak to the shifts in ideals, hopes, and realities that have swept Egyptian society over the past fifty years. Only against a deteriorating social, economic, and political situation in Sadat's and Mubarak's Egypt can one explain, for instance, the resurgence of an almost exclusively romantic view of Nasser since the late 1970s, despite the state-sponsored, far-reaching process of de-Nasserisation that emerged in these eras. Put differently, the proliferation of references to Nasser in the decades following his death can be seen as an attempt to slow down the accelerating processes that are working against his legacy.[48] The particular rapid, shocking, and unforeseen change that Sadat brought to Nasser's Egypt left many Egyptians searching for a shadow of their former leader. It is as though Nasser became a ruin, a *ṭalal*, over which Egyptian writers and film-makers, like their pre-Islamic poet predecessors, lament a bygone epoch, a bittersweet past relation that can nevertheless surpass a decaying reality. The following chapters will show how the late image of Nasser has mostly become synonym for dignity, freedom, and justice, reflecting Egyptians' aspirations for a better, uncorrupted world. I am not saying, however, that, in their works, fiction writers and film-makers merely reflect people's views on Nasser. Rather, their productions are as much *shaped by* as they are *shaping* the public discourse on Nasser. Palestinian critic Muhammad Siddiq shows how the Egyptian novel, for instance, possesses both a *mimetic* and a *performative* power where it does not only mirror a pre-existing reality but rather 'posits a reciprocal pattern of relations between culture and literature, in which the novel plays a performative and dynamic role'.[49]

Within this context, Samia Mehrez's argument about the Arab and Egyptian writer as an 'underground historian' proves significant. Borrowing from George Steiner, Mehrez argues that the contemporary Egyptian writer (and, by extension, film-maker) bears 'the responsibility of producing a counter record, an alternative discourse'[50] that opposes the official, state-produced one. For Mehrez, the importance of the role that the writer can play stems from the 'restrictions, limitations, and censorship he or she may encounter'.[51] Against the silencing, chaining measures of the state, the writer inscribes his/her own version of views, testimonies, and memories. Interestingly, Egyptian writers have at times written an understanding of their very role as creators of a counter-archive into their 'fiction'. Analysing three Egyptian novellas which feature immediate and delayed ramifications of the 1974 visit that former United States President Richard Nixon had made to Egypt, Noha Radwan demonstrates how the authors consciously engage in deconstructing the official story of the visit. Rather than claiming a real nature for their narratives, these novellas are more invested in displaying that 'the events inscribed in them, had they really happened, would still have been bound to remain outside of that [official] archive and denied entry into the hegemonic historical narrative'.[52]

Before proceeding with providing brief descriptions of the chapters, a few words about the selection process are in order. As mentioned earlier, this book studies the representations of Nasser in Egyptian novels, short stories, autobiographies, and films. The work that qualifies as an object of study is the one in which Nasser, as a person, is directly or allegorically portrayed, thus excluding broader treatment of the 1952 revolution and its impact on Egypt. Recognising that vast amount of works, however, I inevitably had to make choices and engage selectively with them. Though I ascribe no comprehensive character to it, I contend that this book treats a number of works that are sufficiently representative of the making and remaking of Nasser's image. It is as much concerned with major works, whose statuses were recognised by critics earlier, as it is with unearthing under-represented works of novel approaches. In addition, though sometimes unavoidable, the aesthetic evaluation of a single work as a whole is not the primary goal of this project, nor do I analyse the work in its totality. Rather, my main goal is to unmask the position that Nasser occupies in the work. Other aesthetic, political, or social aspects are significant only insofar as they relate to Nasser.

Chapter 1, 'Writing to Nasser', explores the position of Nasser as a readership. It argues that the Egyptian public, rather than being conceived as passive, docile followers of, and listeners to, the president, has occasionally reversed roles with Nasser, situating him in a place where he has to be the addressee. Nowhere can this be better recognised as in writing letters to Nasser. The chapter will trace the emergence of a 'tradition' of epistolary literature between Egyptians and Nasser. Motivated by a certainty that Nasser does not know what befalls them, Egyptians invoke in these letters the very ideals, hopes, and dreams about which Nasser has constantly spoken – they, in other words, write to Nasser precisely because they are empowered by a belief in him. The chapter examines the implications of Nasser's position as a reader: absent or present, distant or near, friend or official. In addition, it seeks to question whether Nasser can fit the role of what Janet Gurkin Altman calls 'the active confidant', in which the addressee's 'voice is *heard* within the hero's letters through quotation or paraphrase'.[53] As for the letter and its originator(s), the chapter wonders about the kind of 'capital' – linguistic, intellectual, or moral – the senders possess; the gender of the senders; and whether the letter was a product of individual or collective writing.

The second chapter, 'Nasser as Fiction', analyses the novels in which Nasser emerges as a protagonist. Explicitly or allegorically, he features as a fictive character that lives and interacts with other invented ones in the work. Despite sharing several aspects with the real figure, Nasser as fiction still significantly differs from his historical reference outside the text, adding to, altering, or contradicting it. In other words, there is no realist fictional account of Nasser in Egyptian literature. Rather, the four works which the chapter analyses all seek to reimagine alternative episodes in Nasser's life. By introducing him as an intellectual, an animal, a martyr, and a defendant, each of these works offers its own interpretation of Nasser, fantastically revisiting parts of his life and highlighting certain traits of his character. The chronological order of these works reveals that, contrary to common conceptions, Egyptian writers did not shy from criticising Nasser during his lifetime. What eventually emerges is a shattered imagined Nasser whose very essence is significantly contested. Furthermore, those conflicting interpretations of Nasser speak to his polarising character, which leaves little room for definitive answers, culminating in the position of the 'unfinalised hero' that Mikhail Bakhtin has famously theorised.[54]

The third chapter, on the other hand, locates Nasser's life, words and actions as parts of the background against which the events of the works unfold. Entitled, 'Nasser in Fiction', it considers a different manifestation of Nasser in Egyptian literature, one in which he is not a character, but rather a topic, an idea that is represented through the actions, dialogues, or monologues of the main characters. Whether glorified or undermined, abhorred or admired, Nasser remains a silent figure to whom these works never give a voice. What matters more are the other characters' views of the president. It is here that the otherwise unknowable Egyptian subjects are empowered to speak. In a thematic approach that seeks to highlight largely understudied aspects of Nasser's position vis-à-vis Egyptians, this chapter is divided into two main parts: Nasser and Children, and Nasser and Women. The first part is concerned with the narratives in which a child narrator expresses his/her thoughts on Nasser. It begs for a consideration of a tense relationship between Nasser and the father that inevitably leaves its mark on the child's evaluation of both. In addition, it calls into question the very reliability of the child's story, his torn stance between filiation and affiliation, and his relationship with his older self. The second part engages with three female autobiographical texts, focusing on their respective views of Nasser's gendered identity. It attempts to show whether the often recognised masculinity of Nasser has ever occupied a space in female imaginaries.

The last chapter, 'Nasser on the Screen', traces the treatment that Nasser receives in Egyptian cinema. It asks whether the ubiquitous presence of Nasser in Egyptian life during the 1950s and 1960s was ever translated to the screen. The chapter contends that, contrary to common conceptions, some of the harshest approaches to Nasser in films were produced during his life. Following his death, Egyptian cinema was swept by a series of films that sought to undermine Nasser's regime, reducing it to scenes of torture, prison, and corruption. Widely known as 'cinema of centers of power', the series was motivated by a state-sponsored process of de-Nasserisation, and largely thought to be initiated by Ali Badrakhan's famous 1975 film *al-Karnak*. The personal presence of, or reference to, Nasser in these films, however, was carefully negotiated. The chapter seeks to understand this negotiation through delineating the emergence of Nasser's portrait in Egyptian cinema. The study of the portrait serves also to reveal the romantic comeback of Nasser that has dominated Egyptian cinema since the 1980s. Aside from the portrait, the chapter pays close attention to another Nasser-related theme that recurs in films – the 'resignation speech'. It asks why Nasser was visually and aurally immortalised by, arguably, his most tragic appearance following the humiliating defeat of 1967. The chapter explores some rhetorical aspects of the speech, contextualises its appropriation in Egyptian films, and draws attention to instances in which only Nasser's voice appears.

This book is based on reading and analysing numerous texts and films, the overwhelming majority of which are in Arabic. Unless otherwise stated, all translations in the following chapters are mine. Finally, I should like to recall a sentence that a Tahrir Square revolutionary in 2011 had said to me: 'For me, Nasserism does not mean anything now, but Nasser does.' This book is, in part, a modest attempt to understand why.

Notes

1. Jorge Luis Borges, 'Pierre Menard, Author of Don Quixote', in *Ficciones* (New York: Grover Press, 1962), p. 53.
2. Ahmed Fouad Negm, *Ziyara li Darih Abdel Nasser*, 1970.
3. See, for instance, Egyptian daily newspaper *Al-Tahrir* (No. 79, 19 September 2011).
4. Pierre Nora, 'Between Memory and History: Les Lieux de Memoire', *Representations*, No. 26 (spring 1989), p. 12.
5. Ibid., p. 8.
6. Ibid., p. 9.

7. Andreas Huyssen, *Present Pasts: Urban Palimpsests and the Politics of Memory* (Stanford, CA: Stanford University Press, 2003).
8. Susan Suleiman, *Crises of Memory and the Second World War* (Cambridge, MA and London: Harvard University Press, 2006), p. 5.
9. Cornelius Castoriadis, *The Imaginary Institution of Society*, trans. Kathleen Blamey (Cambridge, MA: The MIT Press, 1987), p. 146.
10. Ibid., p. 147.
11. Ibid., p. 3.
12. Charles Taylor, *Modern Social Imaginary* (Durham, NC and London: Duke University Press, 2004), p. 23.
13. Dilip Parameshwar Gaonkar, 'Towards New Imaginaries: An Introduction', *Public Culture*, Vol. 14, No. 1 (winter 2002), p. 7.
14. Shahid Amin, 'Gandhi as Mahatma: Gorakhpur District, Eastern UP, 1921–2', in *Selected Subaltern Studies*, eds Ranajit Guha and Gayatri Chakravorti Spivak (Oxford: Oxford University Press, 1988), p. 289.
15. Arjun Appadurai, *Modernity at Large: Cultural Dimensions of Globalisations* (Minneapolis, MN and London: University of Minnesota Press, 1996), p. 5.
16. Ibid., p. 7, emphasis mine.
17. Michael Warner, *Publics and Counterpublics* (New York: Zone Books, 2002), p. 65.
18. Ibid., p. 66.
19. See Chapter 1, pp. 23–4.
20. Aziz al-Azmeh, *Muslim Kingship: Power and the Sacred in Muslim, Christian and Pagan Polities* (London; New York: I. B. Tauris, 1997), p. 71.
21. Warner, *Publics*, p. 172. Warner draws heavily here on Claude Lefort's contribution concerning the image of the body. For more on this, see Lefort, *The Political Forms of Modern Society: Bureaucracy, Democracy, Totalitarianism*, ed. John B. Thompson (Cambridge: Polity Press, 1986), pp. 292–306.
22. Yaseen Noorani, *Culture and Hegemony in the Colonial Middle East* (New York: Palgrave Macmillan, 2010), p. 9.
23. Ibid.
24. Ibid., pp. 23–4.
25. Ibid., p. 24.
26. Al-Azmeh, *Muslim Kingship*, p. 73.
27. Suzanne Stetkevych, *The Poetics of Islamic Legitimacy: Myth, Gender, and Ceremony in the Classical Arabic Ode* (Indiana: Indiana University Press, 2002), p. ix.
28. Stefan Sperl, 'Islamic Kingship and Arabic Panegyric Poetry in the Early 9th Century', *Journal of Arabic Literature*, Vol. 8 (1977), p. 34.

29. Al-Azmeh, *Mulsim Kingship*, p. 93, emphasis in the original.
30. See Muhammad Jabir al-Ansari, *Al-Nasiriyya bi Manzur Naqdi: Ayy Durus li al-Mustaqbal?* (Beirut: Al-Mu'assasa al-'Arabiyya li al-Dirasat wa al-Nashr, 2002), pp. 88–105.
31. Aristotle, *Poetics*, trans. John Warrington (London: Alibris, 1963), p. 17.
32. Warner Berthoff, 'Fiction, History, Myth: Notes Towards the Discrimination of Narrative Forms', in *The Interpretation of Narrative: Theory and Practice*, ed. Morton W. Bloomfield (Cambridge, MA: Harvard University Press, 1970), p. 271.
33. Wolfgang Iser, *Prospecting: From Reader Response to Literary Anthropology* (Baltimore, MD and London: The Johns Hopkins University Press, 1989), p. 263.
34. Ibid., p. 282.
35. Ibid., pp. 282–3.
36. Salman Rushdie, 'Imaginary Homelands', in *Imaginary Homelands: Essays and Criticism 1981–1991* (London: Penguin Books, 1992), p. 14.
37. Hayden White, 'The Historical Text as Literary Artifact', in *Tropics of Discourse: Essays in Cultural Criticism* (Baltimore, MD and London: The Johns Hopkins University Press, 1978), p. 82, emphasis in the original.
38. Hayden White, 'The Fictions of Factual Representation', in *Tropics of Discourse*, p. 121.
39. Ibid., p. 125, emphasis in the original.
40. Edward Said, *Orientalism* (New York: Vintage Books, 1979), p. 21, emphasis in the original.
41. Said K. Aburish, *Nasser: The Last Arab* (New York: Thomas Dunne Books, 2004), p. 4.
42. R. Hrair Dekmejian, *Egypt under Nasser: A Study in Political Dynamics* (Albany, NY: State University of New York Press, 1971), p. 97.
43. Ghali Shukri, *Mudhakkirat Thaqafa Tahtadir* (Beirut: Dar al-Tali'a, 1970), p. 409.
44. John Bodnar, *Remaking America: Public Memory, Commemoration, and Patriotism in the Twentieth Century* (Princeton, NJ: Princeton University Press, 1992), p. 13.
45. Ibid.
46. Lila Abu-Lughod and Ahmad H. Sa'di, 'Introduction: The Claims of Memory,' in *Nakba: Palestine, 1948, and the Claims of Memory*, eds Abu-Lughod and Sa'di (New York: Columbia University Press, 2007), p. 6.

47. Bodnar, *Remaking America*, p. 14.
48. See Andreas Huyssen, *Twilight Memories: Marking Time in a Culture of Amnesia* (New York and London: Routledge, 1995), p. 7.
49. Muhammad Siddiq, *Arab Culture and the Novel: Genre, Identity and Agency in Egyptian Fiction* (New York: Routledge, 2007), p. xiii.
50. Samia Mehrez, *Egyptian Writers Between History and Fiction* (Cairo: The American University in Cairo Press, 1994), p. 6.
51. Ibid., p. 7.
52. Noha Radwan, 'A Place for Fiction in the Historical Archive,' *Critique: Critical Middle Eastern Studies*, 17, No. 1 (2008), p. 81.
53. Janet Gurkin Altman, *Epistolarity: Approaches to a Form* (Columbus, OH: Ohio State University Press, 1982), p. 51, emphasis mine.
54. Mikhail Bakhtin, *Problems of Dostoevsky's Poetics*, ed. and trans. Caryl Emerson (Minneapolis, MN: University of Minnesota Press, 1984), p. 63.

1

Writing to Nasser

Throughout his tenure as president of Egypt, Nasser managed to transform the Egyptian public into an audience. Whether in his official processions in the streets of Egypt, on his visits to factories, schools, universities, and companies, or in the mere photographs of him that were ubiquitous in Egyptian society, Nasser was a spectacle to see, a human landmark whose presence in a geographical space would turn it into a Mecca for glances, gazes and stares. Abundant in Nasser's biographies and accounts are descriptions of the passion that would sweep people – men or women, children or adults – upon seeing him. That a few of those encounters were non-verbal – where Nasser would just stand and smile and people would merely look and cheer – only adds more aura to this extraordinary phenomenon. Far from being an exclusively Egyptian phenomenon, however, Nasser was able to turn any Arab people he visited into a similar audience. It is, indeed, his visit to Syria in 1958, upon declaring the formation of the short-lived United Arab Republic, that offered an unprecedented instance of Nasser and the people-as-audience. Muhammad Hasanayn Haykal (1923–2016), prominent Egyptian journalist and Nasser's lifelong confidant, presents the following account:

> The news of Nasser's arrival spread dramatically. People filled the streets between the airport and the palace. And once he arrived, the palace's squares were teeming with thousands, then hundreds of thousands, of people, who expressed their jubilation at Nasser's arrival in unprecedented ways. They would come, one group after another, to greet him, and he would peer from the palace's balcony, then go inside . . . and so on.[1]

It is Nasser's speeches, however, that effectively demonstrate this audience–spectacle relationship. Characterised by their passionate and hyperbolic rhetoric, defiance, and even humour, those speeches punctuated the president's decisions and responses to international and local events – from the nationalisation of the Suez Canal in 1956 to the infamous 'resignation speech' in the wake of the 1967 defeat, to name but the two most memorable ones. They were 'dramatic performance[s]',[2] with the spectators 'looking as if they were seeing something messianic'.[3] I do not intend to dwell here on Nasser's speeches or his voice, for this belongs elsewhere in the book.[4] What merits the attention now, however, is the 'democratic' aspect that a few historians have ascribed to those speeches. Though it could be puzzling to note a shade of 'democracy' manifested in the speeches of someone who is often portrayed as an authoritarian ruler, Lebanese historian Georges Corm (b.1940) argues that 'by thinking loudly before the crowds, using a very simple language, in search of solutions for the various problems of backwardness, dependency, and poverty, and by announcing, at the right moment, the suitable solution he found among all the proposed alternatives',[5] Nasser's speeches were democratic discourses that rectified to a certain extent the crude, despotic practices of his regime. Put differently, the audience, by listening approvingly, if passively, to their leader, bestowed a certain kind of legitimacy on the process of decision-making, whereupon Nasser's speeches could be perceived as both monological and dialogical.

Furthermore, the story is not one-sided. For the crowds, whose love for Nasser was unqualified, occasionally exchanged positions with him, rendering Nasser himself an audience. This was most apparently manifested by writing letters to Nasser, where he would be put in a place to receive, read, and, occasionally, act. By reversing the equation, the people, empowered as they were by 'a belief in Nasser personally',[6] emerged as voiced agents who voluntarily assumed a reciprocal relationship with Nasser, where they could be at once an addresser and an addressee. As is often noted in any hierarchical exchange, one can hardly fail to see the inequality between the sender and the recipient.[7] Yet it is this very same hierarchy that compels one to ponder the kind of 'capital' that those people possessed in order to imagine Nasser as an audience.

This chapter will reflect on some remarkable incidents of writing to Nasser. Those correspondences, manifested as both independent letters as well as letters-in-narrative, will be representatives of a much larger corpus that has often been overlooked by Nasser scholars. I argue that writing to Nasser poses him as an *active confidant*. In her important book on epistolarity, Janet Gurkin Altman establishes confidentiality as a main feature of epistolary literature. If writing letters is an act of confiding in someone, it is the nature of this confidant that would characterise him as a passive or active one. Having clarified how the former merely fulfils his minimal function by listening to stories and confessions, Altman proceeds to define the active confidant as:

> rarely a purely passive listener. Even in letter narrative that includes no letters from the confidant, his voice is *heard* within the hero's letters through quotation or paraphrase. There are varying degrees to his activity, according to whether he merely contributes information relevant to the hero's story or actually influences it.[8]

As will be demonstrated, letters to Nasser took Nasser's words, slogans, beliefs, and deeds as their points of departure. By personalising their relationship with him, and consequently separating him from the regime that he himself had created, the audience of Nasser regularly opted to remind him of the rights about which he himself had frequently spoken. In other words, writing to Nasser expressed the senders' dismay: not at Nasser's acts but at their own life conditions or situations that they assumed would never meet Nasser's approval. It is the discrepancy between the ideals, dreams, and hopes of which Nasser spoke, and the facts on the ground, that the letters were seeking to rectify.

Equally revealing in this context is the dual way in which Nasser emerges in the letters – present and absent. Franz Kafka (1883–1924) once declared that letter writing 'is truly a communication with specters, not only with the specter of the addressee but also with one's own phantom'.[9] Several scholars have noted that, particularly in love letters, the addressee is assumed to be absent: 'if the beloved were present, there would be no need to write'.[10] This view is oversimplifying, however, for it not only takes for granted the transparency of what a 'love' letter is (a letter to Nasser could be based on a certain 'love') but also has an exclusively functional perspective on letter writing. In love, as in other relationships, one can write to the beloved because writing is at times like touching – it is a physical act, exhilarating and fulfilling for many, so much so that one does not need the 'addressee' to be absent in order to write to him or her.

Janet Gurkin Altman offers a more comprehensive paradigm. While acknowledging that letters occur between 'two distant points', she maintains that the sender can 'emphasise either the distance or the bridge'.[11] In the case of Nasser, letters are predicated upon a negotiation between his presence and his absence. On the one hand, the absence is acknowledged by the need to establish a rapprochement through letters. Yet, it is the very ubiquity of Nasser, his voice, words, and deeds that are invoked in them. It is as if the absence of Nasser is shown inconceivable in those letters precisely because he *ought to be* present. Hence the senders' attempts to 'reclaim' Nasser, ever to *Nasserise* him by demanding that their situations be accorded a *Nasserite* level, one that could match Nasser's own visions and aspirations.

Pertinent also in this regard is the fact that letter writing to Nasser eludes the two principal slots that are often ascribed to the addressee: the lover or the friend.[12] Nasser could be both; or neither. After all, he was the president of the republic. The case of Nasser as an addressee begs consideration precisely because it destabilises the notion of formality between a citizen and a president – in one letter, to mention a brief example, a woman ascribes to Nasser an 'angelic voice'.[13] This chapter will be concerned with the way in which Nasser was addressed, the titles that were used, and the respectful words (or lack thereof) that featured in the letters. This will be discussed in relation to the sender's gender, education, age, and political orientation.

It is beyond the scope of this chapter to offer an exhaustive analysis of all the letters that were sent to Nasser. Rather, it will engage a select number of two kinds of letters. The first letters are those that were written to Nasser by journalists, intellectuals, or activists, and were published either in newspapers and other periodicals during Nasser's life or in book form after his death. The second are fictional letters; letters in narratives that employ the epistolary form in order to establish a correspondence with Nasser. I am not suggesting, however, that the first group possesses a more authentic value than the second, nor am I implying that an actual exchange had, in fact, occurred – with a few exceptions, we are uncertain if any letter was received or even sent. The categorisation I am following can merely shed light on the historical context in which those intellectuals felt compelled to write to Nasser. In other words, it is the need to write a letter, its content, and the process of writing, rather than the letter's outcome, that interest me the most. Moreover, by grouping works of fiction together, one can scrutinise its dialogue with history, and the emergence of a mode, its continuities, and discontinuities.

A Journalist Intervention

In his now classic thesis on the emergence of the public sphere in Europe, German philosopher Jürgen Habermas describes the eighteenth century in Europe as 'the century of the letter'.[14] According to him, privatised (that is those who became part of the private sphere) European individuals saw themselves as independent agents who can establish 'purely human' relations with one another. Those relations were better negotiated through letter writing; it is there that 'the individual unfolded himself in his subjectivity'.[15] Interestingly, however, Habermas does not see a contrast between subjectivity, which he calls 'the innermost core of the private', and the public, for the former is 'always already oriented to an audience';[16] hence Habermas's connection between the letter and other eighteenth-century media, such as the novel and the diary. Needless to say, Habermas's view on the relationship between the letter and the public sphere has found a warm reception among scholars. Ann Goldberg notes how 'we, today, in Western liberal societies still, to a large extent, retain a conception of letter-writing that derives from the eighteenth century'.[17]

Obviously, Habermas's thesis is mainly concerned with a European context and may not be unquestioningly transferred to other human experiences – including the Arab one. Aside from letter writing that was flourishing in classical Arabic literature – about which one can only anachronistically employ Habermas's terminology – the 'modern' Arabic experience has witnessed the kinds of letter writing that do not fall into the European paradigm. Prominent Egyptian sociologist Sayyid 'Uways (1903–88) has worked on examining Egyptian letters that were sent to the dead. In his attempt to explain why so many crimes in Egypt were not reported to the police, 'Uways finds that several Egyptians had chosen to report those tragic events to dead religious figures like al-Shafi'i (767–820), the renowned Muslim jurist. Though dead, those blessed figures were believed to have some supernatural power that could heal, help, and improve people's conditions. To 'Uways's astonishment, those letters were not only left at al-Shafi'i's shrine, a practice which he had noticed when he was a child, but were also sent by post to the shrine's address, and were then collected by the shrine's servant.[18] Upon his request, the letters were handed over to 'Uways.[19] The scholar was so enthralled by his study that he referred to it in most of his later works. Commenting on his findings, he maintains how this 'clearly underscores a rise in the position that the irrational cultural aspects occupy in some people's lives'.[20] In addition, he sees in this practice a continuity in a tradition of writing to the dead that featured throughout Egyptian history, implying that 'contemporary' Egyptians 'behave, regarding certain issues, in light of a specific set of old social values that had been carried over time, and which emanated from the conditions of Egyptian society'.[21]

Nevertheless, Habermas's model of interpretation can still offer insights into the practice of generations of 'liberal' Egyptians, those who were highly enchanted by the principles of the European Enlightenment, liberal democracy, and individualism. His reference to a reader-oriented letter, together with his emphasis on the role that newspapers and novels had played in forming the modern subject, are worth considering as we delve into analysing the first incident of letter writing to Nasser. It is precisely a letter *in public*, a letter for both Nasser and a readership, and, more importantly, a letter by one of the leading journalists in Egypt, that had ushered in the phenomenon of writing to Nasser. Surprisingly overlooked by most of Nasser's biographers, the letter was penned by Ruz al-Yusuf (1898–1958) on the pages of her famous weekly periodical of the same name. Sent as early in Nasser's career as 1953, the letter is invaluable not only for its content, or its initiation of a tradition, but also because it was a rare instance in which Nasser himself felt compelled to respond.[22]

Ruz al-Yusuf was born Fatima al-Yusuf in Tripoli, Lebanon.[23] After her mother died giving birth to her, her father, a merchant who used to travel across several Middle Eastern countries, left the child in the custody of two friends of the family. The vague information which was reported by al-Yusuf's biographers stated that the custodians, a Christian couple, began calling the child 'Ruz', a name that would accompany her throughout her life. Al-Yusuf's move from Lebanon to Egypt resembles a fairy tale. Accounts had it that, with the disappearance of her father, al-Yusuf's life with the new family proceeded miserably. One day, a friend of the family, who was preparing himself to migrate to Brazil, suggested that he would take al-Yusuf with him. To the child's astonishment, the family warmly welcomed the proposal. Egyptian historian Ibrahim 'Abdu maintains that, on that day, al-Yusuf's nanny revealed to her that those were not her original parents, and, more surprisingly, that her name was actually Fatima.[24] The accounts left unanswered the reason why al-Yusuf decided to stick to her 'Ruz' name. Also unmentioned was her age at the time of leaving Lebanon. The story resumed with the travellers' stop at Alexandria where, surprisingly, al-Yusuf decided to stay for good and, more surprising still, her company allowed her to do so.

Al-Yusuf had had a flourishing acting career in Cairo before she decided to found her own periodical *Ruz al-Yusuf* in 1925 upon noticing the ill-informed coverage of art and artists in Egyptian media at the time. The new-born publication, a weekly magazine, was not exclusively dedicated to art, however. Politics were, naturally, unavoidable and al-Yusuf needed to find herself an alliance among the several political parties and rivals of that era. As for her private life, she married three times, had two children [one of whom, Ihsan, would become the celebrity journalist and novelist Ihsan Abdel Quddous (1919–90)] and enjoyed a successful career that turned *Ruz al-Yusuf* into one of the biggest media institutions in Egypt to the present day.

Unlike the case of her son Ihsan, we seldom find any mention of a special relationship or even encounters between al-Yusuf and Nasser. True, she dedicated her magazine to supporting the nascent revolution of 1952, given the antagonistic stance that it was taking towards the monarchy, particularly after Ihsan's influential features on what became known as the issue of *al-asliha al-fasida* (the defective weapons). First published in *Ruz al-Yusuf* in 1949,[25] the story 'electrified the already tense atmosphere of the country',[26] with many considering it a major reason behind the mobilisation of the Free Officers (the nickname given to the officers who overthrew the monarchy in Egypt in 1952) and the move towards overthrowing the monarchy.[27] That support, however, was not unequivocal for al-Yusuf was critical of the several censorship laws that the young officers had imposed on the media. It is in that context of choking journalists' freedom of expression that the al-Yusuf–Nasser exchange occurred.[28] Mustafa Abdel Ghani (b.1947) locates the exchange within the few months in which the revolution did loosen its grip on writers and journalists.[29] Indeed, al-Yusuf's letter was as much a writing *for* freedom as it was a writing *as* freedom, an attempt by a woman of letters to persuade a man of power that the role of dissent was no less salubrious to his rule than consent. The exchange, which took place in 1953, revealed yet again the keen perception of al-Yusuf, who realised early in Nasser's career (when Muhammad Naguib was still the president of the newly born republic) the position that the young officer would later occupy in the political and intellectual history of Egypt.

Entitled 'Khitab Maftuh ila Gamal Abdel Nasser' (An Open Letter to Nasser), the letter is bereft of formal structure, particularly in the opening paragraph. There is no mention of names nor titles. The letter, rather, opens thus:

> Freedom is the only lung through which people can breathe.
> You are as much in need for disagreement as you are for unanimity.
> Salutations to your youth that you put into danger and the efforts that you expended for the sake of this homeland. Salutations from a woman who has experienced numerous events and extracted their essence.[30]

Though it is apparently meant as an endearment, the reference to Nasser's youth is immediately contrasted with the seniority and maturity of the older al-Yusuf, thereby creating a condescending tone towards the predictable recklessness of a youth. Al-Yusuf, who was twenty years older than Nasser, emphasises her life experience before she confesses her happiness with the new, young officer who was trying to lead Egypt. Her invocation of age difference and experience at the beginning of the letter could be meant to establish her 'capital' before power. It has been noted in several incidents of letter writing that the sender, particularly women, would seek a specific capital that would bestow on them 'an appropriate epistolary voice'. Lynne Magnusson shows how some poorly educated women would search for more 'linguistic' capital and rhetorical sophistication by searching for a ghost author.[31] No linguistic capital is needed, however, in the case of an educated journalist. Rather, it is deemed sufficient to remind Nasser of the sender's experience and background.

The letter then unfolds as demonstrating at once a belief in Nasser's good intentions and in the fact that he himself will not be capable of handling things alone; hence the need to hear others' voices:

> I know a lot about the hours that you spend working incessantly, your nights of no sleep, and your thorough investigations into every matter in

order to make the right decision. But you – *alone* – will not be able to do everything, not even with the sincere aid of those brothers, friends, and acquaintances of yours that you trust. For you must also seek the aid of those you do not know, those who live in an atmosphere quite different from yours, are influenced by factors other than those which affect your friends, and live through various, different experiences that cannot be all experienced by one, nor tens, nor a thousand people![32]

Having emphasised the obvious need for plurality in any nascent regime, al-Yusuf then reminds Nasser that those different voices might abstain from emerging when they see that the regime is looking for one singular formula for the future. Nor will they dare to speak when they sense the various obstacles, barriers, and laws that bar them from expressing their ideas freely.

Al-Yusuf, however, is keen to display a sympathetic understanding of why Nasser resorts to censorship and limiting people's freedom of expression. It is as though she suggests that she knows he is forced to do so, given that he is 'fearful of snakes' fangs and ships' mice, of the tendentious and corrupt exploitation of freedom'.[33] Yet, she precisely proposes that only in an atmosphere of fear, censorship, and absence of freedom do such people find a great opportunity for corruption and sedition, for 'only free people can benefit from freedom'.[34] Also revealing is al-Yusuf's grasp of Nasser's anti-colonial aspirations at the time which she sees as also compelling him not to allow absolute freedom so that voices 'of defeat and disintegration' will not sneak into the scene with their subversive calls. Yet again, she employs a pleading, friendly voice to convince Nasser that freedom of expression will not stand in the way of Egypt's path towards independence and liberation:

> But, believe me, this will not occur, for those defeatists had an influence in the past only because strong parties were protecting them. Had they been left unprotected, they would not have survived long. *True* freedom can always eradicate its enemies, as the light of the sun kills the earth's worms.[35]

What constitutes true freedom is left unsaid, however, for al-Yusuf's arguments are less concerned with offering a comprehensive view of freedom than with assuring Nasser that 'freedom' should not be seen antagonistically.

As mentioned earlier, her thesis constantly oscillates between a belief in Nasser, and the good intentions that stand behind his apprehension of freedom on the one hand and, on the other, the desire to show him not that his apprehension is unjustified but that it nevertheless should not lead him towards suppressing freedom of expression. Furthermore, she employs several rhetorical modes to corner Nasser, leaving him with very few options to defend the outcome of controlling the media at the time: 'You are surely fed up when you skip through the daily newspapers every morning to find that they sound as if they are one copy, differing only in titles'.[36]

Astonishingly, the letter ends with a prophetic insight. Having credited Nasser for his announcement that any maltreated journalist could take his grievance directly to him, al-Yusuf insists on the impracticality of this approach. It is the personalisation of the relationship between people and Nasser, the reduction of the whole regime's institutions and apparatuses into the single person of Nasser, and ignoring the role of the public sphere, courts, and the legal system as a whole that al-Yusuf is implicitly warning against. After all, she posits, Nasser is but a single individual who has plenty of concerns about which to care, and that approach would be unfair 'to you, journals, and the grand causes that you are busy working for. *Did not I tell you that you alone cannot do everything?*'[37] Prescient, indeed, for it is precisely this view of an omniscient, omnipresent, and omnipotent Nasser that would continuously inspire people to write to him. Never mind the existence of a whole government, of various apparatuses, and of a hierarchical system, Nasser would always be both exempted from and invoked against the misdeeds of the very regime he established. It is as though al-Yusuf's letter is a letter on the potentiality of forthcoming letters if Nasser's public image does not change – which, after all, it did not.

Interestingly, there is no gendered importance attached to the sender. That a woman has written this letter can add very little to our understanding of it. It is not a 'feminist' letter but, rather, a liberal call for abolishing censorship and moving towards a real public space where private individuals, like herself, can freely pour their hearts out before an audience. If it has been noted that the letter is a 'feminine mode par excellence',[38] it is with al-Yusuf less about her or her female readers' specific needs than about those of every Egyptian. It was probably her desire to involve her readership in a debate on freedom of expression that propelled al-Yusuf to publish the letter. She could have quite easily reached Nasser in another way. Yet, I argue that, in her mind, an implied reader (read: ordinary Egyptians) occupied a space next to Nasser's. It is unfortunate that we have no account of how such public advice to Nasser was received by the magazine's readers.

What we do have, however, is a reply written by none other than Nasser himself. In a rare incident of an open reciprocity between the political power and the media in modern Arabic writing, the very next issue of *Ruz al-Yusuf* carried Nasser's response, entitled, 'Al-Khayt al-Rafi' bayna al-Hurriyya wa al- Fawda' (The Thin Line Between Freedom and Chaos). Much shorter than al-Yusuf's (563 vs 942 words), Nasser's letter follows a similar structure of omitting titles and formality, if more vehemently. Whereas al-Yusuf's letter mentions Nasser's name once in the letter's title, thereby adding some personal tone to it, Nasser's title thrusts right into the subject, relegating al-Yusuf's name to the background of the intellectual debate. More importantly, the title here serves tersely to summarise the gist of the previous letter, consisting of an indirect charge of promoting chaos, if not against al-Yusuf herself, then against a potential reading of her advice.

Also telling is the way in which Nasser replies to al-Yusuf's opening paragraphs. Responding to her first three paragraphs, including the greeting, Nasser impatiently moves from a short sentence to the second, maintaining a style of only touching upon what has been brought in her letter:

> As for your greeting, I thank you for it. As for your experience, I am sure it rests on the lessons of life. As for your appreciation of the efforts I make, I am grateful you feel that way. As for your opinion that I alone cannot do everything, this is also my opinion and the opinion of all of my colleagues, the Free Officers.[39]

Nasser not only does not return al-Yusuf's greeting, sufficing instead to thank her for hers, but also attempts to deprive her letter of one of its basic merits by explicitly stating that he never acts alone nor does he seek to do everything by himself. The Arabic sentences are punctuated by the use of the conjunction *amma*, roughly rendered 'as for'. The conjunction is generally used in the context of detailing things, or moving from one point to the other, something that Nasser precisely, and hastily, does here.

The response is predicated upon an attempt to strip al-Yusuf's letter of any genuine, original view it may possess. It does so in two ways. First, it denies any implicit charge that is levelled by al-Yusuf at the new regime and at Nasser personally. Aside from refuting the claim that Nasser seeks to act individually, the response goes further as to dispel the very core allegation of al-Yusuf's letter, namely, the suffocation of freedom of expression. Having shown the damage that absolute freedom could inflict upon a society, Nasser rhetorically wonders:

> However, where is this freedom that [you claim] we restricted? You yourself know that criticism is allowed, and that we insist on our demands for guidance and tutorship. Nay, we even welcome any attack against us if it was meant for the sake of the homeland and the building of its future – and not meant to destroy, ruin, or merely incite.[40]

Second, Nasser appropriates al-Yusuf's opinions themselves, claiming them as his own, only to show that they justify whatever approach to freedom he adopts. The need for disagreement, for example, is something, he says, 'I believe in, and trust that it is of the core foundations of freedom'.[41] But if al-Yusuf herself understands the fear of giving infiltrators a chance to exploit freedom, then she unintentionally gives Nasser a pretext on which to capitalise:

> You yourself said that you know how much I am afraid of allowing freedom lest it would harm the solid position of the country were its waves infiltrated by advocates of defeat and disintegration. As such, you expressed *parts* of what I feel, but allow me to add something more: I am not afraid of allowing freedom. Rather, I fear it would be a commodity that is bought and sold, as it was before 23 July.[42]

The letter ends with Nasser underscoring once again that whatever he does is meant for the sake of the *watan* (homeland). Nasser, as an individual, is not averse to being subject to criticism and accountability, for 'I believe none of us is beyond criticism or infallible'. What matters, after all, is Egypt. Nasser can 'place his head in his palms', a metaphor for sacrificing the self, but cannot do so with 'the interests and the sanctities of the homeland'.[43]

It is worth noting how Nasser meticulously traces each of al-Yusuf's main phrases and arguments, replying to, agreeing with, or refuting them. He understands the nature of the epistolary exchange, where 'the *you* of any *I–you* statement can, and is expected to, become the *I* of a new text'.[44] Janet Gurkin Altman shows how this *I–you* relationship in epistolary exchange differs from any other first-person narrative, such as memoir and diary, in which 'there is no reified addressee'.[45] The 'you' of Nasser in al-Yusuf's letter is a physical 'you', a specific address to a real person who, in turn, understands this message and acts accordingly. He reclaims his voice, turning his former 'you' into a present 'I' in less than a week. In so doing, Nasser is not objecting to his role as reader, for he never questions al-Yusuf's right to address him. What he actually rejects is to remain as such, as a listening 'you', a mute partner who does not engage in personal negotiations over what should and should not be done. By posing as a responder in the realm of reciprocal writing, Nasser at once offers his blessing to an emerging tradition but warns future interlocutors that his status as an audience can be promptly reversed.

As was argued earlier, al-Yusuf's letter can be seen as prescient in the sense that it foreshadows a history of Egyptians overriding institutions and regime apparatuses in an attempt to reach Nasser directly in order to present a grievance or demand a right. This attempt was based on a personal trust in Nasser and a belief in his ignorance of these travails. What ensued afterwards was a corpus of letter writing that would combine those two elements.

A Son Following Suit

In 1980, ten years after the death of Nasser, famous Egyptian novelist, short story writer, and journalist, Ihsan Abdel Quddous, published *'Asif Lam A'ud Astati'* (Sorry, I No Longer Can). The book contains seven short stories, one of which bears the title of the collection. As is the case with most of Abdel Quddous's literary output, it had women as protagonists, centred on love and sexuality, and, more importantly, went almost unnoticed in Egyptian and Arabic critical circles. Critics have often treated Abdel Quddous's writings as sensational, superficial, and flat. Famous and prolific as he was, Abdel Quddous and his literary career were rarely taken seriously and often left out of the Egyptian literary canon. The writer himself complained about critics' disregard and neglect of his works, considering himself 'one of the most unfairly treated writers by critics'.[46] Nevertheless, he has mostly found a warm reception among the public, his novels selling more than those of most of his contemporaries, including the critically acclaimed Naguib Mahfouz (1911–2006), so much so that he was awarded the title of 'the First Writer, in a popular poll conducted by the American University of Cairo regarding the most beloved writer of 1952'.[47]

Abdel Quddous's 1980 collection includes a piece that could otherwise have found an important place in the debate around Nasser, particularly the latter's relationship with writers. Subtitled, 'Seven Short Stories and a Letter', the book, in fact, opts to open with the letter, preceded by a short preface in which Abdel Quddous elucidates its *story*. He begins thus:

> The Charge was:
> - Sex
> - Atheism
>
> I discovered a letter I had written to Nasser in 1955. I was astonished, for I do not ever recall writing a letter to any president. This could have been the only one that I wrote, then forgot. I even forgot whether I had actually sent it to Nasser, or only wrote it before throwing it into the drawer of oblivion.[48]

Abdel Quddous subsequently tells us the story of this 'forgotten' letter. It was in the context of publishing his collection *Al-Banat wa al-Sayf* (Girls and the Summer) serialised in *Ruz al-Yusuf*. 'It seems', Abdel Quddous goes on, 'that Nasser was reading [it] . . . and he sent me his disapproval of what was being published, or at least his dissatisfaction.'[49] The letter itself states that it is Nasser's confidant, Muhammad Hasanayn Haykal, who conveyed Nasser's opinion to Abdel Quddous, probably at the first's behest. As indicated by its title, the collection revolves around stories of Egyptian girls during the summer, including one that apparently stirred the 'strictly conservative' Nasser, as Abdel Quddous characterises him,[50] which features scenes of what takes place inside the cabins of Alexandria beach.

But it was not only the free depiction of sexual rendezvous that upset Nasser, for the incident coincided with another provocative publication in the magazine. It was Mustafa Mahmud's (1921–2009) articles on religion that were not welcomed by the president. Though Abdel Quddous did not elaborate on the nature of those articles, one could guess their critical approach to God and Islam, given Mahmud's interests at the time.

The story confirms my argument about the extent to which Egyptians' relationship with Nasser was personalised, so much so that he himself internalised it. There exist several incidents in which Nasser's taste and opinion became the gauge of what could or could not be published or screened, coupled with his personal interference for the ban or authorisation of a specific cultural product. Realising this, Egyptian intellectuals and artists would turn to Nasser as the last resort, ironically against his own system and (possibly) ruling. The case of Kamal El Sheikh's (1919–2004) film *Miramar*, which was based on Mahfouz's novel, remains the most notorious one. Joel Gordon, who describes this 1969 film as being the first openly to criticise the system without resort to symbolism or allusion, relays how the solicitation of Nasser's personal approval was a prerequisite to show the film.[51] In Abdel Quddous's case, the situation is more puzzling because Nasser himself initiated the exchange. It is also an incident in which Nasser the president intersects with Nasser the man, for Abdel Quddous did, in fact, have a personal relationship with him.

As mentioned earlier, Abdel Quddous was known to Nasser prior to the revolution, his features on the 'Defective Weapons' having turned him into a renowned journalist. Accounts had it that Nasser used to frequent Abdel Quddous's office at *Ruz al-Yusuf*, finding him a source for news.[52] Their friendship became so close that Abdel Quddous nicknamed Nasser 'Jimmy'.[53] It was during the turbulent year of 1954, and what was historically known as the 'March Crisis', that the two men's friendship received a harsh blow. Abdel Quddous's son tells us how his father's article in *Ruz al-Yusuf* on 'The Secret Society that Rules Egypt' led to him to spending three months in jail.[54] Whether the punishment was at the behest of Nasser is difficult to ascertain, though he certainly knew about it. Abdel Quddous even mentioned to Mahmud Murad that Nasser himself had called him in prison and apologetically said, 'What can I do, Ihsan?'.[55] Undoubtedly, the incident left an indelible strain between the two, with Abdel Quddous changing even the way he addressed Nasser after his release:

> A few minutes after my release, and upon arriving at home, Nasser called me, apologised again, and spoke about what he was doing during that severe crisis. He then invited me over for dinner ... I remember very

well that when I arrived, he came to welcome me and see me to the salon, saying '*Itfaddal,* Ihsan' so that, being a guest, I could enter before him. But I stopped motionless and said, 'Excuse me, *ya efendim,*[56] *Itfaddal,* your Excellency.' My reply was surprising, for I used to call him 'Jimmy' before. He then said, 'What happened, Ihsan? You have completely changed.' But I repeated, '*Itfaddal, ya efendim*'.[57]

The letter's preface confirms the distance that grew between the two men after 1954, though Abdel Quddous based it on his inability 'to fulfil the demands of men in charge'.[58] This, together with his desire not to rely on mediators, was the reason behind choosing the letter as a medium for communication. Whether he had actually sent it remains uncertain, for it was equally plausible for Abdel Quddous that he had merely 'written it then thrown it into oblivion'.[59] If that is the case, then why did he publish it when he did? Sensing the readers' potential misgivings around it, Abdel Quddous rushes to offer his own answer: the letter responds to a controversy that surrounded one of this current collection's stories (though he did not specify it), speaks to a debate that was still taking place in Egypt, and articulates several topics that were yet to be resolved.

Questions remain, nonetheless. If we were to take the claim regarding the actual sending of the letter without a grain of salt, it would still be unconvincing that Abdel Quddous only found the letter ten years after the death of Nasser. Naturally, between the date of writing (1955) and that of publishing (1980), the tradition of writing to the president had been revealed in many books, stories, magazines, and memoirs. Was Abdel Quddous seeking to find himself a place in that archive? More puzzling is the fact that he chose to publish the letter in a book of fiction. Indeed, the letter would have probably been more suitable in one of Abdel Quddous's compilations of political writing, such as *Khawatir Siyasiyya*[60] (Political Reflections), which was published by the same publishing house only a year earlier. By opting to include the letter in a short story collection, Abdel Quddous, I would argue, adds something 'fictional' to it. In fact, as if to raise more suspicions about it, he himself acknowledges in the same preface that the letter is not meant to be read as part of his memories, autobiography, or diaries, for he has already published all his memoirs. 'Whatever I find myself unable to publish in an article,' he explains, 'I publish it as a story, disguising myself behind a character of my imagination.'[61]

Furthermore, if Nasser had not actually received the letter, a possibility that Abdel Quddous proposes, then the title 'Did Nasser Read this Letter?' becomes completely rhetorical. But, if Nasser did not read it, we, the readers, would. The title – the paratext in Gerard Genette's well-known terminology – serves to seduce us into devouring the text which Nasser could have read or missed with equal probability. We will find ourselves replacing the 'Nasser' of the title, seeking to reply affirmatively to the proposed question. If Nasser did read it, then we would be the second reader. If he did not, then we would be the first to read a letter that was not written for us (or was it?). Unlike his mother's letter, which was a public correspondence with Nasser, Abdel Quddous's was not initially meant to be. Whether he did not want to be received as merely imitating his mother, or whether he saw disadvantages in publicising the letter in 1955, remains in the realm of speculation.

The letter can be seen as Abdel Quddous's self-defence against the two unfavourable comments that he heard Nasser was making against him. First, there is the free depiction of sexual relationships in his *Al-Banat wa al-Sayf*. Interestingly, he does not seem radically different from Nasser's social conservatism, for he only defends the writer's right to reflect honestly the reality that he sees in a society. As for those realities, he acknowledges that what was taking place in Egypt was 'decadence'.[62] He perceives it as his and other writers' duty explicitly to approach this moral decay, refusing to sugar-coat it. After showing that writers all over the world have done exactly this, from France's Balzac to Italy's Moravia, he declares that he was following what great Egyptian writers, including Tawfiq al-Hakim (1898–1987) in his *Al-Ribat al-Muqaddas* (The Sacred Bond) and Ibrahim al-Mazini (1889–1949) in *Thalathat Rijal wa Imra'a* (Three Men and a Woman), had done before. But a defence will not be complete without invoking Nasser himself. Abdel Quddous reminds him – and perhaps us – of a conversation that had occurred between them on the 'great role that narrative literature could play',[63] and that he has, under Nasser's patronage, contributed to the animation of literary life in Egypt. In other words, Abdel Quddous seeks to take Nasser to his own words, showing that he was doing precisely that which Nasser had already approved.

At stake also is the religious dimension of Nasser's comments. And it is only here that Abdel Quddous's confessions become so personal that we forget he is addressing a president. Having acknowledged that some of those articles on religion published in *Ruz al-Yusuf* might have exceeded the limit of what is permissible, he then turns the letter into a confessional:

> I believe in Allah, Mr President. I am not an atheist. You may not know that I pray. I do not do so ostentatiously or hypocritically, for none of the aspects of my life may suggest that I pray. But I do pray, because it makes me feel comfortable. Yet, I believe that our religion is dominated by several superstitions and absurd interpretations, which the clergy uses to keep the people in darkness so that they can easily exploit and dominate them. Had our religion been purified from this . . . it would have made it easier for *you to lead the people in the path you had drawn for them*.[64]

Once again, Nasser's aspirations are employed in Abdel Quddous's defence, characterised by the notion that he acts only in accordance with what is beneficial to the revolution and its leader. It is astounding, nonetheless, to see Abdel Quddous's pleading regarding his prayer to a president who seldom, if ever, attached himself to religious manifestations. In fact, Haykal himself avoided answering an interlocutor about whether Nasser was praying or fasting.[65] It is significant, however, for it further obfuscates the question of the letter's intended readership and the nature of the epistolary relationship between Nasser and Abdel Quddous.

In fact, the way Abdel Quddous addresses Nasser underscores the ambivalent view that he had about the president. True, there is no longer a nicknaming of Nasser, Jimmy or otherwise. Yet the first three lines of the letter tellingly combine formality and informality:

> Mr President, Gamal Abdel Nasser,
> Dear Mr President,
> A greeting of love and longing.[66]

Abdel Quddous's choice of the word *hubb,* or love, might have been intentional, compelled by an incident he relays in the preface. He used to present a radio programme at the time, concluding it with *tusbihuna 'ala khayr, tusbihuna 'ala hubb,* or 'Good Night, Good Love'. Nasser objected, and suggested the use of the less sexually loaded word for love, *mahabba*. Abdel Quddous, however, did not conform, reasoning that he wanted to spread the correct use of the word *hubb*, whatever that means. Though he stopped presenting the programme, his resorting to the same word in the letter could serve as an implicit reference to that incident.

The body of the letter sees Abdel Quddous addressing Nasser only as 'President', 'Mr President', or 'Your Excellency'. Towards the end of the letter, however, he rearticulates his intentions behind writing to him: 'Mr President, what I intended with this letter is to retain your trust. I need you, *as a supporter and a brother.*'[67] It is signed *al-Mukhlis* (the sincere), Ihsan Abdel Quddous.

Compared to other occasions of writing to Nasser, Abdel Quddous's letter stands out as the one whose very author casts doubts on its status. It is situated in a space between fiction and non-fiction. More importantly, it is the quickest answer to al-Yusuf's prophetic view in her previous letter. Ironically, it was none other than her son, Ihsan Abdel Quddous, who would so soon resort to Nasser, asking for more freedom of speech.

Declaring Allegiance: If Only You Knew How Much We Loved You

The end of the 1950s would offer us yet another peculiar case of writing to Nasser against one of the most notorious incidents to take place in Egyptian prisons. On 15 June 1960, prominent Egyptian communist intellectual, Shuhdi 'Atiyya al-Shafi'i (1911–60), was murdered at the hands of his inquisitors and jailers. A year earlier, al-Shafi'i wrote a letter to Nasser, declaring his allegiance, expounding his and his comrades' stance towards the regime, and pleading for their release. The particularity of this letter stems from the fact that it was published posthumously in 1975 in an issue that the leftist Egyptian magazine, *Al-Tali'a*, dedicated to al-Shafi'i.[68] In addition, there was no record to testify whether al-Shafi'i managed to send the letter or that Nasser knew about it. Nor do we even know how the letter was recovered. The letter is only part of the story of a legend in the making; the epitome of a communist's suffering during Nasser's regime, rivalled only by his Muslim Brother counterpart, Sayyid Qutb (1906–66).[69]

Al-Shafi'i's case occurred during the most intense and violent campaign against communists in Nasser's Egypt, a period in which 'one of the dark pages of modern Egyptian political history would be written',[70] to quote one of its now famous victims, Sonallah Ibrahim (b.1937). It began in 1959 and lasted until 1964. Much has been written about the reasons behind the campaign, and the larger story of communists under Nasser.[71] The crisis occurred in the context of what Malcolm Kerr calls 'shifts in alignments'[72] that characterised Nasser's policies at the time. Nasser's receptive treatment (though not necessarily view) of Egyptian communists in the wake of their positive role during the Suez Canal crisis would come to an end in 1958. Two incidents caused this. First, there was the unification with Syria and the emergence of the United Arab Republic (UAR) in February, of which the Syrian Communist Party was not in favour. Though Egyptian communists first welcomed the union, they were later influenced by the stance of their Syrian comrades, particularly after Nasser dissolved the Syrian Communist Party.[73]

The worst was yet to come, however. In July of the same year Abdel Karim Qasim led a *coup d'état* in Iraq that overthrew the Hashemite monarchy and established the republic. The coup was supported by Iraqi communists who, together with Qasim and their comrades in the UAR, opposed unity with Egypt and attacked Nasser. The last, who was seen by communists as a symbol of Egyptian bourgeoisie attempting to impose its vision on Syria, was disenchanted with the Iraqi revolution, after initially hoping it would bring Iraq to join the UAR. What ensued was a 'Cairene crusade against communism and communists. The largest-scale arrest in the history of Egyptian communists occurred on 28 March 1959.'[74] Indeed, it was a great opportunity for Nasser to halt the growth of one of his two biggest enemies among the political parties, second only to the Muslim Brotherhood. After all, 'communism . . . was not simply an ideology differing on this and that point from Nasser's brand of revolutionary nationalism, but something much worse; an organised movement in competition with his own, and outside his control'.[75]

A turbulent year it was, its repercussions going far beyond the Middle East to include realignments and shifts in the stance towards the United States and the USSR. Not all Egyptian communists viewed unity unfavourably, however, and al-Shafi'i was a notable example. Indeed, all the writers who documented the case of al-Shafi'i agreed unanimously on his support for and belief in Nasser. Sonallah Ibrahim relays this dialogue between al-Shafi'i and one of his jailers:

> 'Are you a communist, you bastard? Say: I am a woman.'
>
> 'This is shame, and your behaviour harms the regime. We are nationalist forces, and we are not against the government. Even if we were, you could not just act so monstrously. We have opinions, we support the revolution, and President Nasser himself knows that.'[76]

Exempting Nasser, that is. This attitude by which Nasser is distanced from the excesses and abuses of his regime is typical of the attitude of Egyptian communists who suffered from their impact. Unlike the Muslim Brothers, who believed Nasser was an evil,[77] most Egyptian communists who were imprisoned and tortured between 1959 and 1964 remained faithful to Nasser and the revolution, so much so that, after their release, they chose to dissolve their party and opted to work within the state's organisations. True, dozens of books were written levelling harsh criticism against the officers and intelligence apparatus but Nasser himself remained, for the most part, beyond suspicion. Egyptian journalist 'Adil Hammuda (b.1948), commenting on suppressing the students' movement in 1968 by then Secretary of State, Sha'rawi Jum'a, expresses this somewhat incredible belief in Nasser, rather emotionally:

> We were not against Nasser. We never attacked him, never chanted '*Irhal*', never demanded his fall . . . What we only wanted was to send him an urgent 'telegram', from his sons in the University of Cairo to his house in Manshiyyat al-Bakri . . . Alas, the telegram did not reach him, or it was maybe distorted, after the apparatuses had added a line or scratched another.[78]

Communists' faith in the revolution was unfathomable to some, given the amount of torture and suffering they faced at the hands of its actors. They were accused of being masochists who 'find pleasure in the torment that was poured on them'.[79] The justification was that Nasser's revolution could not just be reduced to torture and prisons, even though they themselves were among its victims. Rather, positive and negative aspects should all be contextualised to inform a better understanding of Nasser's movement, transcend its shortcomings, and continue its progressive projects.[80]

Still, the case of Shuhdi al-Shafi'i reached a mythical vindication of Nasser. He and forty-eight of his incarcerated comrades (the most famous of whom is Sonallah Ibrahim) were sent to court in what was referred to as the 'Case of the Forty-Eight', for they all were members of HADITO, the Democratic Movement for National Liberation.[81] The trial took place through the first half of 1960, with the defendants making several appearances in court. It was al-Shafi'i who delivered a self-defence speech before the court on 8 March. *Al-Tali'a's* issue on al-Shafi'i left us with a few passages from the transcript of this speech, in which al-Shafi'i declared:

> Am I on trial merely for embracing communist principles, as the prosecution goes? Would I be charged for that, even if it was proved to the court that I support the regime and do not seek to overthrow it? It is impossible. No state would charge people for their principles. President Nasser himself said that there could not be a trial for one's beliefs and principles.[82]

Al-Shafi'i and the other defendants were moved from al-Wahat into Abu Za'bal prison where, on 15 June, he died owing to severe torture at the hands of prison officers.

'He died while screaming, "For Nasser's sake, please".'[83] Thus record most of the accounts of al-Shafi'i's final words before he was pronounced dead, overheard by those who were close to his cell. Ever since that time, al-Shafi'i was referred to as the martyr 'who died while chanting, "long live Nasser!"'[84] He was killed 'while defending the regime and the leader of the regime'.[85] The news of al-Shafi'i's death was shocking and frightening, no less than the accounts of his belief in Nasser right up to the last. It was perhaps in a subconscious attempt to fathom such an opaque relationship with Nasser that Sonallah Ibrahim writes, in one of his random diaries in prison:

> A large number of old Bolsheviks who were detained and mistreated remained certain that they were persecuted without [Stalin's] knowledge. They never recognised that it was Stalin himself who ordered their arrest. After returning from torture sessions, many of them would write with their blood, on the walls of their cells, 'long live Stalin'.[86]

It was thanks to al-Shafi'i's wife, Roxani Petredes, that the news of his death was made public. Petredes followed the prison car that moved the inmates to Abu Zaʻbal prison, and learnt about her husband's fate from the prison guards.[87] Five days later, she was able to publish an obituary in none other than the regime's own paper of record, *al-Ahram*.[88] At the time, Nasser was on an official visit to Yugoslavia. There are different accounts regarding how Nasser learned of the incident. Tahir Abdel Hakim, himself a prisoner during the same era, reports that al-Shafiʻi's wife sent a telegram to Nasser, protesting at her husband's death.[89] Unfortunately, no record of that telegram was kept. On the other hand, Muhammad Hasanayn Haykal says it was he who first relayed the news to Nasser.[90] Worse still, other accounts have Nasser completely surprised when some Yugoslavian journalists asked him about al-Shafiʻi's death. Egyptian journalist Mahmud al-Saʻdani (1928– 2010) even says that 'Nasser, attending a parliament session in Yugoslavia, was astonished when a member asked for a minute of silence, mourning the activist Shuhdi ʻAtiyya who fell as a martyr in one of Egypt's prisons'.[91] At any rate, Nasser's public reaction was instantly to order an investigation. His more private one, however, was reported by Haykal:

> Having heard the story, Nasser's outrage was overwhelming. He picked up the phone and called the secretary of state, relaying to him what he had learnt from me, before adding verbatim, 'if this could happen in the time of the revolution, then it would be more honest to end this and go back to our homes. By Allah, King Farouk's era would be seen as better.'[92]

Whether Nasser had heard of al-Shafiʻi prior to the latter's death is left to speculation. Also uncertain are the circumstances of the unrequited epistolary between them. Did al-Shafiʻi try to sneak the letter out of prison with some guards? Did it reach Nasser's hands or, for that matter, any of his men? Haykal does not say a word, nor does he even allude to the letter. Aside from mentioning there was a letter, Sonallah Ibrahim and other eyewitnesses, who were al-Shafiʻi's prison mates at the time, offer no more. Unlike Abdel Quddous's letter, for which we have the sender's full disclosure regarding its circumstances, little, if anything, is known about al-Shafiʻi's, apart from the date (September 1959, a few months before the beginning of his trial), and the text of the letter.

Interestingly, the letter begins by negotiating the meaning of writing to Nasser. After addressing the letter to 'Mr President Gamal Abdel Nasser', al-Shafi'i, an advocate of democracy and the rule of law, seems aware of the separation of power that is (should be?) ruling the Egyptian political scene. 'The decision in my case must be left to the court,'[93] he writes, adding that it is only because he senses a bigger conspiracy against all progressive forces in Egypt and, consequently, the revolution itself that he seeks to write to Nasser. Al-Shafi'i is keen to show that he does not perceive the whole case personally, for it is 'not merely a trial for one individual charged with a punishable act by the penal code'.[94] He feels 'compelled to write', the letter goes on, 'whatever risk this may incur'.[95] What kind of risk comes with writing to Nasser is undeclared, though it could be guessed that he fears the letter might be intercepted by the guards before reaching Nasser, as will be shown below.

The letter then proceeds with a detailed exposition of the circumstances: the dispute between Iraq and Egypt, the role of reactionary forces in incitement against communists, and the last's stance through it all. Al-Shafi'i's main objective is to affirm the identification between Nasser's and Egyptian communists' views, so much so that someone who is accustomed to Nasser's rhetoric and terminology could see him in the letter. It is 'the reactionary forces' who sow the seeds of discord: 'imperialism', 'Zionism', 'the followers of colonialism', 'the Saudi regime', and 'the Hashemites of Jordan' who, among others, are spreading lies about 'the most sincere supporters of the national regime, and the most enthusiastic who call for the people to unite around Nasser's leadership, not only of the republic, but of the entire Arab East'.[96]

Interspersed in the letter are references to several of Nasser's decisions and speeches that al-Shafi'i glorifies. Whether it is 'your wonderful speech in the conference of November 1958', or 'your remarkable law on limiting companies' profits that was issued early 1959', al-Shafi'i appears eager to prove both his acquaintance with, and endorsement of, Nasser's actions.

Al-Shafi'i's strategy of declaring allegiance to Nasser follows other patterns. For instance, he seeks to prove that the only people who benefited from the crackdown on Egyptian communists were the communists' and Nasser's shared enemies, both locally (the feudalists, the Right, reactionary periodicals such as *Akhbar al-Yawm*) and regionally (Jordanian, Saudi, and Tunisian regimes). More significantly, al-Shafi'i enumerates the communists' basic views and principles, one by one, only to show that 'this is our politics, and that is its application. It perfectly complies with your liberational, nationalist policies, for we are not concerned now with applying socialism, but rather with carrying out what the July Revolution started'.[97]

Nowhere in the letter does al-Shafi'i attribute the crackdown, arrest, or torture to Nasser personally. The letter is not meant to tell Nasser that what *he* had done is wrong and unjustified. Rather, al-Shafi'i mostly employs the passive voice in order to describe that he 'will be presented to the court', or that communists 'are placed under accusations'. Nasser's agency is only invoked towards the end of the letter when al-Shafi'i affirms that it is only the former who can rectify the situation, 'put an end to our trial, and stop the campaign against us'.[98] Nor does al-Shafi'i even allude to any possible transformation in the communists' stance towards Nasser and the regime after their arrest. Doubtless, they had grievances but this would never change their convictions about the righteousness of Nasser. 'What was our position', al-Shafi'i wonders rhetorically,

> despite being arrested, despite all the violence and the fatigue that we went through? Was not this an ordeal, a harsh ordeal? Yet, this did not budge our belief in your patriotism, and our confidence in you as a leader for this Arab East. Our policies and principles are the same, untouched, based on uniting people around you and your national rule.[99]

The closing paragraph epitomises very well al-Shafi'i's ultimate belief in Nasser, personalising the exchange to its maximum. Having acknowledged his uncertainty regarding the identity of the first person who would read the letter, al-Shafi'i wonders beseechingly whether Nasser 'could send a trusted delegation so that I could confide in him what is there in my heart, the gratitude that I cannot scribe in such a letter'.[100] Al-Shafi'i is seeking to bring Nasser closer to him by meeting one of Nasser's men whom the communists could trust. He realises the limitations of the letter as a medium, worrying that an unwanted party could interfere. He therefore wishes to move from writing into speaking to the president – or any of the president's men, at least, trusting that such an opportunity would surely draw a swifter end to his suffering. Alas, al-Shafi'i's suspicion about the letter's limitations was proven true. Yet, although it did not save him, as he wished, the letter remained evidence of a desperate attempt to reach Nasser, turn him into an audience, and, more significantly, tell him: if only you knew.

Letters in Fiction

Unlike other traditions, in which 'a full-length story consisting of nothing but letters'[101] exists, modern Arabic fiction hardly witnessed an epistolary novel. There is no Arabic equivalent of Choderlos de Laclos's *Les Liaisons Dangereuses*, Goethe's *Die Leiden des jungen Werthers*, or Saul Bellow's *Herzog*, to name a few prominent examples. Nor do letters feature frequently in Arabic fiction.[102] In fact, the tradition of employing the letter form as a narrative vehicle has significantly abated across cultures throughout the twentieth century. Whereas the letter was seen as a valuable narrative strategy in the eighteenth and nineteenth centuries, 'a thoroughly and consistently employed epistolary method has little chance of heightening the illusion of reality in a novel of our own time'.[103] In fact, one of the most notable incidents in modern Arabic literature where a fiction writer was involved in letter writing occurred outside the 'strict' realm of fiction. In 1993, famed Syrian writer Ghada al-Samman (b.1942) revealed what she claimed to be love letters that the late Palestinian writer Ghassan Kanafani (1936–72) had penned to her.[104] As for her responses to Kanafani, al-Samman said she did not possess copies of them, and that the originals were held by an unknown third party following the assassination of Kanafani in 1972.

There are, however, a few notable occurrences of employing the letter form in modern Arabic fiction. Among them, writing to Nasser features, where a character in a novel or a short story feels the need to pen a letter to the president. Those works emerged long after al-Yusuf's letter, which was discussed earlier, with the first occasion taking place – strangely enough – in 1967. A major question then arises: were those fiction writers influenced by previous non-fiction letter writing to Nasser? If so, what were the main sites of influence: format, theme, and so on? Although those works are presented as fiction, Nasser does not come out reimagined or fictionalised. Rather, he is the same historical Nasser. In other words, Nasser here is a flat character, born developed and complete. Invoking Nasser is therefore invoking all the associations that his name suggests.

In what follows, I shall examine three remarkable examples in Egyptian fiction where Nasser features as an addressee: Abdel Rahman al-Sharqawi's (1920–87) *Al-Fallah* (the Peasant); Salwa Bakr's (b.1949) *Zeinat fi Janazat al-Ra'is* (Zeinat at the President's Funeral); and Radwa Ashour's (1946–2014) *Faraj*. I am less concerned with discussing the work as a whole than with approaching the position that the letter writing occupies. My reading, therefore, is meant to be specific, highlighting the letter, its structure, sender(s), and their views on Nasser.

Let's All Write to Nasser

The publication of Abdel Rahman al-Sharqawi's novel *Al-Fallah* (the Peasant) in 1967 marks the first incident of turning Nasser into an audience in a work of fiction. Legitimately, one can wonder why it took so long before the already known mode of writing to Nasser inspired fiction writers. We need not forget, however, that Nasser in fact rarely appeared in a work of fiction during his life. Whether it was self-censorship, the ambivalent stance that writers had towards him, or the feeling that his experience was not yet *fictionalisable*, fiction writers in the 1950s and the 1960s have by and large avoided explicit reference to Nasser.[105]

Al-Fallah is al-Sharqawi's fourth and last novel.[106] Interestingly, but surely unintentionally, both al-Sharqawi's first and last novels coincided with the two most significant years in Nasser's life: 1952 and 1967. It is the 1952 one, however, *Al-Ard* (the Land), that established him as a leading fiction writer. Adapted into a celebrated Egyptian film by Youssef Chahine (1926–2008) in 1969, *Al-Ard* was a major intervention in modern Arabic literature for, with it, 'and perhaps for the first time in Arabic literature, the *fallah* is written as a revolutionary historical agent and as the fully articulated subject of narrative'.[107] The novel was an instant critical success, hailed as a fine example of social realism. It was al-Sharqawi's only novel to be translated into English.[108]

But if *Al-Ard*, which represents the pre-1952 village, reinterprets it as a site of social struggle in a feudal system, *Al-Fallah* revisits the same geographical entity, albeit differently. It features the village as a space for struggle between the real, committed revolutionary peasants on the one hand and, on the other, those who are remnants of the old system, the counter-revolution figures, and the beneficiaries who pretend to be on the side of the 23 July movement but who are, in fact, among its worst outcomes. The novel is narrated by an intellectual who returns to his village after years of living in Paris. Punctuated by the various attempts of the peasants to complain and protest against the behaviour of the revolution's men in the village, the novel opens with the unnamed narrator meeting his cousin, Abdel 'Azim, in Cairo where the latter seeks to meet the Minister of Agrarian Reform. It is in that first encounter that the narrator realises the progressive transformation that occurs in the consciousness of the semi-literate Abdel 'Azim after the revolution. Reflecting on Abdel 'Azim's repeated use of words such as 'reactionary', 'production', 'socialists', 'the mother land', among others, the narrator frequently asks himself, 'What is all this, Abdel 'Azim? Where did you learn that?'[109] The major event of the narrative occurs when Abdel 'Azim, along with another peasant, Abdel Maqsud, go to the city to meet its subcommittee of the Socialist Union. They disappear for months which leads the peasants to embark on a collective search for them.

Where does Nasser stand between those two warring groups? Following the same approach that was eminently manifested in al-Shafi'i's letter, the narrative discourse believes there are two governments competing to rule Egypt. The first is that of Nasser and the faithful men surrounding him, while the second consists of 'the remnants of feudalists, some members of the Socialist Union, and the security apparatus, who all compose a new class that receives high salaries and expresses interests that are radically antithetical to the new government's'.[110] The narrative abounds with this differentiation, as well as with the belief in the sincere intentions of Nasser, pronounced not only by the leaders among the peasants, such as Abdel 'Azim and Abdel Maqsud, but also by ordinary peasants like Um Insaf: 'How come all this could happen when we live in Nasser's time';[111] and Salim who, engaging in a heated dispute with the representative of the Socialist Union in the village, asks him, 'What are you going to do? Crucify me on a palm tree? This is something from the past. The president says, "Raise your head, brother".'[112]

Those same ordinary peasants back the idea of writing a letter to Nasser. The incident occurs in the midst of the village's aforementioned concerns about the fate of the two disappeared men. The news both enrages and worries the peasants who begin muttering about the possible reasons behind the disappearance, the kind of people whom the two men may have met in the city, and the potential danger they are probably encountering now. Unable to offer an answer, the peasants *collectively* suggest 'a quick telegram to President Gamal Abdel Nasser'.[113] The sentence opens a new passage in the novel, acting like a magic phrase that is surely seen to bring an end to the helplessness of the peasants' situation. What proceeds highlights not the letter per se but *the process* of writing it. If the dominant concept of the letter posits it as a private site 'where the inner-life achieves self-expression in the search for truth',[114] then the peasants' action is a *collaborative act*, a public aggregation of efforts, money and, more significantly, words, all combined towards writing a letter to Nasser.

The first issue that the peasants raise is the obstacles that they have to overcome to send the letter: that is, how to send the letter undistorted. Owing to the fact that their village has no post office, the peasants suggest going to the neighbouring one, only to remember that 'the employee could reject [sending] the telegram', or that 'he could play with its words'.[115] The suggestion then is for the peasants themselves *collectively* to keep him under surveillance. In the midst of this, however, the semi-literate peasants encounter a more serious difficulty: who will write the letter for them? They first suggest that they should seek the assistance of some secondary school students, thereby unintentionally seeking to transform the letter writing from a 'solitary endeavor'[116] into an act of *writing by proxy*. They decide against it, however, empowered by the few literacy classes they take. The peasants then immerse themselves in discussions about what to write, introducing throughout other issues related to writing to the president. Curiously, their complete belief in Nasser notwithstanding, the peasants are also aware that only grave grievances should be sent to him – for minor problems, it is enough to inform the police. At first, the hierarchy impedes them, forcing them to reconsider the whole issue, with some backing the idea of writing to 'the Secretary of State'.[117] Nonetheless, Nasser, the person, triumphs eventually, for the overwhelming majority of the peasants decisively declare:

> We are writing a telegram to Nasser. Period. We have no one but him. We will complain to him about the guy who came from Cairo and claimed to represent the government, about the supervisor, and about the cooperative's employee. We will demand an urgent investigation. Needless to say, we will mention the disappearance of Abdel Maqsud and Abdel 'Azim. Of course. They have probably been kidnapped. Who knows? Maybe they arrested them. We will tell him everything. Other than Allah, we have no one but him.[118]

At play here are two capitals. First, the peasants' determination to send a telegram to Nasser reveals their moral capital, their profound belief not only in Nasser but in the legitimacy of their attempt to reach him. In other words, the peasants here do not beg, nor do they ask for gratuitous support from Nasser. Rather, they 'negotiate their status and rights as subjects of the state'.[119] As such, the peasants have a 'clear sense of entitlement'[120] to address Nasser. Contrary to this, however, the peasants lack the financial capital that will allow them to write freely to Nasser. If they are encouraged by their belief in Nasser, the way they view their relationship with him, and the legitimacy of their cause, to detail all the grievances in one telegram imposes a financial cost that bars them. They then have recourse to writing 'under erasure', as Linda Kauffman, commenting on Jacques Derrida's *The Post Card*, calls it.[121] It is not censorship, internal or external, nor political surveillance that obliges the peasants to erase some of their choices. Rather, it is their financial inadequacy that forces several among them to say, reacting to the statement quoted above: 'This would be too many words. You think these telegrams are free? Where could we get all the money that is needed for this? We shall say three word only: Oppressed, help us.'[122]

At the post office, the employee there still finds the need to correct the language errors in the telegram before telling the peasant that the money they have allows them up to fifteen words. To the reader's surprise, the novel does offer us the text of the actual telegram. Does it matter? It surely does but the collective negotiation and discussion that occupy the process of writing the letter enable us to predict it. Nor are we to find a direct reference to the letter afterwards. We merely read the narrator observing that 'the village sent a telegram to complain'.[123] Does the telegram reach Nasser? This is also left unanswered but we discover later that the disappeared men are released because of the great efforts that the village's students who live in the city exert in search of them.

Apart from the personal belief in Nasser, the peasants' letter seems antithetical to the previous, intellectual letters that we discussed earlier. If each of those letters was sent by one individual, the peasants' was a product of a collective endeavour, so much so that, when the post office employee asks them for their identification cards, he finds that 'no one has an ID'.[124] If the previous letters were pages, this was merely fifteen words. If earlier letters were written by intellectuals, this was scribed by semi-literates who first thought of asking for students' assistance. There was only one thing in common: Nasser. Trust in Nasser is what all of these letters boil down to – a trust, at the same time, in him and in their right to turn him into their reader.

Zeinat; or: Thanks for Responding, Nasser, but That Was Not Enough

Salwa Bakr's first short story collection, *Zeinat fi Janazat al-Ra'is* (Zeinat at the President's Funeral) (1986) announced the arrival of both a talented writer and the first Egyptian short story to revolve entirely around writing to Nasser. Bearing the title of the collection, *Zeinat fi Janazat al-Ra'is*, the story 'describes Zeinat's attempts to contact the president of the republic in order to obtain a government pension that she is legally owed'.[125] It is notable for what would become Bakr's major narrative attributes: her 'fascination with the practical problems faced by women like her mother: widows, divorcees, women who have never married, or women who are emotionally alienated from their husbands';[126] her 'articulation and dissemination of the suppressed discourse of women';[127] and her fusion of colloquial and standard Arabic in a way that renders the former 'proper' and the latter 'colloquialised', thereby producing what Ferial Ghazoul calls *balaghat al-ghalaba* (the rhetoric of the have-not).[128]

Set shortly before the death of Nasser in 1970, the story is inspired by Bakr's own observations of her mother's gathering with other widows in Cairo during the 1960s. Bakr relays how 'the old women, mostly illiterate, would ask a youth to write a letter on their behalf and send it to Nasser'.[129] What was fascinating, Bakr recalls, was the kind of requests and demands the women made. 'Tell Nasser that the train does not come on time. This does not help,' one woman would say. Still more personal, another would implore, *'winnabi*, my leg hurts me. What shall I do?' Bakr describes a mythical Nasser in which those old women believed, someone who was capable of performing miracles, healing sufferers, and bearing responsibility for every single detail of Egyptians' lives, however trivial.

The story features Zeinat, a poor, illiterate, lonely woman whose name, we are told, is always wrongly pronounced Zanat. She 'embodies the disappointment and broken dreams of a generation that hung its hopes on the revolution's promises'.[130] Zeinat seeks to overcome part of her destitute life by sending letters to Nasser. Resorting to letters, however, is a substitute for the impossible endeavour of reaching Nasser personally. Zeinat dreams of 'the chance to speak to him, and to tell him personally all that she wanted to'.[131] She first attempts to attain a middle ground whereby she can both write a letter and deliver it personally to Nasser. Knowing the streets that he passes by every Friday, she decides to approach him directly, and to give him a very brief letter, written on her behalf by a student, that states: 'Zeinat says hello and wants to find out what you did about the previous matter'.[132] It proves equally impossible, however, and her striving goes unrealised for, at the last minute,

> when she imagined that the president's car was close enough for her to step forward and quickly catch his attention, shake his hand, and deliver the note, she was taken aback by scores of rude hands of policemen and others in plain clothes who appeared in a flash, as if they had dropped from the sky, and shoved her away from the car and the procession. She fell on the ground and was surrounded by feet which Zeinat noticed were mostly covered with high leather boots, and some of which concealed enough guns to massacre a whole country.[133]

Unquestionably painful, the incident still does not affect Zeinat's love of Nasser and belief in him, as it surely 'had happened *behind the president's back*, and if he ever got wind of the doings of those bastards who prevented her from greeting him and delivering her letter, he would have undoubtedly banished them to a god-forsaken place'.[134] Only after the incident does Zeinat give up on both meeting Nasser and delivering a letter personally to him. Her third option is to request the assistance of her apparently only friend, 'Abdu the barber. Similar to the peasants' case in al-Sharqawi's novel, Zeinat establishes a paradigm of writing by proxy, whereby 'Abdu writes the letters, and Zeinat signs them by 'Abdu's '[careful] steadying [of] the pen between her fingers. He firmly held her hand with his own and moved both hands at the same time, so that she would actually have signed her own name.'[135]

Unique in this narrative is the fact that Zeinat's requests of the president are met. After a few months of anticipation, Zeinat 'had been granted a special pension, the sum of three pounds'.[136] Though we do not read them, the letters prove fruitful, and Zeinat now, 'brimming with confidence and proud of herself and of the president',[137] can go, at the beginning of every month, to receive her allowance. Not forgetting 'Abdu's invaluable assistance, she decides to present him with a 'pair of hefty chickens and a bottle of rose sherbet'.[138]

The correspondence does not end here, however. Now empowered by her successful endeavour, and fully aware of the influence of words, Zeinat determines to continue sending letters to Nasser. Advised by the second author of those letters, 'Abdu, Zeinat decides to 'magnify her grievances, to demand an increase in her pension on the grounds of being a lonely woman without a single soul to support her in the whole wide world, to listen to her grievances – except God and the president of the Republic'.[139] She acts accordingly, with 'Abdu outdoing his previous letters, this time by sharpening 'his wit, squeezing out the sap of his rhetorical talents in an attempt to induce the president to issue the necessary mandate to raise Zeinat's pension'.[140] Nonetheless, the letters go unheeded and, after sending nine of them, the narrator, who often adopts Zeinat's perspective, thinks that it must be 'the quality of 'Abdu's writing'[141] which is not persuasive enough to influence the president.

Nowhere in the letters that were studied earlier does the issue of language and formality emerge as urgently. Zeinat is not a passive author of her letters; she is an agent who fully participates in the way her ideas will take shape on the pages. In so doing, she prevents 'Abdu, the man, from dominating the sphere of writing, her inability to perform the actual writing down notwithstanding. In the process of writing the tenth letter, there emerges a disagreement between Zeinat and 'Abdu. While he 'tried to punctuate the conventional preamble he wrote each time – which consisted mainly of expressions of gratitude and laudatory remarks about the president of the Republic – with some of his own views on current political issues',[142] Zeinat refuses, offering a more direct way to address Nasser. As Hoda Elsadda observes, Zeinat

> questions the validity and sincerity of the formal stylised language used by 'Abdu, the barber, in writing letters on her behalf. In her last letter to the president she insists on telling her story in her own words, honestly and without recourse to formal stereotypes.[143]

Zeinat's perspective on the unnecessary embellishment of the letter is informed by her personalised relationship with Nasser, developing through sitting, day after day in front of the president's pictures that fill her shack, and talking to him. She does not see why she has to modify her way of addressing Nasser when her words are put down in a letter and, therefore, decides to 'come right out and tell him her innermost thoughts'.[144]

Justified as it may be, this view has still to appeal to 'Abdu, the actual scribe of the letter. He rejects it at first, considering this 'an affront to his own special skills',[145] before complying eventually, driven by a feeling that Zeinat's own words might actually find an ear. He therefore decides to write down 'every word Zeinat wanted to say to the president'.[146] The letter does not appear directly in the story but, rather, is reported by the narrator. Zeinat indulges in a semi-monologue, telling her story completely. Towards the end, she explains her motive behind writing to Nasser:

> She also told him that she was a lonely soul, and she would never extend her hand and beg for help, no matter what. She was asking him – the way a sister would ask her brother, the way children would ask their father, the way a person in need would ask a generous man of means – to raise her pension a little just to enable her to meet the bare necessities of life.[147]

Zeinat is not a beggar, then, for you do not beg when you ask money from your father. She seems 'to have taken paternalism for granted as a "natural" form of relations between the state and its subjects'.[148]

Assuming her letter reaches Nasser in the way her own words reach his picture, she intends to tell him what happened to her in his procession after that Friday prayer. This, however, requires the intervention of 'Abdu who, aware of the potential censorship, refuses to write these words and explains that 'if the letter were opened and read by someone else, it might not reach the president'.[149] The dynamics between their positions as author and scribe are further complicated towards the end of the letter when 'Abdu attempts once again to add some colour, this time a few verses of poetry that he still remembers from primary school. Zeinat, for her part, does not approve, reasoning that Nasser 'would understand the plain language, just the way it was – there was no need for poetry'.[150] 'Abdu has to agree, acknowledging again that he is not writing only for himself. In relation to this last letter, they both 'partook in writing it'.[151]

To Zeinat's astonishment, this earnest outpouring of the heart still does not bring a reaction from the president. Upon sending it, she seems assured of her success, 'certain that the president would respond and take the necessary measures to grant her request'.¹⁵² After all, what she sends him is '*kalam ma ba'dahu kalam*', the final words with nothing further to add. It is as though she believes this is the last time she will need to write to Nasser.

Indeed. A few days after Zeinat sends her last letter, an 'ominous day' befalls her and her fellow Egyptians. It is noteworthy that Zeinat is informed about Nasser's death through none other than 'Abdu himself. Instead of delivering the news which Zeinat is anticipating, that is, receiving a reply from Nasser, Zeinat observes 'Abdu running through the street 'with a blood-drained face, striking his face *like a woman* in mourning . . . 'Abdu screamed, "The man is dead! Listen everybody, the president is dead."'¹⁵³ If 'Abdu screams the news like a woman, Zeinat, on the other hand, subverts her conventional gender role in turn, chooses not to wail, and instead seizes 'Abdu's collar, saying, 'Shut up! Hold your tongue! Do not say these accursed words.'¹⁵⁴ Remarkably, the story juxtaposes Zeinat's full agency as author of her last letter to Nasser with the death of Nasser, 'her father and brother' as she refers to him earlier. Clearly, Zeinat does not kill the father nor does she under any circumstance intend to. The sheer synchronism of the two incidents, however, coupled with her and 'Abdu's reactions to Nasser's death, destabilises the gendered roles that are assigned to Egyptians in their relationships with him.

The death of Nasser is disastrous enough for Zeinat, as it is for most Egyptians at the time. It is more heartbreaking, however, that Zeinat never hears the voice of Nasser replying to her only attempt to write a letter on her own terms. Only through these lenses, I argue, do we gain a better understanding of the troubling scene at Nasser's funeral in which Zeinat, suddenly recalling her letter and pension,

> ran towards the coffin. She knocked against shoulders, arms and heads, but she had decided to take a close look at him, to touch him with her hand. The coffin came in sight and grew bigger and clearer. She threw herself forcefully between people, pushing away one here and another there, quite heedless of what might befall her. When she was just an inch away from the coffin, hands reached out to strike her, to prevent her. Suddenly, she felt the taste of salty blood on her lips and thought that she had lost her nose.¹⁵⁵

Is she only reacting to the fact that she will never get the pension of which she has been dreaming? The narrative itself suggests another possibility, when Zeinat recalls months (or years) later that what she had in mind at that moment is 'her long wait for his procession after the Friday prayers and what had happened to her then'.[156] Zeinat sees the funeral as her last chance to get an answer from Nasser. If she cannot talk to Nasser anymore, she can at least attempt to see him closely, to touch his body, itself a speaking entity that Egyptians have long been able to read and interpret in various ways.

Interestingly, the death of Nasser marks the end of Zeinat's resort to letters. Writing requires an addressee, a reader, a space that only Nasser is trusted enough to fill. With Sadat, words cease to help, change, or provoke. Ironically, Sadat, who often referred to himself as the Father of Egyptians, never sees his presumed children talking to him. Instead, the end of the story shows Zeinat's political awareness that 'leads her to take part in the Bread Riots of 1977, but she continues to pray for Nasser, clinging to the symbol of dreams and hopes and thereby representing the crisis of an entire generation.'[157] Whereas Zeinat's impoverished living conditions in the past are thought of as something personal, compelling her to write to Nasser and ask for individual help, they are now considered part of a collective crisis where words and letters do not belong, where only physical, somewhat violent, protests can cause the 'father' to hear. But, while 'talking' to Sadat in her own way, Zeinat, now detained at the police station for participating in the protests, ends her last words in the story with a tribute to Nasser: 'May God have mercy on your soul, our dear love'.[158]

I am Illiterate, *Ya* Abu Khalid

A more recently published example of fictionally writing to Nasser appeared in Radwa Ashour's 2008 novel, *Faraj*. It features a protagonist/narrator, Nada Abdel Qadir who, in a non-linear narrative, tells fragments of her story against the historical background of Nasser's, Sadat's, and Mubarak's eras. Like most of Ashour's works, where there appears to be a 'blend of history and literature, and private and public events',[159] *Faraj* is full of references to real people who exist and interact alongside its supposed fictive characters. Whether with Abdel 'Azim Anis (1923–2009), a famed communist thinker whom Nada describes as her father's cellmate in prison[160] or with Arwa Salih (d.1997), a major figure in the Egyptian students' movement of the early 1970s who tragically committed suicide in 1997, *Faraj* 'links the specifics of characters' inner worlds with major social and economic phenomena and political events'.[161] Only in the last chapter of the novel does its title, Arabic for 'relief' or 'salvation', become explicable. In line with the fragmented nature of the narrative, the last chapter moves us suddenly to the notorious Tazmamart prison in Morocco where prisoners are surprised to find a small pigeon in their cell. Optimistically, they call it 'Faraj', feed it, and intend to set it free once it gathers its strength. And eventually, it does.[162]

It belongs elsewhere to discuss the representations of Nasser in this novel.[163] What is relevant to this chapter is the letter that is addressed to him. In fact, letters appear frequently in *Faraj*, often as a means to bridge the gaps, 'the constant separations endured by her characters'.[164] Nada receives a letter from Gerard, a French man she once met in Paris and liked;[165] she constantly pens letters to her French mother, now in Paris following her divorce from Nada's father;[166] and she writes, but does not send, a letter to Hazim, her university boyfriend, exactly four months and ten days after his death, melancholically wondering why he could not have lived to see the day that Israel withdrew from South Lebanon.[167] Moreover, a chapter in *Faraj* is entitled 'A Letter Incomplete' in which we read a long letter that Nada's mother means to send to her daughter, except that she never finishes it.[168] An attempt to explain the mother's decision to withdraw from Nada's life, to turn inwards and never contact her daughter again, the letter is found among the papers that Nada collects after her mother's death.

The letter to Nasser, on the other hand, is sent by her illiterate aunt, protesting against the arrest of her brother (Nada's father), Dr Abdel Qadir Salim, in 1959. In that sense, the letter is meant to suggest that Salim was jailed along with Shuhdi al-Shafi'i. Yet, unlike the case of al-Shafi'i, we never hear Dr Salim speaking to Nasser. Instead, well into the second half of *Faraj*, and years after her brother dies, Nada's aunt, whose name is not disclosed, reveals to her niece that she once wrote a letter to Nasser. The news comes as a surprise to Nada who asks her aunt if she still has a copy of it. She does not but, amazingly, she still knows it by heart. It was argued earlier that, unlike the letters that were sent to Nasser by journalists or activists, the fictional works that we discuss in this chapter feature illiterate people asking others' assistance in writing to Nasser. *Faraj* is no exception. Unlike Zeinat, however, Nada's aunt writes a letter only once. If Zeinat personally intervenes and partakes only in writing the tenth letter, demanding a change in its cliché phrases and formality, Nada's aunt seems aware from the onset of the need to address Nasser unconventionally. She informs her niece:

> I dictated it to four persons. I asked each one of them to read me what he had written, and found *kalam jarayid*, the speech of newspapers and radios. I do not work in a radio station nor in a newspaper. They wrote what I had not said: now the 'immortal leader', another 'the leader of the millions', still other big words that I do not understand. I said, 'Hey, kids, these are not my words.' I then called the youngest kid who was in elementary school, and said, 'Write my words verbatim. Write them *bi al-nahwi*, [in grammatically sound Arabic] but do not add or delete a word.'[169]

Entering the realm of writing, the old woman reveals an understanding that Egyptian colloquial does not belong. The reason behind preferring the standard over the colloquial is never explained by the aunt; it is, in fact, surprising, given that Nasser himself has frequently addressed his people in Egyptian dialect. Possibly, the aunt feels a need to add more 'linguistic capital' to her letter. This sole impersonal element in the letter is nonetheless disclosed to Nasser towards the end of it when the aunt admits, in a precedent unseen in all the letters we have discussed thus far, that she is actually illiterate. To dispel any doubts Nasser may have about the authenticity of the letter, the aunt quickly adds, 'I dictated this letter to my youngest son, who transformed it, with my approval, to the *nahwi*, not adding or deleting anything from it. I then asked him to read it, to make sure he conveyed my words honestly.'[170]

Aside from the illiteracy of the sender, the aunt's letter differs from Zeinat's and the peasants' in the ambivalent stance it adopts towards Nasser's responsibilities. If the peasants fully believe that Nasser does not know about the injustice that some of his men are inflicting upon them, and if Zeinat takes Nasser as her sole supporter in this world save God, the aunt is somewhat less certain. While she strongly demands that Nasser scrutinises 'the justice of the judge who ordered [her brother's] arrest and the validity of the documents that considered what he did a crime punishable by imprisonment',[171] thereby indicating that Nasser has nothing to do with it, she nevertheless holds Nasser accountable:

> I am the sister of Dr Abdel Qadir Salim, who first went to the *kuttab*, then learnt in schools, then entered the university, before going abroad to France, pursuant to the Holy Prophet's saying, 'seek knowledge, even if it is in China'. When he came back, and began teaching in the university and taking part in what is in the country's interests, *you* put him in prison.[172]

In yet another instance, she accepts that Nasser becomes the arbitrator in the issue, justifying it, interestingly, by stating, 'I accept you as a president of the country. How would not I accept your judgment in my brother's case?'[173]

Also unique to this letter is addressing Nasser with his *kunya*, Abu Khalid. The *kunya* usually adds intimacy to a conversation, indicating both respect and friendliness. Abu Khalid occurs three times in the letter, the first of which is in the first line:

> President Abu Khalid, Gamal Abdel Nasser.
> Son of Bani Murr, President of Egypt and Syria.[174]

The 'Bani Murr', mentioned above, is the name of the village where Nasser was born in Asyut. The letter cunningly juxtaposes the fact that Nasser comes from this tiny village with the prestige of his current position as president of the United Arab Republic. It reminds him of his simple past, obliquely suggesting that he is a normal Egyptian, 'one of us', with no special merits that place him above any of his subjects.

Unlike Zeinat, who seeks a purely personal aid from Nasser, the aunt is keen to expose that she is not only concerned with her brother's arrest. On the contrary, reminiscent of the letter of Ruz al-Yusuf, it is the desire to assist 'Abu Khalid' that compels her to write: to assist him so that he 'will not bear the burden of an unjust judge nor a haughty officer'[175] but, more importantly, to assist Egypt as a whole. 'My brother, along with the other young prisoners, are good for the country,' she states.[176] How then, she asks, can Nasser put them in jail, barring them from offering their knowledge to their country?

The letter is short, precise, and to the point. It does not indulge in personal details nor does it implore Nasser or employ sentimental words. The president does not appear here as a mythical figure. His pictures are not hung in the aunt's house. Rather, the aunt treats herself as an equal part of the correspondence, explicitly stating that 'we never lower our heads save for our creator, and only request that which is our right'.[177] Yet, she still cannot conceal her belief that Nasser will surely cause the truth to triumph. When Nada asks her if Nasser has responded to her letter, she says that she has received a reply from his office, stating that they will investigate the issue. 'I waited,' she continues, 'after a long wait I said, "Either he received the letter and got too busy, or *they* withheld it from him."'[178] She confesses to Nada that that was her wishful thinking at the time, for she loves Nasser. She further admits that this is just 'an excuse I came up with to forgive him!'[179]

Conclusion

Rather than being exclusively listeners to Nasser, Egyptians have occasionally assumed the role of the addresser, turning their president into an audience. Empowered by a personal belief in Nasser, they employed the letter as a medium to establish contact with him. Interspersed in these letters were references to the ideals, hopes, and aspirations about which Nasser himself frequently spoke. As this chapter has demonstrated, these letters often separated Nasser from his regime, whereby he was sought to rectify the injustice that the senders have experienced at the hands of the regime. Similarly, Nasser was believed to be unaware of those abuses, and Egyptians presented their letters as sources revealing a reality otherwise unknown to him. Seldom did any of these senders hold Nasser responsible for their maltreatment nor did they announce their disenchantment with him. Rather, they often invoked Nasser's sincerity, decency, and integrity as incentives that compelled them to consider him as their audience.

As the previous pages have shown, there were two kinds of letter writing to Nasser. First, independent letters that were written by intellectuals, journalists, and activists, and were published either as a public correspondence during Nasser's life or in book form following his death; second, letters employed as a technique by protagonists in Egyptian fiction in order to reach Nasser. The six instances of letter writing that have been analysed in this chapter did not fall into one single format. While some letters were sent by an individual, others, such as that of the peasants in Abdel Rahman al-Sharqawi's *Al-Fallah*, were the product of a collective endeavour. In addition, whereas the intellectuals obviously wrote their letters themselves, fiction letters were all examples of *writing by proxy*, where the illiterate sender seeks someone to write on his/her behalf. Still more divergent is the extent of formality or informality that the letters followed, with some, such as the aunt in Radwa Ashour's *Faraj* going so far as to resort to terms of endearment in addressing the president. What all these letters shared, however, was Nasser – a man in whom the senders can believe, trust, and confide. As Nasser and his legacy have been significantly reinvigorated in the past few years in Egypt,[180] one waits impatiently to see if the tradition of Nasser as an audience will live on and inspire still more instances of writing to him.

Notes

1. Fu'ad Matar, *Bi Saraha 'an Abdel Nasser: Hiwar ma' Muhammad Hasanayn Haykal* (Beirut: Dar al-Qadaya, 1975), p. 140.
2. Robert Stephens, *Nasser: A Political Biography* (New York: Simon and Schuster, 1971), p. 195.
3. Aburish, *Nasser: The Last Arab*, p. 296.
4. For more on Nasser's 'resignation speech', see Chapter 4, pp. 187–96.
5. Georges Corm, *Infijar al-Mashriq al-'Arabi: min Ta'mim Qanat al-Suwis ila Ijtiyah Lubnan* (Beirut: Dar al-Tali'a, 1987), p. 27.
6. Marina Stagh, *The Limits of Freedom of Speech: Prose Literature and Prose Writers in Egypt Under Nasser and Sadat* (Stockholm: Almqvist & Wiksell International, 1993), p. 128.
7. See David A. Gerber, 'Epistolary Masquerades: Acts of Deceiving and Withholding in Immigrant Letters', in *Letters across Borders: The Epistolary Practices of International Migrants*, eds Bruce S. Elliott et al. (New York: Palgrave Macmillan, 2006), p. 151.
8. Altman, *Epistolarity*, p. 51, emphasis mine.
9. Franz Kafka, *Letters to Milena*, quoted in Altman, *Epistolarity*, p. 2.
10. Linda S. Kauffman, *Discourses of Desire: Gender, Genre, and Epistolary Fictions* (Ithaca, NY and London: Cornell University Press, 1986), p. 17.
11. Altman, *Epistolarity*, p. 12
12. Ibid., p. 69.
13. See the letter that poet 'Afifa al-Hisni wrote to Nasser in the appendix of her elegiac collection of poems, *Shahid al-Tadhiyat* (Cairo: Matabi' al-Nashir al-'Arabi, 1070), pp. 68–70.

14. Jürgen Habermas, *The Structural Transformation of the Public Sphere: an Inquiry into a Category of Bourgeois Society*, trans. Thomas Burger (Cambridge, MA: The MIT Press, 1991), p. 48.
15. Ibid.
16. Ibid., p. 49.
17. Ann Goldberg, 'Reading and Writing across the Borders of Dictatorship: Self-Censorship and Emigrant Experience in Nazi and Stalinist Europe', in *Letters Across Borders*, p. 166. For more on Habermas, the letter, and the public sphere see Taylor, *Modern Social Imaginaries*, pp. 84–99, and Warner, *Publics*, pp. 46–56.
18. Shrines of religious figures are often found in mosques, and the people who look after mosques are referred to as *Khadim al-Masjid*, or the 'servant of the mosque'.
19. See Sayyid 'Uways, *Min Malamih al-Mujtama' al-Misri al-Mu'asir: Zahirat Irsal al-Rasa'il ila Darih al-Imam al-Shafi'i* (Cairo: Al-Markiz al-Qawmi li al-Buhuth al-Ijtima'iyya wa al-Jina'iyya, 1965), pp. 19–29.
20. Sayyid 'Uways, *Al-Khulud fi Hayat al-Misriyyin al-Mu'asirin* (Cairo: Al-Hay'a al-Misriyya al-'Amma li al-Kitab, 1972), p. 26.
21. Sayyid 'Uways, *Hadith 'an al-Thaqafa: Ba'd al-Haqa'iq al-'Ilmiyya al-Mu'asira* (Cairo: Maktabat al-Anjlu al-Misriyya, 1970), p. 60.
22. For more on the role of epistolary art in the emergence of an Egyptian public sphere see Boutheina Khaldi, 'Epistolarity in a "Nahḍa" Climate: The Role of Mayy Ziyadah's Letter Writing', *Journal of Arabic Literature*, Vol. 40, No. 1 (2009), pp. 1–36.
23. See Ibrahim 'Abdu, *Ruz al-Yusuf: Sira wa Sahifah* (Cairo: Mu'assasat Sijill al-'Arab, 1961), and *Ruz al-Yusuf: 80 Sanat Sihafa*, ed. Khalid 'Azab (Alexandria: Maktabat al-Iskandariyya, 2006).
24. 'Abdu, *Ruz al-Yusuf*, pp. 19–21.
25. See Amirah Abu al-Futuh, *Ihsan Abdel Quddous Yatadhakkar* (Cairo: Al-Hay'a al-Misriyya al-'Amma li al-Kitab, 1982), p. 82.
26. Aburish, *Nasser*, p. 33.
27. Yusuf al-Qaid, *Muhammad Hasanayn Haykal Yatadhakkar: Abdel Nasser wa al-Muthaqqafun wa al-Thaqafa* (Egypt: Dar al-Shuruq, 2003), pp. 69–70.
28. Mustafa Abdel Ghani, *Al-Muthaqqafun wa Abdel Nasser* (Kuwait: Dar Su'ad al-Sabah, 1993), pp. 411–12.
29. Ibid.
30. Ruz al-Yusuf, 'Khitab Maftuh ila Gamal Abdel Nasser', *Majallat Ruz al-Yusuf*, Cairo: No. 1300 (11 May 1953).

31. See Lynne Magnusson, 'Widowhood and Linguistic Capital: The Rhetoric and Reception of Anne Bacon's Epistolary Advice', *English Literary Renaissance*, 31, No. 1 (2001), pp. 3–33.
32. Al-Yusuf, 'Khitab Maftuh,' emphasis mine.
33. Ibid.
34. Ibid.
35. Ibid., emphasis mine.
36. Ibid.
37. Ibid., emphasis mine.
38. Linda S. Kauffman, *Special Delivery: Epistolary Modes in Modern Fiction* (Chicago, IL and London: University of Chicago Press, 1992), p. 103.
39. Gamal Abdel Nasser, 'Al-Khayt al-Rafi' bayna al-Hurriyya wa al-Fawda', *Majallat Ruz al-Yusuf*, Cairo: No. 1301 (18 May 1953).
40. Ibid.
41. Ibid.
42. Ibid., emphasis mine.
43. Ibid.
44. Altman, *Epistolarity*, p. 121.
45. Ibid., p. 117.
46. Muhammad Misba'i, *Surat al-Mar'a fi Riwayat Ihsan* Abdel Quddous (Algeria: Dar al-Qasaba li al-Nashr, 2000), p. 18. For more on Abdel Quddous's fiction, see, for example, 'Isa al-Na'uri, *Udaba' min al-Sharq wa al-Gharb* (Beirut: Manshurat 'Uwaydat, 1977); Ghali Shukri, *Azmat al-Jins fi al-Qissa al-'Arabiyya* (Beirut: Dar al-'Afaq al-Jadida, 1987); and Mahmud Amin al-'Alim and Abdel 'Azim Anis, *Fi al-Thaqafa al-Misriyya* (Egypt: Dar al-Fikr al-Jadid).
47. Yahya Haqqi, *Khatawat fi al-Naqd* (Egypt: Maktabat Dar al-'Uruba, 1961), p. 171.
48. Ihsan Abdel Quddous, 'Hal Qara'a Abdel Nasser Hadhihi al-Risala?', in *'Asif Lam A'ud Astati'* (Cairo: Muntasir, 1980), p. 6.
49. Ibid., p. 7.
50. Ibid., p. 6.
51. Joel Gordon, *Revolutionary Melodrama: Popular Film and Civic Identity in Nasser's Egypt* (Chicago, IL: Middle East Documentation Center, 2002), p. 225. For more on this, see Chapter 4, pp. 172–7.
52. Abdel Rahman Abu 'Awf, *Ihsan Abdel Quddous bayna al-Sahafa wa al-Riwaya* (Cairo: Al-Majlis al-A'la li al-Thaqafa, 2006), p. 145.

53. Mahmud Murad, *I'tirafat Ihsan* Abdel Quddous: *al-Hurriyya . . . al-Jins* (Cairo: Al-'Arabi li al-Nashr wa al-Tawzi', 1980), p. 52.
54. Muhammad Abdel Quddous, *Hikayat Ihsan* Abdel Quddous (Cairo: Al-Hay'a al-Misriyya al-'Amma li al-Kitab, 2011), pp. 95–7.
55. Murad, *I'tirafat Ihsan*, p. 50.
56. A Turkish word that means 'sir'.
57. Murad, *I'tirafat Ihsan*, p. 52.
58. Abdel Quddous, 'Hal Qara'a Abdel Nasser Hadhihi al-Risala?', p. 6.
59. Ibid.
60. See Ihsan Abdel Quddous, *Khawatir Siyasiyya* (Cairo: Muntasir, 1979).
61. Abdel Quddous, 'Hal Qara'a Abdel Nasser Hadhihi al-Risala?' p. 7.
62. Ibid., p. 9.
63. Ibid., p. 10.
64. Ibid., p. 11, emphasis mine.
65. Matar, *Bi Saraha*, pp. 179–80.
66. Abdel Quddous, 'Hal Qara'a Abdel Nasser Hadhihi al-Risala?' p. 8.
67. Ibid., p. 12, emphasis mine.
68. See *Al-Tali'a*, No. 1 (January 1975), pp. 82–113.
69. Qutb, arguably the most influential and controversial Islamist thinker of the twentieth century, was executed in Egypt in 1966. For a brief discussion of his thought, see Hamid Algar's introduction to Qutb's *Social Justice in Islam* (Oneonta, NY: Islamic Publications International, c.2000).
70. Sonallah Ibrahim, *Yawmiyyat al-Wahat* (Cairo: Dar al-Mustaqbal al-'Arabi, 2004), p. 27. Ibrahim was one of al-Shafi'i's inmates in prison. He would later dedicate a celebrated work of his, *Najmat Aghustus*, to the memory of al-Shafi'i.
71. On that specific campaign against Egyptian communists, see Ibrahim's *Yawmiyyat al-Wahat*; Ilham Sayf al-Nasr, *Fi Mu'taqal Abi Za'bal* (Cairo: Dar al-Thaqafa al-Jadida, 1977); Al-Sayyid Yusuf, *Mudhakkirat Mu'taqal Siyasi: Safha min Tarikh Misr* (Cairo: Al-Hay'a al-Misriyya al-'Amma li al-Kitab, 1999); and Fawzi Habashi, *Mu'taqal Kul al-'Usur: Hayati fi al-Watan* (Cairo: Dar Mirit, 2004). On Nasser and Egyptian communists see Tariq Y. Ismael and Rifa'at El-Sa'id, *The Communist Movement in Egypt, 1920–1988* (Syracuse, NY: Syracuse University Press, 1990); Selma Botman, *The Rise of Egyptian Communism, 1939–1970* (Syracuse, NY: Syracuse University Press, 1988); and Fakhri Labib, *Al-Shuyu'iyyun wa Abdel Nasser: Al-Tahaluf wa al-Muwajaha* (Cairo: Sharikat al-Amal li al-Tiba'a wa al-Nashr wa al-Tawzi', 1990).

72. Malcolm H. Kerr, *The Arab Cold War: Gamal 'Abd al-Nasir and His Rivals, 1958–1970* (London and New York: Oxford University Press, 1971), p. 18.
73. Anouar Abdel-Malek, *Egypt: Military Society, the Army Regime, the Left, and Social Change under Nasser*, trans. Charles Lam Markmann (New York: Random House, 1968), pp. 270–2.
74. Khayri 'Aziz, 'Abdel Nasser wa al-Ittihad al-Suvyati', in *Abdel Nasser wa ma Ba'd*, ed. Anis al-Sayigh (Beirut: Al-Mu'assasa al-'Arabiyya li al-Dirasat wa al-Nashr, 1980), p. 252.
75. Kerr, *The Arab Cold War*, p. 19.
76. Ibrahim, *Ayyam al-Wahat*, p. 228.
77. See my discussion of Zaynab al-Ghazali's autobiography in Chapter 3.
78. 'Adil Hammuda, *Azmat al-Muthaqqafin wa Thawrat Yulyo* (Cairo: Maktabat Madbuli, 1985), pp. 14–17.
79. Abu Sayf Yusuf, 'Likay la Yandam Ahad 'ala al-Haya,' appendix to Shuhdi 'Atiyya al-Shafi'i, *Tatawwur al-Haraka al-Wataniyya al-Misriyya, 1882–1956* (Cairo: Dar Shuhdi, 1983), p. 329.
80. See what Mahmud Amin al-'Alim, one of the most prominent Egyptian communists and intellectuals of the past century, and himself a prisoner during Nasser's era, had to say on this in 'Misr Abdel Nasser,' in *23 Yulyu: Khamsat Ab'ad* (Beirut: Dar al-Quds, 1974), pp. 29–52.
81. Labib, *Al-Shuyu'iyyun wa Abdel Nasser*, p. 417.
82. *Al-Tali'a*, p. 85.
83. Ibrahim, *Ayyam al-Wahat*, p. 228.
84. Salah 'Isa, *Muthaqqafun wa 'Askar* (Cairo: Maktabat Madbuli, 1986), p. 35.
85. From a letter sent by al-Shafi'i's wife to the head of the court on 1 July 1960. See *Al-Tali'a*, pp. 89–90.
86. Ibrahim, *Ayyam al-Wahat*, p. 83. In the footnotes, which were written at the time of publishing this book in 2004, Ibrahim, commenting on the entry above, says, 'Were I mindful, at the time when I wrote this, how much it could be applied to our situation in al-Wahat?' See p. 258.
87. Ibid., p. 33.
88. See the foreword that Sha'ban Yusuf wrote for al-Shafi'i's literary works which were published posthumously in a book entitled *Harat Umm al-Husayni wa Qisas Ukhra* (Cairo: Al-Majlis al-A'la li al-Thaqafa, 2009), pp. 5–6. Sonallah Ibrahim alludes to the fact that the censorship of newspapers did not include the obituaries section which therefore may have enabled Petredes to publish the obituary. See *Ayyam al-Wahat*, p. 33.

89. Tahir Abdel hakim, *Al-Aqdam al-'Ariya: al-Shuyu'iyyun al-Misriyyun, Khams Sanawat fi al-Sujun wa Mu'askarat al-Ta'dhib* (Beirut: Dar Ibn Khaldun, 1974), p. 184. Abdel Mun'im al-Ghazali, in the preface to *Al-Tali'a*'s issue, seconds this. See *Al-Tali'a*, p. 86.
90. Muhammad Hasanayn Haykal, *Li Misr, la li Abdel Nasser* (Cairo: Tawzi' al-Akhbar, 1976), p. 46.
91. Mahmud al-Sa'dani, *Al-Tariq ila Zimsh* (Cairo: Dar Akhbar al-Yawm, 1993), p. 176.
92. Haykal, *li Misr*, pp. 46–7.
93. The letter in *Al-Tali'a*, p. 91
94. Ibid.
95. Ibid.
96. Ibid., p. 92.
97. Ibid., p. 93.
98. Ibid.
99. Ibid.
100. Ibid.
101. Vivienne Mylne, *The Eighteenth-Century French Novel: Techniques of Illusion* (Cambridge and New York: Cambridge University Press, 1981), p. 144.
102. I am speaking here solely about modern Arabic fiction, and it belongs elsewhere to discuss the epistolary genre in classical Arabic literature. For more on this, see Thomas Hefter, *The Reader in al-Jahiz: The Epistolary Rhetoric of an Arabic Prose Master* (Edinburgh: Edinburgh University Press, 2014); and J. D. Latham, 'The Beginnings of Arabic Prose Genre: the Epistolary Genre', in *Arabic Literature to the End of the Umayyad Period*, eds A. F. L. Beeston et al. (Cambridge: Cambridge University Press, 1983), pp. 154–79.
103. Bertil Romberg, *Studies in the Narrative Technique of the First-Person Novel* (Folcroft PA, Folcroft Library Editions, 1974), p. 49.
104. See *Rasa'il Ghassan Kanafani ila Ghada al-Samman* (Beirut: Dar al-Tali'a li al-Tiba'a wa al-Nashr, 1999).
105. For more on this, see next chapter.
106. Mustafa Abdel Ghani, *Abdel Rahman al-Sharqawi: al-Dalala wa al-Shahada* (Cairo: Al-Majlis al-A'la li al-Thaqafa, 2010), p. 15.
107. Samah Selim, *The Novel and the Rural Imaginary in Egypt, 1880–1985* (New York and London: Routledge Curzon, 2004), p. 127.
108. The translation appeared as *Egyptian Earth* and was published by the University of Texas, Austin Press in 1990. It was translated by Desmond Stewart.

109. Abdel Rahman al-Sharqwi, *Al-Fallah* (Tunis: Mu'assasat Ibn 'Abdellah, 1975), pp. 5, 8, 19, respectively.
110. Samah Idris, *Al-Muthaqqaf al-'Arabi wa al-Sulta: Bahth fi Riwayat al-Tajriba al-Nasiriyya* (Beirut: Dar al-Adab, 1992), p. 83.
111. Al-Sharqawi, *Al-Fallah*, p. 109.
112. Ibid., pp. 128–9.
113. Ibid., p. 150.
114. Gerald MacLean, 'Re-sitting the Subject', in *Epistolary Histories: Letters, Fiction, Culture*, eds Amanda Gilory and W. M. Verhoeven (Charlottesville, VA and London: University of Virginia Press, 2000), p. 176.
115. Al-Sharqawi, *Al-Fallah*, p. 150.
116. Kauffman, *Special Delivery*, p. 55.
117. Al-Sharqawi, *Al-Fallah*, p. 153.
118. Ibid., p. 154.
119. Vadim Kukushkin, 'To His Excellency the Sovereign of all Russian Subjects in Canada: Emigrant Correspondence with Russian Consulates in Montreal, Vancouver, and Halifax, 1899–1922', in *Letters across Borders*, p. 295.
120. Ibid.
121. Kauffman, *Special Delivery*, p. 84.
122. Al-Sharqawi, *A-Fallah*, p. 154.
123. Ibid., p. 160, emphasis mine.
124. Ibid., p. 155.
125. Caroline Seymour-Jorn, *Cultural Criticism in Egyptian Women's Writing* (Syracuse, NY: Syracuse University Press, 2011), p. 26.
126. Ibid., p. 22.
127. See Hoda Elsadda's introduction to her own translation of Bakr's stories in *Such a Beautiful Voice, and Other Stories* (New Delhi: Kali for Women, 1994). I shall be relying on Elsadda's translation of '*Zeinat*'.
128. Ferial Ghazoul, 'Balaghat al-Ghalaba', in *Al-Fikr al-'Arabi al-Mu'asir wa al-Mar'a* (Cairo: Dar Tadamun al-Mar'a al-'Arabiyya, 1988), pp. 107–24.
129. In discussion with the author in Cairo, October 2011.
130. *Arab Women Writers: A Critical Reference Guide, 1873–1999*, eds Radwa Ashour et al. (Cairo and New York: The American University Press, 2008), pp. 139–40.
131. Bakr, '*Zeinat*', p. 22.
132. Ibid., p. 23.
133. Ibid.

134. Ibid., p. 24, emphasis mine. 'A godforsaken place' is how Elsadda renders *wara' al-shams*, the phrase that was commonly used to refer to the unknown destiny facing those who were imprisoned in Nasser's Egypt.
135. Ibid., p. 22.
136. Ibid., p. 25.
137. Ibid.
138. Ibid.
139. Ibid., p. 26.
140. Ibid.
141. Ibid.
142. Ibid., p. 27.
143. Elsadda, 'Introduction', in *Such A Beautiful Voice*, p. xix.
144. Bakr, '*Zeinat*', p. 27
145. Ibid.
146. Ibid., p. 28.
147. Ibid.
148. Kukushkin, 'To His Excellency the Sovereign', p. 295.
149. Bakr, '*Zeinat*', p. 28.
150. Ibid., p. 29.
151. Hoda Elsadda strangely leaves this phrase untranslated. See the Arabic in Salwa Bakr, *Zeinat fi Janazat al-Ra'is* (Cairo: s.n., 1986), p. 83.
152. Bakr, '*Zeinat*', p. 29.
153. Ibid., p. 30, emphasis mine.
154. Ibid.
155. Ibid., pp. 30–1.
156. Ibid., p. 31.
157. *Arab Women Writers*, eds Ashour et al., p. 140.
158. Bakr, '*Zeinat*', p. 31. The Arabic text actually reads, 'the beloved of all people'. See Bakr, *Zeinat fi Janazat al-Ra'is*, p. 85.
159. *Arab Women Writers*, eds Ashour et al., p. 136.
160. Radwa Ashour, *Faraj* (Cairo: Dar al-Shuruq, 2008), pp. 17–18.
161. Seymour-Jorn, *Cultural Criticism*, p. 111.
162. Ashour, *Faraj*, pp. 215–19.
163. See Chapter 3, pp. 125–9.
164. Seymour-Jorn, *Cultural Criticism*, p. 109.
165. Ashour, *Faraj*, p. 61.
166. Ibid., p. 66

167. Ibid., p. 173.
168. Ibid., pp. 140–5.
169. Ibid., p. 120.
170. Ibid., p. 121.
171. Ibid.
172. Ibid., p. 120, emphasis mine.
173. Ibid., p. 121.
174. Ibid., p. 120.
175. Ibid., p. 121.
176. Ibid.
177. Ibid.
178. Ibid., emphasis mine.
179. Ibid.
180. See the Epilogue, pp. 252–9.

2

Nasser as Fiction

Across the corpus of Egyptian literary narratives, one can identify two major approaches in which Nasser is inserted into the narrative. In the first approach Nasser is featured as part of a historical background against which the narrative unfolds. Interspersed in these narratives are references to Nasser, his legacy, physical and moral attributes, as well as his perspectives on matters concerning both Egypt and the rest of the world. These references are put forward in the dialogues that occur among the protagonists of the work, in their streams of consciousness, or by the omniscient narrator that the work may adopt. Nasser remains part of the historical setting, however, and does not enter the narrative as one of the characters. In other words, in these works Nasser is described, debated, denigrated, or glorified, yet he is not reimagined or fictionalised. Rather, his image is constructed insofar as the main protagonists' lives interact with, relate to, or are concerned with his. Falling into the famous dictum of Georg Lukács, these narratives represent Nasser 'as only a minor character compositionally, a figure described from the outside, in action, whose character is not developed throughout the novel, but whose presence, words, and actions have a significant effect on the other fictional characters'.[1]

In the second approach, Nasser himself is a main, if not *the* main, protagonist. Living side by side with other invented characters, Nasser emerges as a fictive figure whose external reference outside the text is recognisable yet whose actual representation in the text may drastically add to, differ from, or contradict this reference. By way of introducing him, explicitly or allegorically, these narratives open up a space for Nasser as fiction, as a literary character whose life becomes subject to 'conscious distortion of history through omissions, exaggerations, and anachronisms'.[2] In so doing, each narrative in this category may give us a Nasser of its own, a revised figure that is inevitably coloured by the perspectives of its producers. Shattering the essence of the historical figure that we claim to know, these narratives consequently contribute to the abolition of 'the mythic conquest of personal identity'.[3]

This chapter will consider the narratives that belong to the second category where Nasser, symbolically or explicitly, features as a protagonist of the text. I have found that in Egyptian literature there are not documented historical narratives on Nasser. As Joseph W. Turner notes, this kind of historical narrative is a space where actual people from the past occur, emphasising their direct links with recorded history.[4] Egyptian fiction does not offer a realist fictional account of Nasser, nor does it attempt to reconstruct his entire life within a historical perspective. Rather, it occasionally alters the historical record of the president in order to reimagine specific parts of his life. In so doing, it adopts a fantastic and surreal approach to Nasser in which reality itself, and the possibility 'of ascertaining the true nature of . . . history'[5] are called into question. Put differently, Nasser as fiction offers models of interpretation of the president, his actions, and legacy. These interpretations have less recourse to documented episodes in Nasser's life than to obviously fictitious accounts. It is as though the fictional interpretation of Nasser can be realised only through subverting, distorting, and reimagining the historical events themselves, whereby Nasser can be reproduced fantastically.

Notably, these models of interpretation are in constant struggle over the legitimate representation(s) of the president. As is commonly the case with larger-than-life historical figures, several aspects of Nasser's life remain 'unresolved and unassimilated in the national psyche',[6] hence the difficulty of fixing his image in one exegetic paradigm. The multiple, at times contradictory, depictions of Nasser in narratives are evidence of his enigmatic aura, his fluid character, and his inexplicable actions. This chapter will demonstrate how Nasser as fiction is fragmented into multiple Nassers, each a product of a specific attempted interpretation of him, but all eventually contributing to the construction of 'a site of litigation over the meaning of the past'.[7] The abundance of surreal representations of Nasser, I argue, stems partly from his polarising character which, by urging for a passionate engagement, leaves little room for the disengaged style of historical fiction that was described earlier. In addition, similar to that which Xenia Gasiorowska has to say about

Tsar Peter the Great, one can convincingly argue that 'there are no indifferent, middle-of-the-road, or simply objective creators' of Nasser's image; 'there are only admirers and detractors'. It is as though Nasser's own feelings 'were so intense that he could not inspire lukewarm feelings in others'.[8]

In tracing the depictions of Nasser as a protagonist in Egyptian narratives, I shall present a selection of works written both in Nasser's life as well as after his death. As will be demonstrated, studies on Egyptian literature have paid little attention to some of these narratives, particularly to the way they approach the character of Nasser. By and large, whereas the allegorical presence of Nasser in narrative was a feature of the 1950s and the 1960s, his explicit emergence as a protagonist occurs only after his death. This is not to suggest, however, that symbolic takes on Nasser ceased to exist after 1970 – they surely did not. For Nasser allegorised was not only an attempt to circumvent the restrictions on freedom of expression during Nasser's lifetime but also a literary medium that best served a specific model of interpretation that a writer sought to adopt.

In fact, the ubiquitous influence that Nasser's character and policies had on multiple aspects of Egyptian life, together with the potentially various explanations that his character may inspire, have at times made it common to see him symbolically represented in various Egyptian literary and artistic productions. Whether in literature, cinema, or music, Nasser has been a favourite site of reference not only for the creators but also for the recipients of those works. As Margarit Litvin articulates it,

> The degree to which Nasser's 'face' dominated Egyptian and Arab stages, screens, podiums, and loudspeakers would have a fateful effect on Arab arts as well as politics. Audiences internalised the syllogism 'Nasser is the sole authority; Nasser is represented everywhere.' Its converse was that nearly every ruler or authority figure depicted on stage or film, regardless of context or period, was assumed to represent Nasser. Theatre critics saw Nasser's features in sultans, drug lords, railroad stationmasters, honey-tongued charlatans, and mythical kings.[9]

Remarkably, even songs of love were at times understood as hinting at him. The classic *al-Atlal* (The Ruins), for instance, which was written by poet Ibrahim Naji (1898–1953) long before the 1952 revolution, acquired an altogether different reception when the legendary Umm Kulthum (1898–1975) performed it. Released in 1966, parts of this poem/song, which has been heard in Egyptian and Arab cities over the years, were charged with political connotations, stemming perhaps from the flaming social and political context of the 1960s in Egypt. Thus, Virginia Danielson shows how the song's arguably most famous line, *a'tini hurriyyati atliq yadayya* (Give me my liberty, untie my hands), was 'linked by listeners variously to the struggles of the Palestinians and Arabs against the West and of Egyptian citizens against 'Abd al-Nasir's oppressions'.[10]

Interestingly, those assumptions of a Nasser allegorised in narratives were at times advanced by none other than Nasser himself. Tracing the official reception of Naguib Mahfouz's 1966 novel *Tharthara Fawqa al-Nil* (Adrift on the Nile), for instance, Samia Mehrez shows how the book 'brought Mahfouz into direct confrontation with the president himself'.[11] The novel, depicting a society of defeatism and decadence as has been rarely done in Nasser's Egypt, was read as a blow to the ideals of the nation. True, no character in the novel was assumed to refer personally to Nasser. Yet the whole approach was disturbing to Nasser and his entourage, so much so that the president had to seek the opinion of his then Minister of Culture, Tharwat 'Ukasha. Naguib Mahfouz recounts the rest of the episode:

> Tharwat 'Ukasha, who was preparing a trip to Europe, was asked by Nasser, 'Have you read *Tharthara Fawqa al-Nil*?' He answered, 'No, not yet.' Nasser said, 'Read it and let me know what you think.' So Tharwat 'Ukasha took it with him on his trip. After he read it he understood the reason for Nasser's question. It had been an angry question. Tharwat feared that I might be in trouble, that I might be dismissed or transferred, so upon his return, he went to see the president. He said to him, 'Mr President, I tell you frankly that if art is not allowed this kind of freedom, it will not be art.' So Nasser said calmly, 'Very well, consider the matter closed.'[12]

In line with the common horizon of expectations, allegorical approaches to Nasser during his life were predominantly negative. Egyptian writers, living as they were in an era of 'severe censorship and the emergence of evasive jargons among the intellectuals',[13] sought to find their own way to voice their occasionally harsh criticism, not only against the repressive measures of the regime but also against Nasser himself. Mahfouz's first novel to appear after Nasser's revolution, *Awlad Haratina* (Children of Gebelawi), though notoriously remembered for igniting heated discussions among Egyptian religious circles for its assumed depiction of God and prophets, was also received as a 'symbolic history of Egypt after the revolution',[14] with Gebelawi himself seen as a critic of Nasser. In fact, almost all of Mahfouz's post-1952 literary productions can be interpreted as 'a barrage of bitter criticism aimed at a revolution that has abjectly failed to deliver the goods'.[15] Equally revealing are the approaches of Yusuf Idris (1927–91) to the character of Nasser, one of which will be discussed at length below; suffice it to say for now that, perhaps more than Mahfouz, Idris has often been invoked whenever a discussion on Nasser allegorised arises. Indeed, as Gabir 'Asfur notes, Idris's allegories functioned as trials of the 'illusions of the fifties'. Not exempting the people, whom his stories presented as accomplices, they nevertheless cast their major attention on the 'leader himself [Nasser] who hides behind the allegory in "*A Kana la Budda an Tudi'i al-Nur Ya Lili?*" (Did You Have to Turn on the Light, Lili), "*Al-'Amaliyya al-Kubra*" (The Biggest Operation), and "*Al-Khud'a*" (Delusion).'[16]

If that was the case, then one could only label as misrepresenting what Tawfiq al-Hakim depicts in his infamous post-Nasser memoirs '*Awdat al-Wa'i* (The Return of Consciousness). Writing in 1974, al-Hakim, who was one of Nasser's early inspiring men of letters, describes a society of followers who were nothing short of obedient, docile individuals mesmerised by Nasser's magical power. When Nasser spoke, 'no one argued, checked, verified, or commented. We could not help but believe, and burn our hands with applause.'[17] That al-Hakim himself had produced well-known critical allegories of Nasser a decade earlier seemed to pose no puzzle to him. Commenting on such self-contradiction and rather exaggerating, oversimplifying statement, prominent Egyptian intellectual Luis 'Awad (1915–90) argues that al-Hakim himself 'was in the forefront of honest writers who voiced their opinions in the heyday of Nasser's era. He expressed them in *al-Sultan al-Ha'ir* (The Sultan's Dilemma), *Bank al-Qalaq* (Bank of Anxiety), as well as in some other works.'[18]

Doubtless, this is not to render Egyptian literary and artistic productions in Nasser's era predominantly dissident. Rather, it is to demonstrate that, despite the sweeping popularity that Nasser had among the masses, whose manifestations in literature and film this book engages, Egyptian writers and, for that matter, film-makers were not unequivocally tools of the regime. On the contrary, one can barely find, across the prominent productions of that era, a novel, short story, or film that can be described as propagandist. The puzzling aspect of Egyptians' relationship to Nasser, as this book endeavours to show, lies not as much in their positive depictions of him as in their personalised, intimate view of the president that has survived *despite* the well-known failures of his regime.

As mentioned earlier, allegories to Nasser were not only emerging during his life. In fact, one of Yusuf Idris's late works was perhaps among the harshest appropriations of the president. First published in the Egyptian magazine *October* in 1987, *Abu al-Rijal* (The Father of Men) easily yields itself to allegorical interpretation. As Joseph Massad demonstrates,

> An allegory about President Nasser, to whom it alludes but never explicitly names, the novella is a cruel denouncement, not of Nasserism as such, but of Nasser himself . . . it exposed Nasser himself as a 'pseudoman' whose status everyone knew but could not say due to their 'hypocritical manners'.[19]

Earlier than Idris's work, Gamal al-Ghitani (1945–2015) had engaged in prominent allegorical approaches to Nasser, best recognised in his 1974 celebrated work *al-Zayni Barakat* (Zayni Barakat). But, if al-Ghitani here disguised Nasser behind the medieval character of al-Zayni, he opted for a more contemporary figure in his lesser known short story *'al-Zuhur Tatafattah'* (Flowers are Blossoming). Written in 1976, and published two years later in his short story collection *Dhikr ma Jara* (Recounting What Happened), the story closely follows the early measures of defaming Mao Zedong that took place a few months following his death. A conveniently recognised allegory to the de-Nasserisation that was synchronous to the time of its publication, the story, as al-Ghitani himself informed me, 'is about Nasser in every detail'.[20]

The above overview was not meant to offer an exhaustive listing of all the allegorical approaches to Nasser. Rather, it sought to draw attention to major literary incidents in which Nasser was differently appropriated. In what follows, however, I shall offer a critical engagement with what I perceive as textual models of interpretations of Nasser. These works, symbolically or otherwise, will feature Nasser as a protagonist. Beginning with Yahya Haqqi's (1905–92) *Sah al-Nawm* (Good Morning), it will be demonstrated that, contrary to al-Hakim's aforementioned claims, the literary response to the figure of Nasser began early, perhaps prematurely, with the rising leader of the 1952 revolution facing a writer's imagination in 1955.

Nasser as an Intellectual

Yahya Haqqi's[21] creative writing career, which spans more than six decades, did not leave us with voluminous collections. With only one novel, a novella, and six short story collections, Haqqi stands in contrast to his contemporaries, such as Naguib Mahfouz, Tawfiq al-Hakim, and Yusuf Idris, whose *oeuvres* cover thousands of pages. In fact, Haqqi, who died in 1992, ceased to write long before, with his last book released in 1972. Those few works, however, were sufficient to establish Haqqi's reputation as 'one of the greatest short story writers in the Arab world'[22] and 'the Grand Old Man of Egyptian literature'.[23] No anthology of modern Arabic literature, Egyptian narrative, or public intellectual figures in Egypt can afford to miss him.

Among the several factors that contribute to this salient position, Haqqi's novella *Qindil Umm Hashim* (The Lamp of Umm Hashim)[24] surely stands out. Published in 1944, the narrative demonstrates the relationship between the East and the West through the story of a young ophthalmologist, Ismail, who studies medicine in Europe, immerses himself in its worldly pleasures, and returns to Egypt to face the traditional values of his society. The novella is a milestone in the literary attempts to narrativise the encounter between the Arab world and the West, which would later evolve to be a salient theme in twentieth-century Arabic literary production, perhaps best epitomised by Tayeb Salih's (1929–2009) magnum opus *Mawsim al-Hijra ila al-Shamal* (Season of Migration to the North). Similar to Salih's book, *Qindil* became Haqqi's best-remembered work, so much so that 'people seem to think that he has not written anything else'.[25]

The novella could also be seen as Haqqi's first attempt at symbolic writing where the lamp has been interpreted by many as a symbol for the established norms of society. This use of symbolism, which Taha Hussein (1889–1973) finds 'an obvious tendency'[26] in Haqqi's writing, would eventually find a broader space in his only novel, *Sah al-Nawm* (Good Morning).²⁷ Published in 1955, the book was among the first literary responses to the 1952 revolution to come from an established writer. Sensing the possible repercussions of (mis)understanding his message, Haqqi himself oversaw the process of publication, where he not only bore its costs but also managed to guarantee a limited distribution. Miriam Cooke explains the process thus:

> Haqqi decided to finance publication of this novel himself so that he could dictate the format in which it was to appear. The presentation was to be sober: the cover title was to be printed and not written in fancy calligraphy; there should be no women on the cover . . . Five thousand copies were distributed to Cairo's newspaper stands, where they remained on sale for two weeks for a price of ten piasters. Then the volumes were withdrawn and Haqqi made his way to the printer (*al-Akhbar*) to see how the enterprise had fared – his precautions against the casual reader had worked only too well: 125 copies had sold.²⁸

This novel excepted, Haqqi has had no significant engagement with the Egyptian revolution – nor, for that matter, with Nasser. In fact, the writer's biographies do not provide information as to whether Haqqi had officially met Nasser. Aside from the fact that he had assumed a few official positions – the most prominent of which was Director of the Department of Fine Arts – Haqqi was not part of the regime's men of letters, nor could he be classified as dissident or controversial.

The novel is divided into two unequal parts. The first is 'Yesterday', in which an anonymous narrator describes an unnamed Egyptian village prior to the arrival of *al-Ustadh*.²⁹ Divided into nine sections and punctuated by the introduction of a few of the village's inhabitants, this part revolves mainly around the village's tavern where the characters mingle and interact. Owned by a man who is merely referred to as 'the tavern keeper',³⁰ the tavern represents a space where people can dispense with the artificial behaviour of the outside, thus allowing the tavern keeper 'to see [them] as they really are, naked as the day they were born'.³¹ Mainly frequented by men, it shows a village whose men escape their familial commitments, finding in the tavern a getaway from their wives. The women, on the other hand, are presented as either complacent with, or dismissive of, their men's way of life. Among the second group is a crippled woman who abruptly visits the tavern to look for her husband. Slightly acquainted with foreign culture, the woman shows an understanding of the deficiencies of the post-colonial society, where the natives reproduce the behaviour of the colonials. In one of her visits to the tavern, she verbally assaults the tavern keeper, saying,

> Thou art the source and cause of the ills of this good village. Because of thy deeds thou hast become the butt of the district's jokers. Woe to thee! Art thou not ashamed? Before it was the *foreigners* who had opened taverns in our countryside, thus corrupting our tribe, stealing its money through wine and usury. Then we gave thanks to God for freeing us of them and their evil and their influence. So what has come over thee, one of us, that thou shouldst emulate their ways and harm thy people? Does thy religion not prevent thee from acting in this way?[32]

Not all the village's inhabitants immerse themselves in drinking, however. The narrator tells that the young artist, for instance, does not drink nor find any inspiration in drinking. He joins the group only because he feels 'warm and alive here just like out in the fields and the flowers'.[33] In fact, the narrator himself refrains from partaking in the people's ritual pleasures. He even admits that 'my friends accuse me of observing and not participating. With head bent as though blind, I listen to conversations, rarely taking part.'[34] In a section entitled, 'A Break', the narrator seems fully aware of the recording aspect of his job. Declaring himself a writer, he does not hide the nature of his mission: 'To document a historical event that had serious repercussions on Egyptian political life'.[35]

Equally important is the narrator's acknowledgement that he finds interest only in a few of the tavern clients, ignoring the others. His proposed justification is that the former's 'lives presented a moral. They are the eccentrics doomed to suffer. They are the most representative, because they are the first to be shaken when society is hit.'[36] Subscribing to the narrator's explanation is Miriam Cooke who argues that those characters – who include the butcher, the dwarf, the station-sweep, the cart driver, and others – are 'not representative of the labourers, but are potential victims of modern society'.[37] In his instant reception of the novel at the time of publication, however, Taha Hussein notes that those characters are, in fact, far from representing an Egyptian village and that the tavern, with its rituals, resembles more a European setting than an Egyptian one.[38]

At any rate, the narrator's explicit motivation behind telling the story is to show how much reform the village requires. Aside from those eccentric characters, the rest merely wonder 'when injustice would cease'.[39] Taha Hussein himself sees in Haqqi's depiction of the village in the first part a space 'utterly miserable, in dire need of amelioration'.[40] An ambivalent stance towards the conditions of the village's inhabitants could be noticed here, however. While the majority of them are, indeed, poor, it remains unclear whether a *modern* reform is actually required. In fact, the narrator mentions that the village has a bitter memory of encountering the outside world, when a tragic event befell it upon the arrival of a travelling circus.[41] The novel also shows that the characters in the village cannot be categorised according to a given formula, thus defying the presumed necessity of conforming to modern criteria about people's conditions. True, the village seems detached from the 'modern' world, not even having a bank, but part of its population is satisfied and indifferent to the manifestations of modernity. In a telling incident, the narrator describes how, one day, the village's *'Umda* receives a form from the capital, demanding a list of the villagers' jobs, the number of unemployed, and the reason behind their idleness. The *'Umda* writes down the name of the cripple's husband. The narrator then goes on to declare: 'Had the government had a heart, it would have added another column asking the unemployed whether they were happy. Had it done so, with our unanimous approval, the *'Umda* would have written by the name of the cripple's husband: "Very happy".'[42]

The transition from the first part 'Yesterday' to the second, shorter 'Today' is initiated by the arrival of the *Ustadh*. While he is first mentioned in the second page of the novel, where the narrator tells that the village hears about him and his studies in the capital but has not actually seen him, the *Ustadh* is not mentioned again until he suddenly re-emerges. On his entrance into the scene, he notices the poverty around him and says, 'That will go. That will go.'[43] Expectedly, the novel proceeds towards showing the effects of change on the village brought about by the *Ustadh* and his assistants. The first part ends with the narrator leaving the village for more than a year, and it is this absence that enables him on his return to notice the starkness of the difference.

Stereotypically, the second part of *Sah al-Nawm* sheds light on the people's dissatisfaction with the post-reform era, thus highlighting the shortcomings of the *Ustadh*'s programme. One could recognise, however, yet another incident of ambivalence, as the narrative ambiguously embraces and subtly criticises both the *Ustadh* and the people. This ambivalence, which pervades the narrative, has led to different readings of the novel, based on the view a critic may have towards top-down reform. Miriam Cooke perceives the novel as a document full of sympathy towards the village's people. Those peasants are 'blissfully oblivious to the threat which contemporary society held for the harmony of their lives'.[44] Significant in this context is the peasants' indifference to the railway project that was to pass through their village. Abruptly encountered with a forceful change in the second part, the peasants' transformation discloses the tragic effect 'that the modern era has on a remote village'.[45] The post-*Ustadh* village is now subject to a secular view of the world, where ethical norms (represented by closing down the tavern) are forcefully imposed; where official religion and disciplinary measures were to take place; in sum, where 'culture killed nature'.[46]

Other readings, however, tend to empathise with the *Ustadh* and his relentless efforts to bring about change to the village. Following such reception, the novel has been read as a work tinged with optimism, essentially premised on the belief that 'reforming a society is possible with some effort and firmness from the rulers'.[47] Naturally, individuals differ significantly in their ability and readiness to change. Thus, even when the vicissitudes of society shake the old norms, a calm conformity of people is hardly guaranteed. Rather, reluctant individuals furnish the background of a society in flux, whether by intentionally resisting reforms or by their inability to cope. For those, change is tantamount to death.[48]

Those two readings, however, are predicated upon a timeless, spatially unbound understanding of the unnamed village, thus missing the not-so-subtle reference to the 1952 revolution in the novel and, more significantly, to Nasser himself. I would argue that *Sah al-Nawm* is less about modernising forces and their effects on the Egyptian village than about the 1952 revolution and Nasser. This reading finds support in the fact that modernisation in Egypt had begun long before the writing of the novel. Additionally, the symbolic nature of the work, the time of publication and, more particularly, the unnamed *Ustadh*, are rather lucid signs that invite this alternative reading. As will be demonstrated below, I read the *Ustadh* as the first attempt in Egyptian literature to *narrativise* Nasser, to fictionalise his character, his revolution, and his ideas, albeit allegorically.

Seldom did any of the novel's reviews following publication touch upon a resemblance between the *Ustadh* and Nasser. Na'im 'Atiyya goes even so far as to suggest that the novel should not be read 'politically . . . Rather, Haqqi celebrates the human condition regardless of the system in which it emerges.'[49] There were, however, suggestions that 'the village stands as a symbol for Egypt, the tavern for corruption, "Yesterday" for pre-revolution, and "Today" for the revolution'.[50] In other cases, the *Ustadh* was credited for enjoying 'idealist traits that resemble the features of the revolution's leader who guides his country through the path of socialism'.[51]

The temporal circumstances against which the novel emerged, three years after the revolution and the rise of Nasser's position and popularity – which culminated in the nationalisation of the Suez Canal – might have rendered it infeasible for critics publicly to announce a fictionalised Nasser. Interestingly, only one figure in the literary field, with an authority prodigious enough to compete with Nasser's political one, was able to come close to demystifying the otherwise apparent symbolism of the novel. It was none other than Taha Hussein, arguably the most influential Egyptian intellectual of the past century, who enunciated this relationship between Nasser and the *Ustadh* – still without spelling out Nasser's name. He tells us:

> It is obvious that the writer's village is Egypt, and no wonder we find there a tavern and its clients. And it is obvious that the miracle-maker is the leader of the revolution, his friends, and his assistants. And it is finally obvious that the writer aspires to make us satisfied with the reform that has been done in Egypt, and to console us regarding its shortcomings . . . for Paris, according to the French, was not built in a night.[52]

Hussein, however, criticises the second part of the novel for being dull and incoherent, preferring the literary beauty of the first part. In other words, he chooses the marvellous depiction of what he sees as a miserable village over the trite take on a reformed society – the literary merit of the text over its message. Elucidating the reason behind this noticeable disparity in the aesthetic value of the text, Hussein very intelligently raises the following point:

> It is easy to explain this [disparity]; the Egyptian revolution has not yet constituted a theme for high literary narratives, as it has yet to reach its end. We live it; we do not *dream* about it. And if we talked about it, we would opt for honest exhortation and pure advice, and would impose on ourselves motives that are foreign to fiction.[53]

Put differently, Hussein maintains that the Egyptian revolution and its leader are not *fictionalisable* yet, for they are part of a reality that has not yielded itself to literary imagination. They are still a history unfolding, continually adding details to their (then) incomplete, potential story. Only when the story ceases to exist in reality can it become literature.

The novel abounds with references that link the *Ustadh* to Nasser. Upon his arrival in the village, for instance, the *Ustadh* is first seen by the carriage driver whose vehicle is the village's only means of transport. Moments before he recognises the *Ustadh*, it is the latter's physical traits that capture the driver's attention:

> The man appeared to be a huge, powerful giant to the driver. His outline was clearly defined like a charcoal drawing on a sheet of the horizon and the mist . . . he looked at him for a while as he stood there. Despite their simplicity his clothes were elegant and well-fitting. He held his head high on a long neck, which would not submit to injustice. This impression was enhanced by a perfect nose, which was not too thin nor too snub nor too weakened by vicissitudes. Under his broad, powerful shoulders was a straight back that would bow only to God.[54]

Obviously, the voice of the narrator (read: the author) can be easily recognised. Not only do these attributes match Nasser's but the paragraph works as though to adopt Nasser's call for pride and dignity, evoking his famous slogan: *irfaʿ raʾsak ya akhi* (Raise your head, my brother). Later in the novel, during a meeting with the *Ustadh*, the narrator devotes a full paragraph to describing his smile, and how it reflects the *Ustadh*'s mentality: 'Originally, the smile had indicated a determination to overcome tyranny and obstacles ... But today it seemed to indicate a deep understanding of human aspirations'.[55]

The aspirations and the actions of the *Ustadh* resemble those of post-1952 Nasser. As mentioned earlier, the determination to eliminate poverty is what the *Ustadh* first expresses upon his arrival. More significantly, the novel presents the first speech that the *Ustadh* delivers in the village, explaining his reforming agenda. Commenting on the unpleasant conditions in which the villagers live, he maintains that the source is the people's 'sense of inferiority, their submission to injustice, and their predilection for peace and quiet at all costs'.[56] In addition, the speech proposes the *Ustadh*'s vision for improving the peasant's conditions, including the redistribution of land and wealth.

Equally indicative is the reference to the *Ustadh*'s assistants among the youth of the village. On his first encounter with the carriage driver, the *Ustadh*, notwithstanding his long absence, appears fully cognisant of the minute details of life in the village, so much so that the driver wonders 'where on earth does he get his information from? Does he have informants in the village that keep him up to date, without our knowing who they are?'[57] This allusion to the secrecy that engulfs the *Ustadh*'s work prior to the change (read: revolution) that he introduces echoes the historical account of the discrete meetings between Nasser and the Free Officers in preparation for the 1952 coup. The identity of those informants is first disclosed during the *Ustadh*'s first speech, when the narrator notices that: 'The professor stood up with a small group of young men from our village, known for their seriousness, determination, uprightness, and *concealment (kitman)*. I realised that they were the ones who had told him about the secrets of our village.'[58]

Well into the second part of the novel, the narrator once again reflects on the traits of those aides who, by now, make up the majority in the village council. Having realised their competence, efficiency, and trustworthiness, the narrator regretfully admits how the villagers, himself included, underestimated those youths prior to the arrival of the *Ustadh*. Noticeably younger than the other villagers, the latter 'had ignored [them], not realizing that they would be able to shoulder a great burden which needs soundness of mind and body. Some of the elders, who prided themselves on their experience, had not paid them attention.'[59]

The narrator does not completely spare those assistants his criticism, however. Recognising the negative transformation that befalls them after the revolution, he comments, addressing the *Ustadh*, 'When some of your close and highly trusted friends turned from you, you rejected them'.[60] As such, the narrative contrasts the *Ustadh* with his aides, whereby the former is not only exonerated from their misdeeds but also credited for standing against them once he realises that they betray his ideals. In so doing, the narrative sets an early fictional example in Egyptian literature of the way in which Nasser is personally separated, and mostly exempted, from the misdeeds of his regime. Nasser's exceptionality, a trait on which successive Egyptian literary productions would capitalise, transforms him into a value, an all-embracing, transhistorical, positive notion that evokes senses of honesty, pride, and modesty. It stems, as *Sah al-Nawm* relays, from the fact that he

> had not given anyone the opportunity to say: 'we were confused by him, because he has two faces'. They had said this of many exceptional *rulers* who opened the door of hope onto torture and suffering . . . But you have only one face to your inner and outer selves. You have protected your people against doubts and shocks. With a guide like you, the wayfarer is sure to reach his destination however long it may take.[61]

Having established the *Ustadh* as a Nasser allegorised, how the latter is reimagined merits attention. The narrative is determined to highlight the intellectual dimension of the *Ustadh*. On his arrival, he spends 'the night in his study reading'.[62] In fact, his whole intent to bring about change is born out of his long devotion to reflection and observation: 'For months I locked myself up in my room, continuously studying and pondering, until the path became clear'.[63] The *Ustadh* is presented more as a wise man than as an army officer. When necessary, however, he will resort to force: 'My friends and I will lead gently at first, and if this should not work, then force will'. The novel shows that the villagers offer the *Ustadh* their allegiance, 'promising to follow him wherever he went and to do whatever he advised'.[64] In so doing, the novel seeks to imagine an alternative history to the 1952 revolution; it attempts to *demilitarise* it, to imagine it as a social movement led by an intellectual whose education is the primary incentive behind his reforming aspirations. This alternative account offers the narrator the freedom to criticise and advise the

Ustadh himself, bestowing, I would argue, a didactic, preaching tone upon the novel. In other words, the narrative creates its own Nasser, a Nasser who admits, as early in his career as in 1955, the down sides of the revolution, and who, equally importantly, is willing to listen receptively to admonition and direction. Thus, in a self-assessing scene that constitutes a precedent in Egyptian literature, the narrative has the *Ustadh*/Nasser acknowledging the mistakes and conceding that his movement might have harmed some people:

> We are turning over a new page, and will not go back even for a second, because this is not possible in our world. One cannot, however, avoid some shadow of that previous page falling over the new . . . you think I am not concerned about what has happened to some people as a result of my programs?[65]

The didactic aspect of the novel is best recognised in the last section, entitled, 'The Meeting with the Professor'. This section, triggered by an invitation that the narrator receives for a private meeting with the *Ustadh*, sheds light on yet another concern of the novel: namely, the relationship between Nasser and Egyptian intellectuals. It reflects the apprehensions that Egyptian writers, particularly the liberal generation to whom Haqqi belongs, had towards a military coup. Interestingly, the publication of *Sah al-Nawm* coincided with the personal letter that veteran Egyptian artist and journalist Ruz al-Yusuf had sent to Nasser, asking for unrestricted freedom of speech. As shown in the previous chapter, the letter would establish a tradition of writing to Nasser. The *Ustadh*'s view on writers, represented by the narrator of *Sah al-Nawm*, is revealed soon after his arrival. Having joined other villagers to welcome him, the narrator seems uneasy upon hearing that the *Ustadh* has actually mentioned him in passing: 'Who is he? This silent, absent-minded fellow? I have no time for the likes of him. I want workers, not *dreamers*.'[66] Favouring action over intellectual theorising, as though to echo Nietzsche's aphorism that 'knowledge kills action; action requires the veils of illusion',[67] the *Ustadh* turns towards the space where actions vanish the most. Reasoning why he intends to shut down the tavern, he declares in a public speech, attended by the narrator, that 'because it is a den of iniquity, luring the men away from their homes. It brings together the misguided and the idle with the disappointed and the dreamers.'[68] The narrator comments that 'while uttering the word "dreamers", the *Ustadh* looks up at me'.[69]

The private meeting with the *Ustadh* is an opportunity for the narrator to offer suggestions and advice to the new political authority in the village. In addition, it shows the narrator that this authority may at times be intrusive, its surveillance measures penetrating the seemingly discrete aspects of intellectuals' lives. Thus, the *Ustadh* takes the narrator by surprise when he informs him that 'I have also heard that you are writing a journal and I have seen some excerpts'.[70] The narrator's reaction shows the anxiety of a writer whose secret work is invaded:

> I was surprised at these words, and I did not know what to say. On the one hand, I was impressed that the professor had acquired news of all my movements, and had come into possession of my papers. On the other, I was annoyed to be exposed after having reckoned that my movements were not being observed.[71]

Corrective and exhortative, the dialogue between the two men examines the positive and negative outcomes of the revolution. In addition, it depicts the *Ustadh* impatiently waiting for intellectuals to intervene, announcing, in fact, that he knows what concerns them. Interrupting a long speech that the narrator makes before him, the *Ustadh* takes the lead and states:

> Shall I complete what you are saying? I know the rest of your speech because I have read your journal. You will remind me (do you think I do not know?) to be tolerant and to respect the rights of the individual first as a human being and only then as a stone in the building of society, and to distinguish between my belief that I am right and that I am absolutely right, and to remember that sincerity and correct opinions are harmonious, if not always found together.[72]

The last section is a twofold invitation. It calls on the political authority to lend an ear to intellectuals, and asks intellectuals in return to approach the authority and advise it. In a kind of wishful thinking for the situation in Egypt at the time, the novel ends with the two men shaking hands, the *Ustadh* putting it forward before the narrator that 'I expect you to do your duty',[73] and the narrator informing the readers: 'and I have'. Apparently, the narrator considers telling this narrative, that is, the novel itself, to be fulfilment of his duty. In so doing, he once again acknowledges the didactic, rectifying nature of his mission. Though harmful to the aesthetics of the narrative, this tone, particularly dominant in the last chapter, succeeds in conveying both the fears and the hopes of the intellectual elite following Nasser's revolution. Which would prevail in successive literary writings on Nasser will be unearthed in the course of this book.

Nasser as a Beast

Unlike Yahya Haqqi, Yusuf Idris had a more volatile, critical, and confrontational experience with Nasser and his regime. Initially supportive of the revolution, he nevertheless became one of its early victims, and was arrested during the infamous 1954 crisis, a month after the publication of his first short-story collection, *Arkhas Layali* (The Cheapest Nights).[74] In the ensuing years, Idris, an idealist, became disenchanted with the outcomes of the revolution, realising that 'few of the aims pronounced so eloquently by the new leader had in fact been accomplished'.[75]

As mentioned earlier, Idris repeatedly approached Nasser in his fiction, producing some of the most powerful allegories about him. In fact, 'Nasser had, by Idris's own account, always been a source of inspiration to him.'[76] Complex and multilayered, Nasser's character posed several dilemmas to the leftist Idris. In an interview with Egyptian intellectual Ghali Shukri, he acknowledged how he began to contemplate the attributes of Nasser during his 1954 incarceration. Sensing the seemingly irreconcilable features of him, Idris declared that he and his comrades

> were baffled. This is a dictator, but he collaborates with socialist states to protect the homeland and build its major productive institutions. He orders agrarian reforms, free education throughout all stages, and the Egyptianisation of foreign banks.[77]

Echoing common feelings that were shared by a sizeable group of Egyptian intellectuals, Idris lacked a singular view of Nasser. His was a mixture of admiration and disapproval, veneration and dismay. These conflicting sentiments were strongest during Nasser's final years. The very same Idris whose post-1967 literary productions were condemning and decrying Nasser personally could nevertheless pen one of the most despondent elegies following the president's untimely death. Writing in his daily column in *al-Ahram* newspaper, Idris lamented:

> O, our father in the earth. O, our compassionate, big heart.
> For the first time ever, the world is without Nasser. We are not accustomed to breathing air that he does not breathe. We cannot sleep except when we are certain he is there, over the al-Qubba Bridge, nor can we wake up if his smiling face does not greet us.[78]

Of all the Nasser allegories that Idris produced, his short story '*al-Khud'a*' (Delusion) stands out. First published in *al-Ahram* newspaper in 1969, the story was included two years later in one of Idris's best-known collections, *Bayt min Lahm* (House of Flesh). In fact, perhaps owing to its temporal circumstances – emerging as it did a year following Nasser's death – a good number of the book's stories were retrospectively read as allegories of Nasser. For instance, '*al-Rihla*' (The Journey), narrating the story of a man carrying the dead body of his father in a car, was widely interpreted as a reference to the then current situation in Egypt, where 'the dead father is intended to represent 'Abd al-Nasir (rendered effectively "dead" by the June War of 1967 and its results), and the message of the story is thus that the time had come to abandon even such a beloved figure as one's own (the country's) father figure.'[79] Indeed, with '*al-Rihla*' first published in *al-Ahram* only three months prior to the actual death of Nasser, it was proclaimed prophetic, attesting to Idris's prescient capacities and his profound vision of the incidents that would soon unfold.[80]

Peculiar to '*al-Khud'a*' is Idris's appropriation of an animal, the camel, as a symbol for Nasser. The story revolves around a camel's head intruding into the life of the narrator and his compatriots. Registering a unique literary incident in Egyptian writing, where an animal stands for Nasser, it should be noted, however, that bestial allegories are generously encountered in Idris's *oeuvre*, be they dogs, as in '*Shay' Yujannin*' (Something to Drive You Crazy) (1961), fish in '*al-Ra's*' (The Head) (1962), birds in '*al-'Usfur wa al-Silk*' (The Bird and the Wire) (1971), or lions in '*Ana Sultan Qanun al-Wujud*' (I am the Lord of the Law of Existence) (1980). Outdoing most of his contemporaries in resorting to this technique, Idris 'presents strong moral, social, political, and religious criticism under the cover of ordinary biological phenomena'.[81]

Presenting human beings as animals 'is effective not only because of the conventional associations we make with various animals but also because it establishes the individual or individuals targeted as other'.[82] In other words, it is an othering discourse, where otherness is not based on race or gender but on species. By satirically turning humans into animals, the discourse is invested in negative theriomorphism where, instead of humanising the animal, it acts as a dehumanisation of the human. Tzvetan Todorov recounts how, during the conquest of America, the natives were looked upon as animals, thus relegating them to a lower status than the conquistadores had.[83]

Still, the selection of the camel in 'al-Khud'a' owes more to linguistic reason than to an intrinsic feature of the animal. Both *jamal*, Arabic for camel, and Nasser's first name Jamal, are derived from the same root. The trilateral root, *J M L*, produces words that are basically related to beauty (*jamal*) and sentence/wholeness (*jumla*). The pun was missed by hardly any of the critics who commented on the story, with some even going so far as to detect another – this time between *ra's* (head) and *ra'is* (president), also sharing the same root.[84] The effortless accessibility of the reference is intentional, and Idris makes no attempt to mystify it. The camel, whose ugly presence in the story serves as a 'scathing satire on Nasser's omnipresence in the forms of portraits in public buildings, in the press, and so on, and through the interference of his security services with the private lives of citizens',[85] is appropriated merely because of its Arabic linguistic connection to Nasser's name, which renders the symbol obviously understood. In other words, the camel in Arabic culture bears no connotations of obtrusiveness, surveillance, or trespassing, nor does it invoke senses of evil and bad omens like the owl or the crow do. In fact, a glimpse at classical Arabic poetry shows the camel, and particularly the she-camel, as the best, most friendly companion to the poet. In addition, the camel was seen as a miraculous creature, whose minute physiological details testify to the omnipotence of God. Thus the Quran combines the camel with the sky, the mountains, and the earth as evidence of the necessary existence of God: 'Will they not look at the camels, how they were created, and at the sky, how it was raised up, and at the mountains, how they were constructed, and at the earth, how it was spread flat?'[86] The fascination with the camel's physiology, together with the animal's frequent nocturnal appearances in the desert, may have conjured an eerie feeling in Arabs' minds, given one of their traditional monikers for camels, *banat al-layl* (daughters of the night).[87] Unable to fathom its uniqueness among animals, 'the old Arabian belief was that the camels were descended from the jinn'.[88]

By subverting the common metaphors that the camel often connotes, the story restructures the readers' literary memories, reorienting them towards a less familiar world. In so doing, it poses Nasser and his era as culpable, as deformers of an otherwise amicable being. The story opens with the narrator recounting the first time he notices the camel's head. The scene is worth quoting in full:

> There must be a first time for everything and the first time was at night. The moon diffuses a silver peacefulness, the spring is limpid, its water flowing unhurriedly, with a tender murmur and, whenever you see the moon melting in the water, freshly melting in front of you, you cannot help feeling thirsty and you try to drink or at least to get a taste of it. I leaned forward with my whole body and stretched out my hand. The cool, sparkling drops almost reached my mouth, and *I almost enjoyed the first taste of it* when I noticed, next to my quivering image, quivering in shades of white and black, and to the tremor of the moon, *the reflection of another head*, protracted to the fore as if an outstretched hand had wrenched all its features violently out of its face, an elongated head ending with an unlimited transversal slit and, as if this were not enough, there was another slit lengthwise. No doubt, the head of a camel. Voiceless. Noiseless. Motionless. Suddenly, there was the head. I was not scared and I did not scream, I just turned round for no reason other than to make sure. *The moon was gone, the spring had vanished as well as the murmur and the silver.*[89]

While the setting is both timeless and not spatially defined, a political reading of this opening is too tempting to resist. The optimistic, colourful atmosphere that the narrator inhabits – the moon, the spring, the flowing of the water – can be interpreted as the hopes that Egyptians possess in the wake of the revolution. These were real, tangible hopes, partially realised and experienced as the narrator seeks the water and, in fact, enjoys 'the first taste of it'. The joy is interrupted, however, when the camel's head emerges in the background, crowding the narrator in his own space that is mirrored in the spring. The juxtaposition of the three images that are now reflected in the water – the narrator, the moon, and the camel's head – establishes a tense, dramatic moment that will determine the future of such context. To the narrator's dismay, 'the moon was gone, the spring had vanished'. No coexistence, that is, as the camel's head leaves no room for poetic imagination.

What is it in the camel's head that causes a sudden disappearance of the moon? The narrator makes it clear that the head is neither harmful nor even noisy. It is as though the mere existence of the head, unmediated, abrupt, and forceful, together with its unpleasant, mutilated features, mark an end for the otherwise idyllic surroundings. It is important to bear in mind that the story was written in the final years of Nasser's life when the ship was already sinking, having received a major blow in the 1967 defeat. Compared to the equivocal, ambivalent stance towards the early years of the revolution that Haqqi's *Sah al-Nawm* adopts, Idris's text, written thirteen years later, is categorical and unwavering, unflinchingly condemning the leadership that brings people's dreams to an end. Whether Idris relates the deformed camel's head only to the final years of Nasser, or labels the whole 1952 movement as monstrous, is hard to ascertain. A few lines later, however, the narrative produces a highly ambiguous scene in which it makes a reference to the 'owner' of the camel, dragging the animal slowly, until,

> without any prelude or any struggle, without there being a doer or a shot or a weapon, without anything at all, the man in the white garment and turban collapses. The owner collapsed. He had been murdered, for around his head thrown on the ground and despite the darkness of the scene, there was a pool of blood. Moreover, the camel did not run away, nor clamor, nor rage, nor did it gurgle.[90]

The scene was read as a further uncovering of the camel's unspecified identity. 'The fact that the camel at one time killed its owner', Cohen-Mor expounds, '[is] a reference to the deposed leader of the revolution, Naguib.'[91] More plausible, I argue, is to see in the camel's owner a silhouette of a people crushed, dreams aborted, and promises unfulfilled. What is left is a camel's head, unrestrainedly wandering among the masses.

The narrative is driven by three recurring motifs. First, it shows the elements of the grotesque as manifested in the camel's head: a head without a body, full of slits; a face with three lips. If 'depicting a human as an animal is indeed a disparaging critical gesture',[92] more so is the case when the animal is disfigured. The uncanny nature of this creature extends to the neck, 'thick, long, curved, sharp at the lower end as if it were a lathe, a neck ending with a head at its fore'.[93] Throughout the story, the narrative is keen to repeat these monstrous descriptions of the head, almost verbatim: 'That high elongated head with features that seem to have been pulled forward considerably, the three huge, swollen lips'.[94]

Second, whenever the head pops into view, the narrator reflects on its haughtiness and indifference to its surroundings. It does nothing, says nothing, and sees nothing. On first noticing it, the narrator tells how it is 'looking on at me from above, and it was not even really looking at me, it was as if it did not see me or as if I had not been there altogether'.[95] When the head appears while the narrator takes a shower, literally standing with him within the curtain, it again pays no attention to the surroundings, leaving the reason behind its existence inexplicably cryptic:

> I went on having my bath and I started looking carefully at the two eyes through the thin wires of water hoping to catch a glimpse of something, hoping to know why it looked on and what it wanted, hoping to feel for a moment that it did see me, but not at all, it just looked on, from above, and also straight ahead.[96]

Even when the narrator begins to discuss the head's appearance with his boss and colleagues at work, the camel partakes in the setting, staring at the nothingness. A complete observer, looking yet not looking, the head's passivity is epitomised in the final words of the story, where it is 'looking ahead motionless, neither angry nor pleased, neither reaching out nor holding back, never doing anything except looking on, just looking on . . .'[97]

More significantly, the narrative demonstrates the way in which the narrator and his fellow citizens react to the existence of the head. Simultaneously, the story shows that the people are helpless in the face of the intrusive presence of the head and have become comfortably accustomed to it. In fact, on his first encounter with the head, the narrator admits that 'the strangest thing was that I was not astonished, and did not question how a neck could spring out of no body'.[98] The narrator becomes surprised when he learns from his colleagues that the head is not new to them, having all constantly seen it before. When he seeks advice for a course of action, they respond,

> Do as people do. I ask them what they do and find that they do nothing at all. Sometimes some try to touch it, pat it, fondle it, sometimes some fly into a rage, are infuriated and curse it; others kick it or butt it, but the camel's head always remains as it is, and people remain as they are. It appears to them in a manner that makes them wonder at first, then they get bored with talking, and soon the eerie presence of the camel's head no longer seems a phenomenon that warrants a pause or even a glance.[99]

Even in the most intimate, private situations, such as sexual intercourse, the narrator and his partner, though obviously irritated by the head's presence, can nevertheless consummate their love, realising that their attempts to expel it from their room are futile: 'It slowly, patiently and persistently sneaked back between us so that it became clear that it was no use pushing it aside'.[100]

At play here is a twofold condemnation. I argue that the narrative exposes Egyptians' lack of agency, denounces their helplessness, and criticises their capacity to coexist not only with the regime's intrusion in their life and their lack of privacy but, as importantly, with a world of ugliness and malformation that beleaguers them. More precisely, Nasser does not only emerge as deformed, he also deforms the psyche of people, turning them into other 'heads' who can normalise their relationship with the otherwise unliveable, uncanny situations. It is no wonder that none of the people in the story ever attempts to kill the camel's head. Even the narrator, taken aback by the inadequacy of people, himself included, cannot resist releasing these thoughts, reflecting, 'Perhaps if we were to be astonished, merely astonished, if we were all of us to be astonished whenever it appeared, it would cease to appear'.[101]

I argue, however, that the essence of the story lies in mockery. Idris ridicules not people but Nasser himself. Despite Nasser's ubiquitous encroachment in every aspect of Egyptians' lives, Idris predicts that Egyptians will not only endure this but will eventually ignore it. As seen above, the presence of the camel does not bar Egyptians from indulging in the most mundane and intimate of activities – it does not even bar them from discussing the issue itself. I read 'al-Khud'a' as an act of confrontation whereby Idris epitomises his personal defiance of Nasser. Astonishingly brave, Idris wrote the story as his first contribution to *al-Ahram* upon joining its staff in 1969 at a time when it was regarded as the regime's official newspaper and was headed by none other than Nasser's closest intellectual and confidant, Muhammad Hasanayn Haykal. Rather than declaring allegiance, Idris opted for a showdown with the president. He not only transformed him into a mere deformed camel's head, whose only power was to watch people from afar, but also rejected hiding his intention behind the already obvious symbolism of '*al-Khud'a*'. Ultimately, the narrator declares in the final paragraph his full awareness that the camel/Nasser must be watching while he writes the story itself. Yet, he will continue writing – nay, he only writes because he knows that the camel is looking at him, thereby emasculating its alleged competence. As for the camel, it is devoid of any real threat – it can look, and only look:

> Had it not been for my awareness of its presence I would have never ventured upon what I am doing right now, for – now – without a hint of astonishment or surprise, and without me raising my head, I am sure that the camel's head is looking on at me, that high elongated head with features that seem to have been pulled forward considerably, the three huge, swollen lips and the regular teeth, large tooth next to large tooth, tightly clenched and without any clefts between them, looking ahead motionless, neither angry nor pleased, neither reaching out nor holding back, never doing anything except looking on, just looking on . . .[102]

Indeed, the message did not elude the president. According to one account, 'the story displeased Nasser, who saw it insinuating at him'.[103] As mentioned earlier, Nasser was an active reader of major literary productions in Egypt, particularly those that were first fully published or serialised in *al-Ahram* by influential writers such as Idris and Mahfouz. Relying on the support and the protection of Haykal, those writers ironically found in *al-Ahram* a safe space for political innuendo. '*Al-Khud'a*' comes as no exception. A few of Idris's biographers point out how he would have been 'barred from writing [for *al-Ahram*] afterwards, had it not been for Haykal's intervention'.[104] The significance of these allegorical readings that Nasser proposes is that he, intentionally or otherwise, accepts to situate himself as a potential subject of literary imagination. Another possible and, in fact, more literal translation of Idris's story title is 'Trick' or 'Deception'. By reading himself in the story, was Nasser tricked into acknowledging a semblance with an ugly reality? His refraining from punishing Idris can perhaps render the allegorical story more truthful for, like the camel's head, Nasser can watch, and only watch.

Nasser as a Martyr

Nasser died from a heart attack on 28 September 1970, a few hours after the conclusion of the extraordinary Arab League Summit that was held in Cairo to negotiate a ceasefire between the Jordanian army and Palestinian guerrilla fighters, in what was referred to later as 'Black September'. Having bid farewell to the emir of Kuwait at the airport, he felt dizzy and began to sweat heavily. He was then

> driven home and the doctors were called. When Heikal reached the residence the end was already near. Nasser lay on his bed in pajamas surrounded by doctors. Heikal was joined by Ali Sabry, Hussein al-Shafi'i and Anwar Sadat who recited some verses from the Quran. General Mahmud Fawzi entered the room in great dismay just as a doctor said: 'Everything is over'. General Fawzi said bitterly: 'No, impossible. Continue your work . . .' All the doctors cried. Tears fell, a deluge of tears.[105]

Nasser's death was obviously from natural causes, and health issues that had befallen him earlier were not news to people. The grief and pain that overtook many Egyptians and Arabs upon hearing the news were overwhelming, and they soon began to search for some agent to hold accountable for their loss. Popularly, the 'fatal heart attack was widely blamed on the stress of recent events, particularly the failure of the Cairo peace talks he [Nasser] convened to try to stop the "Black September" civil war'.[106] Indeed, a certain feeling of guilt spread among some Arabs, having witnessed their beloved leader working day and night, incessantly, against doctors' orders, desperately attempting to bring bloodshed among Arabs to an end. It is as though the president, whose attendance to Arab causes was deemed exceptional, did in fact die for, but equally because of, those very causes. 'Intra-Arab fighting, it was said, had broken Nasser's heart.'[107]

It is within this context that the notion of Nasser as a *shahid* (martyr) began to grow, not only among ordinary citizens but also among writers and intellectuals. Both in Egypt and in other Arab countries, Nasser's death was seen by some as an act of sacrifice, the paragon of a selfless life that was entirely devoted to the welfare of the Arab people. A few months after his death, a Syrian female poet published a collection of poems whose title captured these feelings. Published in November 1970, *Shahid al-Tadhiyat* (The Martyr of Sacrifices) revealed less a poetic prowess than 'the essence of a grieving heart which has been crushed by the catastrophe'.[108] The collection, written in the classical form of the Arabic poem, was prefaced by a dedication to Nasser, who 'died as a martyr while performing the greatest human service to Arabs'. The dedication was signed by the poet al-Hisni who introduced herself as a 'Nasserist Arab citizen from Damascus'.[109]

The two most notable contributions in this regard, however, were those of Fu'ad Haddad (1927–85), Egypt's leading vernacular poet, and Nizar Qabbani (1923–98), the Arab world's most popular poet at the time. In November 1970, Fu'ad Haddad embarked on writing an elegy for Nasser that was tellingly entitled, *'Istishhad Gamal Abdel Nasser'* (The Martyrdom of Nasser). Initially intended as a lengthy piece, Haddad explains that only two parts were completed. Written in Egyptian colloquial, the poem abounds with references to Nasser as a *shahid*, as in 'O God, why did not you give the *shahid* a chance to bid us farewell', or 'Farewell, O father, the most soulful *shahid*'.[110] In addition, Haddad, in line with the prevailing discourse on Nasser's death, alludes to the president's fatally exhausting days prior to his death: 'Keep on doing the right thing, O greatest of Arabs; / Who spent ten days and nights with no sleep.[111]

The second part of the poem, optimistically entitled, *'Lazim T'ish al-Muqawma'* (Resistance Must Live On) more emphatically creates a special connection between Nasser's death and the tragic events that were concurrently befalling Palestinians in Jordan. Thus, 'a Palestinian orphan seeks to confide his sorrows in you;' 'you had to stop the bloodshed in Jordan.'[112] Only Nasser could have healed the wounds:

> O the heart of Nasser
> Stand up for *jihad* and duty
> For the meeting with the kings
> For orphans who hastened to search for you.[113]

But if Haddad shows both appreciation for Nasser's sacrifices and fears about the fate of Palestinians in Jordan after his death, Nizar Qabbani goes so far as to hold Arabs responsible for Nasser's death. For Qabbani, Nasser was metaphorically killed by Arabs, who were unworthy of such a phenomenal man. As such, he was only the last in a chain of prophets and martyrs whose demise was brought about by the very same people whom they served. Characterised by an angry voice and a hyperbolic, condemning diction – common in Qabbani's political poetry – the poem launches an attack against Arabs, the poet included, where 'a relentless rhythm of "we" and "you" casts Nasser as a paternal protector and the Arabs as disloyal children'.[114] It opens thus:

> We killed you, O last of the prophets.
> We killed you. It is not new for us
> To kill the *Sahaba*[115] and the saints.
> For many are the prophets that we have killed . . .
> Many are the imams that we have slaughtered
> While they were praying the evening prayer.
> Our history is a mere calamity,
> Our days are all Karbala.[116]

Naturally, Black September rears its head once more, where the poem sees in Nasser's death his ultimate disillusion with the potential for progress of Arabs who temporally belong to the time of *Jahiliyya* (pre-Islamic era):

> We watered you with the poison of Arabness till you were full
> We threw you in the fire of Amman till you were burnt
> We showed you the betrayal of Arabness till you lost faith.
> Why did you appear in the land of hypocrites?
> Why did you appear? For we are the people of *Jahiliyya*.[117]

Depicting Nasser as a martyr harmonises with the Islamic notion of martyrdom which does not restrict the category to those who die in battle. As Talal Asad notes, 'The Islamic tradition has described several ways of dying as *shahada* that are not connected with war.'[118] Of these ways, natural death is featured prominently, befalling those who die 'either while engaged in a meritorious act such as a pilgrimage or a prayer, or after leading a virtuous life'.[119]

This meritorious act has in the modern time been extended to other mundane, non-religious spheres, such as serving the nation or any other cause in which one believes. As such, the word *shahid* has at times been stripped of its religious connotations and, instead, appropriated by groups, such as communists, who are commonly seen as antagonistic to Islam. This in part explains how, in the context of Palestinian resistance movements, *shahid* was used to designate those who died while engaging in the struggle for Palestine, regardless of the way in which they died. In other words, *shahada*, contrary to common (mis) conceptions, is not only about the faith that leads you to a heavenly hereafter, it is equally, for many, about worldly affairs, social justice, and dignity. It is 'an ideology that could easily thrive in a secular context, where the individual has little hope for the afterlife, but wants to leave behind a lasting legacy'.[120]

With the publication of Gamal al-Ghitani's *Kitab al-Tajalliyat* (The Book of Epiphanies)[121] in 1983, the approach to the theme in literature of Nasser's martyrdom took on an altogether different form. Whereas he was seen earlier as someone who devoted his life to the good of his people, thereby attaining, despite his natural death, the position of martyr, in *Kitab al-Tajalliyat* Nasser's death was fantastically revisited, whereby Nasser himself was resurrected, thrown back into life, and physically killed by his enemy. In so doing, al-Ghitani transformed Nasser into a battlefield martyr, one whose earlier sacrifices for the nation were attested by the blood that flowed from him in war.

Kitab al-Tajalliyat conforms to al-Ghitani's recognised writing techniques where he 'predominantly parodies an archaic Arabic style, which he resurrects from his constant dialoguing with the Arabic literary heritage'.[122] If he imitated the style of medieval historians in his well-known novel, *al-Zayni Barakat*, al-Ghitani turns to Sufi writing in *al-Tajalliyat*. In fact, the title itself relates to Sufism, particularly to the legendary master Ibn Arabi who had, arguably, written a book with the same title before.[123] Ibn Arabi's appropriation of the word *tajalli* added a mystical dimension to its original meaning, which has to do with emergence, clarity, and appearance. For him, *tajalli* means '*ma yankashifu li al-qulub min asrar al-ghuyub*'[124] (that which appears before the heart from the secrets of the unseen). It is more specifically related to 'seeing Allah everywhere, a gift that is primarily bestowed upon prophets and saints'.[125]

Al-Ghitani's work is massive, consisting of intentionally disparate reflections on death, time, martyrdom, and finitude. Its eight hundred pages, divided into three books, constitute a semi-autobiographical narrative in which the author/narrator Gamal retells the contents of a spiritual journey that he has just experienced. What unfolds is an 'associative reminiscing [that] takes the narrator's discourse from one story line to another, then back to the earlier one in a maze-like sequence that is accentuated by the fragmentary structure of the narrative'.[126] The book is triggered by the death of al-Ghitani's father in 1980. The despondent son, who happens to be away at that tragic moment, feels distraught, with an eruptive sense of mortality overwhelming him. Torn between 'a finite existence, and a desire for an infinite one',[127] the narrator seeks to defy death by embarking on a journey that annihilates history, resuscitates the dead, and obliterates the otherwise fixed barriers between past and present, here and there, and self and other. Only through a Sufi concept of *tajalli* can time be suspended, spaces traversed, and ephemerality challenged – hence the narrator's determination to 'see what nobody had seen; to live that which had never occurred to anyone; to be illuminated. To be illuminated. To be illuminated.'[128] As one critic puts it,

> *Kitab al-Tajalliyat* reflects the writer's dream of possessing time and the impossible quest to travel through it. Points of time overlap through *tajalliyat* . . . whereby the narrator witnesses the moment his father was born; sees his father as a child and his mother as a child, a young girl, and a bride; sees the moment he himself was born, as well as the birth of his beloved Lour.[129]

It is in these illuminations that Nasser matters. The loss of the narrator's father is accompanied by a cataclysmic vanishing of the Nasserite dream, manifested in the narrative largely through Sadat's economic policy of *Infitah* and the relinquishment of Egyptians' and Palestinians' rights by signing a peace agreement with Israel. The narrator, unable to fathom these drastic changes, seeks to retain that romantic, Nasserite past or, more precisely, to entwine it with the present so that the dead Nasser can be brought to life again. If Sadat's policies are tantamount to stabbing his predecessor's ideals in the back, the narrative materialises this betrayal by pitting the two men against each other on a battlefield.

However, the pair, Nasser/the narrator's father, acquires a mythological dimension through the appearance of Imam al-Husayn. In fact, the narrative first introduces these three figures together, acting like the focus of a light that dazzles the narrator's eyes. Later on, al-Husayn functions as a guide who leads the narrator through his multiple epiphanies. And it is the martyrdom of Imam al-Husayn in the Battle of Karbala that the narrative employs as a device through which to link the past to the present.

Al-Husayn is perhaps the most significant martyr in Islamic history, and he certainly is for Shi'ites. His killing, together with his immediate family and the few supporters who stood with him, in Karbala in AD 680 at the hands of the Umayyads was a defining moment in Arabic and Islamic history, and the Battle of Karbala would become a symbol for 'righteous struggle against worldly injustice'.[130] In most of the historical accounts,

> Al-Husayn is presented as the paradigmatic heroic figure, who cares for his fallen children, tries to obtain water for the non-combatant women and young ones, and fights nobly until the end. When he dies, he is said to have received at least thirty-three wounds and killed a number of the enemy. His body is treated ignobly; he was trampled under the hooves of the horsemen [sic], and his head was cut off and presented to 'Ubaydullah b. Ziyad, the Umayyad governor, and eventually to the caliph Yazid in Damascus.[131]

The centrality of al-Husayn's martyrdom in Muslim and, particularly, Shi'ite imagination cannot be overstated. Its annual commemoration and mourning on 'Ashura Day, its multiple interpretations, and its relevance to the Islamic Revolution in Iran are but a few manifestations of a tragedy that has been regarded by the Shi'ite community as a 'cosmic event around which the entire history of the world, prior as well as subsequent to it, revolves'.[132]

As Nizar Qabbani's earlier poem shows, Karbala has been invoked in the context of Nasser's death, albeit in passing. Nowhere in modern Arabic literature, however, have the Battle and al-Husayn's martyrdom occupied a larger space than in *Kitab al-Tajalliyat*. This space, I argue, follows what Michael Fischer calls the 'Karbala paradigm', where the Battle and its protagonist function as a 'rhetorical device' that al-Ghitani reworks in a different domain. According to Fischer, the story 'can be elaborated and abbreviated. It provides models for living and a mnemonic for thinking how to live.'[133]

Al-Ghitani stages Nasser's fantastic death as another Karbala, borrows the details of the Battle's original setting, and turns the Egyptian president into a Husayn. In so doing, al-Ghitani engages in a *karbalisation* of Nasser's fate, lending his otherwise natural death an entirely new meaning. Moreover, by appropriating Karbala in a secular setting, featuring as it does Nasser vis-à-vis Israel, the United States, and Sadat, al-Ghitani manages to de-sectarianise al-Husayn, detach him from the Shi'ite vs Sunni debate to which he is often related, and transform him into a humanistic symbol.

The narrative establishes several parallels between al-Husayn and Nasser, a few of which precede the latter's surreal resurrection. For instance, the narrator tells al-Husayn in one *tajalli* how he and his father used to 'pray the Eid prayer at your mosque, where we would see Nasser and his procession'.[134] He mentions his father's frequent visits to al-Husayn's grave in the mosque where it is popularly believed that the Imam's head was buried after Karbala.[135] Interestingly, the homage is reversed shortly, as it is al-Husayn and the narrator who now appear before Nasser's grave. Upon their arrival, al-Husayn draws the narrator's attention to roses that blossom on top of the grave:

> He pointed to small red roses that are penetrated by blue circles, whose centers are in turn occupied by white dots. He said that these roses emanate from him [Nasser], and that he emanates from them.[136]

Such saint-like depiction of Nasser, which permeates the narrative, establishes what one critic describes as a hagiographic discourse in which Nasser appears as a spiritual hero whose life is sanctified.[137] Hagiography is a genre that 'favours the actors of the sacred realm, "saints", and intends to edify, through exemplarity'.[138] Of the hagiographic tales, the martyr's flourishes 'wherever the community is very marginal, confronted with the threat of extinction'.[139] This is precisely the case in *Kitab al-Tajalliyat* where the martyrdom of Nasser is seen as the epitome of a 'phantasmagoric confrontation between the symbols of good and those of evil'.[140]

As mentioned earlier, the narrative conjures up a resurrection of Nasser. In a section entitled *Tajalli al-Mustahil* (The Epiphany of the Impossible), the president is seen by the narrator in the early 1980s, and the encounter takes place in Dokki Square in Cairo. This choice of location is significant for the neighbourhood housed the first Israeli embassy in Egypt. To the narrator's dismay, no one else notices the appearance of Nasser. Their first conversation goes as follows:

> 'How are you? What is up with you?'
> 'You know me?'
> 'Who does not know him who needs no introduction?'
> He nodded his head. I noticed that his hair has turned completely gray.
> 'So I am in Egypt.'
> I was taken aback. He shouted,
> 'I see what should not be seen.'
> He paused for a minute, before muttering words imbued with puzzlement and questions.
> 'Did the Israelis infiltrate the front?'
> 'No,' I said.
> 'Did their army reach Cairo?'
> 'No,' I said.
> 'What is it that I see, then? Explain it to me,' he said.[141]

This emergence establishes the first episode of the Karbala paradigm in *Kitab al-Tajalliyat*. Similar to al-Husayn's travel to Kufa in order to lead the rebellion against the Umayyads, Nasser's return is seen as 'answering the call of those helpless, weak people'.[142] If al-Husayn is betrayed by the people of Kufa, whom the poet al-Farazdaq (641–732) had famously characterised as 'their hearts are with you, but their swords are with the Umayyads',[143] so too is Nasser who is now 'wanted, chased after. He needs to hide and finds no hideout. His followers deserted him.'[144] The conflation of epochs is further intensified when Nasser is captured by an officer whom the narrative describes as working for 'Ubaydullah b. Ziyad, the *wali* of Kufa who orchestrated the crackdown against al-Husayn in Karbala.[145]

Underlying the reason behind Nasser's fantastic return is the ultimate continuity that the narrative establishes between the president and al-Husayn. In a twist that somehow affirms the hagiographic nature of the text, Nasser seeks those who have killed al-Husayn, identifies them, and prepares for a war of retaliation. The enemy turns out to be none other than Sadat himself, backed by Israel and the United States, who, like the

Umayyads before him, amasses thousands of people to face the Karbala-esque meagre number of warriors that Nasser leads. As such, the narrative confirms the cyclic nature of history where every martyr is a Husayn, every enemy is a Yazid, and every battle is a Karbala. Nasser's supporters are killed, one by one, each bidding him farewell moments before they vanish, saying, 'Peace be upon you, O protector of the poor, champion of the homeland'.[146] Eventually, Nasser stands alone, whereupon Sadat – who is never explicitly named but rather referred to as *al-jilf al-jafi* (the blunt ingrate) – approaches him and, at the behest of Americans and Israelis, cuts off his head, thus epitomising the paradigm.[147]

With no more than seventy warriors, Nasser's battle is obviously deemed lost. In fact, one can see in Nasser's act less an attempt to retaliate, as the narrative hints, than a determination to encounter death. Written in the aftermath of Sadat's peace agreement with Israel, the rise of violent Islamic movements in Egypt, and the collapse of the Nasserite project, the narrative is an elegy for a bygone era whose end can only be realised through a bloody rupture. On the other hand, *Kitab al-Tajalliyat* is a fixation on the passive, if heroic, dimension of Karbala. Its view of the struggle for one's rights is fatalistic where Karbala inexorably has to duplicate itself almost verbatim. Unlike the combative interpretation of Karbala, which aims 'to have the martyrdom of the prophet's grandson understood as a call for struggle, and not . . . as a tragic incident that was to be mourned in passive suffering',[148] al-Ghitani's *Tajalliyat* celebrates a valiant loss. Nasser, literally the victorious, empties his name of its content for, as a Husayn, he can only be an inevitably crushed martyr.

Nasser as a Defendant

In 1983, Naguib Mahfouz published *Amam al-'Arsh* (Before the Throne), a book that 'surprised his readers (and presumably himself as well)'.[149] Subtitled, 'A Dialogue with the Rulers of Egypt from Menes to Anwar Sadat', the book's surprise stemmed from the fact that it was Mahfouz's first return to the pharaonic past in a work of literature in more than forty years. While it 'complicates the standard linear development of Mahfouz's career',[150] this return to a pharaonic setting was read as a discourse on the current time, indicative of Mahfouz's 'rediscovering [of] the usefulness of history as a medium for expressing himself on the present'.[151] In addition, it was seen as the writer's attempt 'to remind Egyptian readers of the uniqueness of Egyptian identity – a national identity which precedes Arabism and Islam'.[152]

Furthermore, the book's structure calls into question the literary genre to which it belongs. Consisting of sixty-four dramatic scenes with very minimal narration, the book is a unique experiment in Mahfouz's literary output. Ever since its publication, critics have been divided as to how to label it. 'The real question is whether it falls into the genre of fiction or drama,'[153] as Raymond Stock, who translated the book into English, puts it. While Samia Mehrez unequivocally dubs it as 'not a novel',[154] and Waïl Hassan, perhaps noting a continuity between *Amam al-'Arsh* and Mahfouz's early historical novels, considers it the beginning of 'late pharaonic novels',[155] Menahem Milson, throughout the chapter he dedicates to it, merely refers to *Amam al-'Arsh* as 'the book', implicitly attending to the problem of categorising.[156] Rasheed El-Enany sums up the discussion as follows:

> It is a difficult book to classify, being unlike anything previously or since written by Mahfuz. It certainly is not a historical novel, nor is it a scholarly book of history in spite of its strict adherence to historical fact. Based mainly on dialogue rather than narration, it used a fictitious dramatic situation (i.e. the underworld trial) to bring into focus a certain vision of Egyptian history in its entirety. This however does not make the book a play as it consists of independent scenes held together only by the unities of space, action, and theme without either a plot or character development.[157]

Mahfouz's surprises do not end here, however. For the book, which features a surreal trial of Egypt's men of power from time immemorial, produced an unprecedented characterisation of Nasser in Egyptian literature: the defendant. Borrowing from Egyptian mythology, the book's tribunal is headed by Osiris and Isis. 'Egyptian leaders file in, one by one, and are questioned on their deeds and misdeeds.'[158] Trials follow a chronological order, with Nasser occupying the penultimate section. Mahfouz introduces major modifications to the original ancient setting, however, particularly to the way that the final verdict is passed. The pharaonic myth had it that Osiris, the god of the underworld, was responsible for judging the souls of the dead, aided by his sister–wife Isis, his son Horus, and Thoth, the scribe of the gods. In the judgment hall,

> Osiris sat enthroned surrounded by forty-two judges. (This number evokes the forty-two district rulers of Egypt.) A pair of scales was placed before him to weigh the heart of the deceased against a feather, the symbol of Ma'at. The keeper of the balance was Thoth, the god of magic. Anubis, the guide of souls, led the deceased before Osiris. Nearby, a monster called the 'devourer' stood ready to swallow those who were condemned.[159]

The goddess Ma'at symbolised 'harmony, justice, order, and truth'.[160] Those dead Egyptians who passed the balance test 'were rewarded with immortality'.[161]

Mahfouz's version of the trial, in turn, eliminates the scale, Ma'at, and the devourer. Perhaps influenced by the biblical–Koranic narrative of the hereafter, Mahfouz creates three kinds of verdict: Heaven and Immortality, Hell, as well as a third position which he calls *Maqam al-Tafihin* (The Realm of the Unworthy). In his translation of the novel, Raymond Stock renders this term 'Purgatory'.[162] Also missing from Mahfouz's appropriation are the forty-two judges who are interestingly replaced by whoever is acquitted and finds a space among the immortals. In other words, the book intends to confront Egypt's past leaders with their successors, thereby creating an inter-ruler debate. The two final words are respectively left to Isis, however, who acts as an intercessor, and Osiris, who declares the final ruling.

Legitimately, and perhaps inevitably, one has to consider the reason that compels Mahfouz to resort to a pharaonic medium by which to assess Egyptian history. Much attention has been given to the fact that Mahfouz sees Egypt as primarily pharaonic, thus challenging, among other things, what Menahem Milson calls 'the myth of Gamal 'Abd al-Nasir' and, by extension, the latter's fixation on Egypt's Arab identity.[163] Indeed, *Amam al-'Arsh* shows an essentialist view of Egypt, bestowing less indigenousness on those Egyptians who converted to Christianity or Islam and who, unlike the pharaonic kings, will not be categorically subjected to Osiris' final verdict. Rather, the deity's judgment will be 'a sort of historical appraisal that we hope will be duly considered when the citizen is tried by his proper religious court in the Abode of the Everlasting'.[164] Equally significant is that, by placing him as a defendant among a series of Egyptian leaders, the book strips Nasser of any exceptional status in Egyptian history, rendering him a mere dot in the enormous book of Egypt – as a normal president whose importance is acknowledged yet whose paramount centrality, so commonly believed, is obliterated.

I would like, however, to venture another approach to *Amam al-'Arsh*'s representation of Nasser's character. In his most direct attempt to come to terms with Nasser, following decades of allegorical and less explicit representations of him, Mahfouz opts for the format of trial to evaluate the president. Why? What are the openings and the limitations that such a format offers or imposes? By posing Nasser as a defendant, I argue that the book exemplifies the polyphonic nature of Mahfouz's works whereby the author creates 'a plurality of independent and unmerged voices and consciousness, a genuine polyphony of fully valid voices'.[165] Hence the trial – and, equally significant, the brilliant detail that Mahfouz adds to the ancient setting of allowing the former leaders to engage in arguments with their successors. In the work that culminates 'the problem of neutrality and the refusal to take sides',[166] as Samia Mehrez puts it, Mahfouz, the real occupant of the throne, allows Nasser to speak freely, to defend, refute, attack, and even to apologise – acts that Nasser himself had so long been accused of denying his opponents.

Not surprisingly, Nasser's trial occupies the longest section of the book. Summoned to enter the hall by Horus, he is given the chance to speak by Osiris. Nasser's long defence reads:

> I come from the village of Beni Murr, in the districts around Asyut. I was raised in a poor family, from the popular classes, and endured the bitterness and hardship of life. I graduated from the War College in 1938, and took part in Wafdist demonstrations. I was besieged along with others at Falluja in 1949. The loss of Palestine dismayed me, but what disturbed me even more was the depth of the defeat's roots inside the homeland. Then it dawned on me that I should transfer the fight to within, where the real enemies of the nation were hiding in ambush. Cautiously and in secret, I formed the Free Officers' organisation. I watched as events unfolded, waiting for the right moment to swoop down upon the regime in power. I realised my objective in 1952, then the Revolution's achievements – such as the abolition of the monarchical system, the completion of the total withdrawal of British troops from the country, the breaking up of the big landed estates

through the law of agricultural reform, the Egyptianisation of the economy, and the planning for the comprehensive revamping of both farming and industry to benefit the people and to dissolve the divisions between the classes – came one after another.[167]

Given the historical context of that era, such endeavours certainly cannot pass without the interference of the imperialist forces. 'They', Nasser proceeds, in a style that is redolent of the president's actual speeches,

> lay waiting to spring upon me – and then the detestable defeat of 5 June 1967 descended upon me. The great work was shaken to its foundations, and I was doomed to what seemed like death three years before I actually expired. I lived a sincere Egyptian Arab, and died an Egyptian Arab martyr.[168]

After a few exchanges between Nasser and some pharaonic kings, including Rameses II, Menes, and Abnum, whose brief evaluations of Nasser largely depend on the last's resemblance of them,[169] the book turns to more relevant, contemporary reckoning of the president. Introducing Saad Zaghlul and Mustafa al-Nahhas, the trial turns into a confrontation between the two most significant political movements in twentieth-century Egypt – the Wafd Party and the Free Officers Movement. It is in these heated exchanges that Mahfouz's own voice is best recognised. A lifelong Wafdist, Mahfouz is a forthright admirer of both leaders who are venerated 'in his works wherever that period of modern Egyptian history is invoked, and especially in The Trilogy'.[170] He structures the dialogues between Nasser and the two men in a way that begs for a reconsideration of the 'neutrality' that Samia Mehrez ascribes to *Amam al-'Arsh*. In fact, Mahfouz had once explained his position as an author vis-à-vis the characters of his works, stating, 'My sympathies for a certain character appear one way or the other within the novel . . . when I represent the world with neutrality, I do so without being neutral'.[171]

Indeed! For, while he allows Nasser to defend himself, Mahfouz gives a markedly larger space to Zaghlul's and al-Nahhas's arguments. In addition, a glimpse at Mahfouz's own assessment of Nasser, which was published in several interviews, shows that he hides behind the two men, putting his words into their mouths. For instance, Zaghlul's reproach, 'You attempted to blot my name from existence, along with the name of Egypt',[172] echoes Mahfouz's public statement that 'The first defect of the July Revolution lied in *tanakkur* (repudiating) . . . the Wafd Party, which had been struggling for Egypt's independence from 1919 until 1952'.[173] Similarly, when al-Nahhas shows how Nasser's 'defiance of the world's powers led . . . to horrendous losses and shameful defeats',[174] it resonates with what Mahfouz once said, 'I would not have blamed Nasser for his policies had he had the sufficient economical and military power to confront and challenge the super imperialist powers'.[175] Even the rare instances in which Nasser's accomplishments are acknowledged hint at Mahfouz's known reasons to appreciate the president, particularly with regard to his undisputed attention to the poor of Egypt. While al-Nahhas in *Amam al-'Arsh* remarks in passing, 'I do not deny that you kept faith with the poor',[176] Mahfouz never ceases to elaborate on Nasser's care for lower classes, often considering it his most perennial virtue: 'Nasser was the fairest to the poor. He gave them so much. What he could not concretely realise, he transformed into a hope – hence people will never forget him, because hope never dies.[177]

Equally significant, Nasser is not given the chance to seal the reciprocal arguments. Instead of listening to the defendant offering his final plea, Mahfouz enables Nasser's opponent, Mustafa al-Nahhas, to proceed uninterrupted with his last, long, somewhat rhetorical attack, facing no rebuttal:

> If only you had been more modest in your ambitions, if only you had stuck to reforming your nation and had opened the windows of progress to her in all areas of civilisation. The development of the Egyptian village was more important than the world's revolutions . . . unfortunately, you wasted an opportunity that had never appeared to the country before. For the first time, a native son ruled the land, without contention from a king or coloniser. Yet rather than curing the disease-ridden citizen, he drove him into a competition for the world championship when he was hobbled by illness. The outcome was that the citizen lost the race, and himself, as well.[178]

Obviously, such harsh evaluation is bound to produce an equally harsh judgment by Osiris. Mahfouz leaves the debate on Nasser unsettled, however. In a perfect instance of inconclusiveness in modern Arabic literature, typical of Mahfouz, Nasser eventually proves an unfinalised hero, an 'unfinished dialogue'[179] who, as Mikhail Bakhtin explains, 'is not a final and defined quantity upon which firm calculations can be made.'[180] Mahfouz, an inheritor of Dostoevsky's polyphonic style, engages with Nasser in a 'fully realised and thoroughly consistent dialogic position, one that affirms the independence, internal freedom, unfinalizability, and indeterminacy of the hero'.[181] Hence Osiris' opening line in his verdict, 'If our trial here had the last word in your judgment, we would be compelled to give long difficult consideration to arrive at justice.'[182] It is as though the court (and, by extension, Mahfouz himself) is relieved from the necessity of passing a final ruling on such a multifaceted character. As mentioned earlier, Muslim and Christian Egyptians are not to be decisively judged by Osiris. Nasser is therefore only allowed 'to sit with the Immortals until this tribunal ends. Afterward, you shall go to your final trial with an appropriate recommendation.'[183] A recommendation for which verdict is left to speculation, and Mahfouz dismounts from his throne ambiguously, leaving much to say to future literary imaginations of the president.

Conclusion

Ever since he assumed power in 1952, Nasser has been a notable subject of literary representations. The enigmatic, charismatic, and complex nature of his character, together with the magnitude of his ambitions, achievements, and tragic shortcomings and failures have ignited authors' imaginations, who have approached him in multiple but equally memorable ways. In fact, the enormous presence that Nasser has enjoyed in Egyptian everyday life, particularly during his tenure, has often invited symbolic interpretation of otherwise non-specific literary references. Many critics in Egypt and the Arab world have seen allegories of Nasser in works that introduced characters belonging to the ruling elite, the army, or the intelligentsia. As most of these depictions were negative, they stirred controversies in the Egyptian literary scene, with Nasser himself feeling occasionally compelled to intervene. It was a long while, however, before Nasser explicitly became a protagonist in literary narratives – a fictionalised character whose connection with the real Nasser was mediated, negotiated, and at times obscured.

This chapter studied four Egyptian narratives in which Nasser was allegorically or explicitly introduced as a protagonist. It argued that these representations departed from the historical archive to reimagine alternative episodes in Nasser's life. Far from adopting a singular view of him, these works contributed to the ever-present debate about the legacy of Nasser. By depicting him as an intellectual, an animal, a martyr, and a defendant, these narratives presented models of interpretation of Nasser's character, each producing a Nasser of its own. As the previous pages showed, 'Nasser as Fiction' is a space of literary production that enables Egyptian writers to reflect on the multiple meanings that Nasser still invokes for Egyptians. As such, this space can be regarded as much a commentary on the past as it is a consideration of the future – a present where a man, long dead, is still heard, seen, and felt.

Notes

1. Georg Lukács, *The Historical Novel*, trans. H. and S. Mitchell (London: Merlin Press, 1962), pp. 37–8.
2. Seymour Menton, *Latin America's New Historical Novel* (Austin, TX: University of Texas Press, 1993), p. 23.
3. Fredric Jameson, *The Political Unconscious: Narrative as a Socially Symbolic Act* (Ithaca, NY: Cornell University Press, 1981), p. 153.
4. Joseph W. Turner, 'The Kinds of Historical Fiction: An Essay in Definition and Methodology', *Genre* (autumn 1979), p. 337.
5. Menton, *Latin America's New Historical Novel*, p. 23.
6. Lloyd Hughes Davies, *Projections of Peronism in Argentine Autobiography, Biography, and Fiction* (Cardiff: University of Wales Press, 2007), p. 262.
7. Robert Holton, *Jarring Witnesses: Modern Fiction and the Representation of History* (Hertfordshire: Harvester Wheatsheaf, 1994), p. 165.
8. Xenia Gasiorowska, *The Image of Peter the Great in Russian Fiction* (Madison, WI: University of Wisconsin Press, 1979), p. 120.
9. Margarit Litvin, *Hamlet's Arab Journey: Shakespeare's Prince and Nasser's Ghost* (Princeton NJ, Oxford: Princeton University Press, 2011), p. 44.
10. Virginia Danielson, *The Voice of Egypt: Umm Kulthum, Arabic Song, and Egyptian Society in the Twentieth Century* (Chicago, IL: University of Chicago Press, 1997), p. 168.
11. Mehrez, *Egyptian Writers Between History and Fiction*, p. 26. For the English translation of this novel, see Naguib Mahfouz, *Adrift on the Nile*, trans. Frances Liardet (New York: Anchor Books, 1993).
12. Ghali Shukri, *Naguib Mahfouz: min al-Jammaliyya ila Nobel* (Cairo: Al-Hay'a al-'Amma li al-Isti'lamat, 1988), p. 56. The English translation above is found in Mehrez, *Egyptian Writers between History and Fiction*, pp. 26–7.

13. Sabry Hafez, 'The Egyptian Novel in the Sixties', in *Critical Perspectives on Modern Arabic Literature*, ed. Issa Boullata (Washington, DC: Three Continents Press, Inc., 1980), p. 171.
14. Mehrez, *Egyptian Writers Between History and Fiction*, p. 21.
15. Rasheed El-Enany, *Naguib Mahfouz: The Pursuit of Meaning* (London and New York: Routledge, 1993), p. 25. For the English translation, see Naguib Mahfouz, *Children of Gebelawi*, trans. Philip Stewart (Washington, DC: Three Continents Press, 1988). Peter Theroux's translation was published in 1996 as *Children of the Alley: A Novel* (New York: Anchor Books, 1996).
16. Gabir 'Asfur, 'Hal Yamut Hadha al-Zammar?!' *Ibda'*, Vol. 9, No. 9 (1991), p. 28. Idris's 'Did You Have to Turn on the Light, Lili?' appeared in *The Essential Yusuf Idris: Masterpieces of the Egyptian Short Story*, edited by Denys Johnson-Davies (Cairo: The American University in Cairo Press, 2009), pp. 109–22.
17. Tawfiq al-Hakim, *'Awdat al-Wa'i* (Egypt: Dar al-Shuruq, 1974), p. 50. The English translation was quoted from Litvin, *Hamlet's Arab Journey*, p. 43. Al-Hakim's book was translated into English by Bayly Winder as *The Return of Consciousness* (New York: New York University Press, 1985).
18. Luis 'Awad, *Aqni'at al-Nasiriyya al-Sab'a* (Beirut: Dar al-Qadaya, 1975), p. 33. *The Sultan's Dilemma* appeared in Mahmoud Manzalaoui, *Arabic Writings Today: Drama* (Cairo: Publications of The American Research Center in Egypt, 1977), pp. 89–183.
19. Joseph Massad, *Desiring Arabs* (Chicago, IL and London: University of Chicago Press, 2007), p. 327. For the English translation of the story, see Yusuf Idris, *A Leader of Men*, trans. Saad Elkhadem (Fredericton, NB: York Press, 1988).
20. In discussion with the author in Cairo, October 2011. For the English translation of *al-Zayni Barakat*, see Gamal al-Ghitani, *Zayni Barakat*, trans. Farouk Abdel Wahab (Cairo: The American University in Cairo Press, 2010).
21. There are a few sources in English that offer insights into Haqqi's life and works. See, for example, Miriam Cooke, *Yahya Haqqi: the Anatomy of an Egyptian Intellectual* (Washington, DC: Three Continents Press, 1984). Expectedly, more works can be found in Arabic, including Bushusha Bin Jum'a, *Al-Qass wa al-Tahawwul* (Lattakia: Dar al-Hiwar, 1998); Yusuf al-Sharuni, ed., *Sab'un Sham'a fi Hayat Yahya Haqqi* (Cairo: Al-Hay'a al-Misriyya al-'Amma li al- Kitab, 1974); Naji Najib, *Yahya Haqqi wa Jil al-Hanin al-Hadari* (Cairo: Al-Hay'a al-Misriyya al-'Amma li al- Kitab, 1998); and Na'im 'Atiyya, *Yahya Haqqi wa 'Alamuhu al-Qasasi* (Cairo, Maktabat al-Anjlu al-Misriyya, 1978).
22. Nabil Faraj, 'Sah al-Nawm', p. 205

23. Cooke, *Yahya Haqqi*, p. 12.
24. For the English translation, see Yahya Haqqi, *The Lamp of Umm Hashim: And Other Stories*, trans. Denys Johnson-Davies (Cairo: The American University in Cairo Press, 2004). An earlier translation by Muhammad Mustafa Badawi appeared as *The Saint's Lamp and Other Stories* and was published by Brill in 1973.
25. Cooke, *Yahya Haqqi*, p. 7. Salih's novel appeared in English as *Season of Migration to the North*, trans. Denys Johnson-Davies (New York: NYRB Classics, 2009). For more on this theme, see Rasheed El-Enany, *Arab Representations of the Occident: East–West Encounters in Arabic Fiction* (London: Routledge, 2006).
26. Taha Hussein, *Naqd wa Islah* (Beirut: Dar al-'Ilm li al-Malayin, 1977), p. 154.
27. I am relying on Miriam Cooke's translation of the novel, which appeared in her *Good Morning and other stories* (Washington, DC: Three Continents Press, 1987), pp. 43–112.
28. Cooke, *Yahya Haqqi*, p. 8
29. Arabic for 'teacher' or 'master', the word is rendered by Cooke's translation of the novel as 'professor'. I find this translation limiting, however, for *al-ustadh* refers to any educated or learned man, whether professionally or not.
30. Haqqi, *Good Morning*, p. 46.
31. Ibid., p. 47.
32. Ibid., pp. 61–2, emphasis mine. I recognise that the register of the English translation in this quote is rather odd but I kept it in fidelity to the translator's choice.
33. Ibid., p. 73.
34. Ibid., p. 61.
35. Ami Elad, *The Village Novel in Modern Egyptian Literature* (Berlin: Klaus Schwarz Verlag, 1994), p. 22.
36. Haqqi, *Good Morning*, p. 76.
37. Cooke, *Yahya Haqqi*, p. 50.
38. Hussein, *Naqd wa Islah*, pp. 154–5.
39. Haqqi, *Good Morning*, p. 76.
40. Hussein, *Naqd wa Islah*, p. 157.
41. Haqqi, *Good Morning*, p. 51.
42. Ibid., p. 69.
43. Ibid., p. 79.
44. Cooke, *Yahya Haqqi*, p. 49.
45. Ibid.
46. Ibid., p. 54.
47. 'Atiyya, *Yahya Haqqi wa 'Alamuhu Al-Qasasi*, pp. 94–5.

48. Ibid., p. 95.
49. Ibid.
50. Abdel Hamid Al-Qut, *Bina' al-Riwaya fi al-Adab al-'Arabi* (Cairo: Dar al-Ma'arif, 1982), p. 210.
51. Faraj, 'Sah al-Nawm', p. 208.
52. Hussein, *Naqd wa Islah*, p. 159.
53. Ibid., p. 160, emphasis mine.
54. Haqqi, *Good Morning*, p. 78.
55. Ibid., p. 107.
56. Ibid., p. 82.
57. Ibid., p. 79.
58. Ibid., p. 82, emphasis mine.
59. Ibid., p. 98.
60. Ibid., p. 151.
61. Ibid., p. 111, emphasis mine.
62. Ibid., p. 81.
63. Ibid., p. 82.
64. Ibid., p. 83.
65. Ibid., p. 109.
66. Ibid., p. 81, emphasis mine.
67. Friedrich Nietzsche, *The Birth of Tragedy*, in *Basic Writings of Nietzsche*, trans. and ed. Walter Kaufmann (New York: The Modern Library, 2000), p. 60.
68. Haqqi, *Good Morning*, p. 83.
69. Ibid.
70. Ibid., p. 109.
71. Ibid.
72. Ibid., p. 111.
73. Ibid., p. 112.
74. For the English translation, see Yusuf Idris, *The Cheapest Nights*, trans. Wadida Wassef (Washington, DC: Three Continents Press, 1989).
75. *The Essential Yusuf Idris: Masterpieces of the Egyptian Short Story*, ed. Denys Johnosn-Davies (Cairo: The American University of Cairo Press, 2009), p. 1
76. Dalya Cohen-Mor, *Yusuf Idris: Changing Visions* (Potomac, MD: Sheba Press, 1992), p. 116.
77. Ghali Shukri, *Yusuf Idris: Farfur Kharij al-Sur* (Cairo: Al-Hay'a al-'Amma li al-Isti'lamat, 1992), p. 85.

78. Naji Najib, *Al-Hulm wa al-Haya: Fi Suhbat Yusuf Idris* (Cairo: Dar al-Hilal, 1985), pp. 87–8.
79. Roger Allen, 'Yusuf Idris' Short Stories: Themes and Techniques', in *Critical Perspectives on Yusuf Idris*, ed. Roger Allen (Colorado Springs: Three Continents Press, 1994), p. 26.
80. See Abdel Rahman Abu 'Awf, *Yusuf Idris wa 'Alamuhu fi al-Qissa al-Qasira wa al-Riwaya* (Cairo: Maktabat al-Usra, 2001), pp. 253–4.
81. Cohen-Mor, *Yusuf Idris*, p. 23.
82. Karen L. Ryan, *Stalin in Russian Satire: 1971-1991* (Madison, WI: University of Wisconsin Press, 2009), p. 50.
83. Tzvetan Todorov, *The Conquest of America: The Question of the Other* (New York: Harper & Row, 1982), pp. 153–4.
84. Habib al-Salimi, *Al-Uqsusa al-'Arabiyya wa Matlab al-Khususiyya: Majmu'at Bayt min Lahm li Yusuf Idris Namudhajan* (Qayrawan: Matba'at al-Nasr, 2006), p. 165.
85. P. M. Kurpershoek, 'The Later Stories', in *Critical Perspectives on Yusuf Idris*, p. 43.
86. The Koran, 88: 17–21. For the English translation, see A. J. Droge, *The Qur'an: A New Annotated Translation* (Bristol: Equinox Publishing Ltd, 2013), p. 432.
87. Kamal al-Din Al-Damiri, *Hayat al-Hayawan*, trans. A. S. G. Jaykar (London: 1906), Vol. 1, p. 26.
88. Robert Irwin, *Camel* (London: Reaktion Books Ltd, 2010), p. 68.
89. Yusuf Idris, *'al-Khud'a'* (Delusion) in *Flights of Fantasy: Arabic Short Stories*, eds Ceza Kassem and Malak Hashem (Cairo: Elias Modern Publishing House, 1985), p. 27, emphasis mine. I shall rely on Kassem's and Hashem's translation of the story throughout the chapter.
90. Ibid., p. 28.
91. Cohen-Mor, *Yusuf Idris*, p. 26.
92. Ryan, *Stalin in Russian Satire*, p. 49.
93. *'Al-Khud'a'*, p. 27.
94. Ibid., p. 32.
95. Ibid., pp. 27–8.
96. Ibid., p. 29.
97. Ibid., p. 32.
98. Ibid., p. 27.
99. Ibid., p. 31.
100. Ibid., p. 29.

101. Ibid., p. 31.
102. Ibid., p. 32.
103. Najib, *Al-Hulm wa al-Haya: Fi Suhbat Yusuf Idris*, p. 34.
104. Faruq Abdel Qadir, *al-Bahth 'an al-Yaqin al-Murawigh* (Cairo: Dar al-Hilal, 1998), p. 126. For more on Nasser's reaction to controversial texts that were published in *al-Ahram*, see Yusuf al-Qaid, *Muhammad Hasanayn Haykal Yatadhakkar*, particularly the section on Naguib Mahfouz, pp. 331–40.
105. Stephens, *Nasser*, p. 556.
106. Litvin, *Hamlet's Arab Journey*, p. 122.
107. Joel Gordon, *Nasser: Hero of the Arab Nation* (Oxford: Oneworld Publications, 2006), p. 122.
108. Al-Hisni, *Shahid al-Tadhiyat*, p. 70.
109. Ibid., p. 3.
110. Fu'ad Haddad, '*Istishhad Gamal Abdel Nasser: Misr wa Gamal*', in *Fu'ad Haddad: Al-A'mal al-Kamila*, eds Amin and Hassan Haddad (Cairo: Al-Hay'a al-'Amma li Qusur al-Thaqafa, 2006), Vol. 2, p. 300.
111. Ibid., p. 301.
112. Ibid., pp. 317 and 319
113. Ibid., p. 321.
114. Litvin, *Hamlet's Arab Journey*, p. 123.
115. Plural of *sahabi*, or companion. The term is used to designate Prophet Muhammad's companions.
116. Nizar Qabbani, '*Buka'iyya li Gamal Abdel Nasser*', in *Muhammad Huwwar, Buka' Ramz: Gamal Abdel Nasser fi Marathi al-Shu'ara'* (Beirut: Al-Mu'assasa al-'Arabiyya li al-Dirasat wa al-Nashr, 1997), p. 367.
117. Ibid., pp. 368–9.
118. Talal Asad, *On Suicide Bombing* (New York: Columbia University Press, 2007), p. 49.
119. Etan Kohlberg, *Medieval Muslim Views on Martyrdom* (Amsterdam: Koninklijke Nederlandse Akademie van Wetenschappen, 1997), p. 26.
120. Daniel Brown, 'Martyrdom in Sunni Revivalist Thought', in *Sacrificing the Self: Perspectives on Martyrdom and Religion*, ed. Margaret Cormack (Oxford and New York: Oxford University Press, 2001), p. 113.
121. The late Farouk Abdel Wahab's translation of this novel is titled, *The Book of Epiphanies: An Egyptian Novel* (Cairo: The American University in Cairo Press, 2012).
122. Mehrez, *Egyptian Writers Between History and Fiction*, p. 13.

123. See Ibn Arabi, *Kitab al-Tajalliyat*, ed. Ayman Hamdi (Cairo: Al-Hay'a al-Misriyya al-'Amma li al-Kitab, 2002).
124. Ibn Arabi, *al-Futuhat al-Makkiyya* (Cairo: Maktabat al-Thaqafa al-Diniyya), Vol. 2, p. 485.
125. Muhammad Ghazi 'Urabi, *al-Nusus fi Mustalahat al-Mutasawwifa* (Damascus: Dar Qutayba, 1985), p. 45. In addition to Abdel Wahab's rendition of the title as *The Book of Epiphanies*, other critical studies of the novel, quoted below, referred to it as *The Book of Theophanies*. Still, Khalid Osman, who translated the novel into French, opted for *Le Livre des Illuminations* (The Book of Illuminations).
126. Maha El Marraghi, 'Gamal al-Ghitani's *Kitab al-Tajalliyat (The Book of Theophanies)*: A Deconstructive Discourse' (unpublished MA thesis: Institute of Islamic Studies, McGill University, Montreal, 1992), p. 50.
127. Gamal al-Ghitani, *Kitab al-Tajalliyat: Al-Asfar al-Thalatha* (Cairo: Al-Hay'a al-Misriyya al-'Amma li al-Kitab, 1997), p. 37.
128. Ibid., p. 26.
129. Marwa Mitwalli, *Hadathat al-Nass al-Adabi al-Mustanid ila al-Turath al-'Arabi: Dirasa li Fanniyyat al-Mawruth al-Nathri wa Jamaliyyat al-Sard al-Mu'asir fi Adab Gamal al-Ghitani (1969–2005)* (Damascus: Dar al-Awa'il, 2008), p. 105.
130. Keith Lewinstein, 'The Reevaluation of Martyrdom in Early Islam', in Cormack, ed. *Sacrificing the Self*, p. 80.
131. David Cook, *Martyrdom in Islam* (Cambridge: Cambridge University Press, 2007), p. 57.
132. Mahmoud Ayoub, *Redemptive Suffering in Islam: A Study of the Devotional Aspects of 'Ashura in Tewlver Shi'ism* (The Hague: Mouton, 1978), p. 141.
133. Michael Fischer, *Iran: From Religious Dispute to Revolution* (Madison, WI: University of Wisconsin Press, 2003), p. 21.
134. Al-Ghitani, *Kitab al-Tajalliyat*, p. 38.
135. Cook, *Martyrdom in Islam*, p. 57.
136. Al-Ghitani, *Kitab al-Tajalliyat*, p. 88.
137. See Bashir al-Qumri, *Shi'riyyat al-Nas al-Riwa'i: Qira'a Tanassiyya fi Kitab al-Tajalliyat* (Rabat: al-Bayadir li al- Nashr wa al-Tawzi', 1991), p. 200.
138. Michel De Certeau, *The Writing of History*, trans. Tom Conley (New York: Columbia University Press, 1988), p. 269.
139. Ibid., p. 273.
140. El Marraghi, *Gamal al-Ghitani's Kitab al-Tajalliyat*, p. 152.
141. Al-Ghitani, *Kitab al-Tajalliyat*, pp. 12–13.
142. Ibid., p. 137.

143. Ibid., p. 136.
144. Ibid., p. 201.
145. Ibid., pp. 113–14.
146. Ibid., p. 234.
147. Ibid., p. 235.
148. Friederike Pannewick, 'Passion and Rebellion: Shi'iti Visions of Redemptive Martyrdom', in *Martyrdom in Literature: Visions of Death and Meaningful Suffering in Europe and the Middle East from Antiquity to Modernity*, ed. Friederike Pannewick (Wiesbaden: Reichert, 2004), p. 58. The most prominent advocate of such an interpretation is perhaps Ali Shariati. For a discussion of his thoughts and, more importantly, relevance to the Islamic Revolution in Iran see Hamid Dabashi, *Theology of Discontent: The Ideological Foundation of the Islamic Revolution in Iran* (New York: New York University Press, 1993), pp. 102–46.
149. El-Enany, *Naguib Mahfouz: The Pursuit of Meaning*, p. 42.
150. Waïl Hassan, 'Teaching a Seminar on Mahfouz', in *Approaches to Teaching the Works of Naguib Mahfouz*, eds Waïl Hassan and Susan Muaddi Darraj (New York: The Modern Language Association of America, 2012), p. 34. Hassan refers to critics' continuous attempts to classify Mahfouz's *oeuvre* into rigid stages, such as the romantic, the realistic, and the symbolic periods. For a good study and critique of this approach, see Gabir 'Asfur, 'Naguib Mahfouz's Critics', in *Naguib Mahfouz: From Regional Fame to Global Recognition*, eds Michael Beard and Adnan Haydar (New York: Syracuse University Press, 1993), pp. 144–71.
151. El-Enany, *Naguib Mahfouz*, p. 42.
152. Menahem Milson, *Najib Mahfuz: The Novelist-Philosopher of Cairo* (New York: St. Martin's Press, 1998), p. 94.
153. Raymond T. Stock, *A Mummy Awakens: The Pharaonic Fiction of Naguib Mahfouz* (UPenn Dissertations: Near Eastern Languages and Civilisations, 2008), p. 247.
154. Mehrez, *Egyptian Writers between History and Fiction*, p. 36.
155. Hassan, 'Teaching a Seminar on Mahfouz', p. 34.
156. Milson, *Najib Mahfuz*, pp. 144–55.
157. Rasheed el-Enany, 'The Novelist as a Political Eye-Witness: A View of Najib Mahfuz's Evaluation of Nasser and Sadat Eras', *Journal of Arabic Literature*, Vol. 21, No. 1 (March 1990), p. 82.
158. Mehrez, *Egyptian Writers between History and Fiction*, p. 37.
159. Bojana Mojsov, *Osiris: Death and Afterlife of a God* (Malden, MA: Blackwell Publishing, 2005), p. 48.

160. David P. Silverman, 'Divinity and Deities in Ancient Egypt', in *Religion in Ancient Egypt: Gods, Myths, and Personal Practice*, ed. Byron E. Shafer (Ithaca, NY and London: Cornell University Press, 1991), p. 48.
161. Ibid., p. 49.
162. See Naguib Mahfouz, *Before the Throne*, trans. Raymond Stock (Cairo: The American University in Cairo Press, 2009), pp. 50, 64, and 68. All quotations are taken from Stock's translation of the novel.
163. Milson, *Najib Mahfuz*, p. 153.
164. Mahfouz, *Before the Throne*, p. 80.
165. Mikhail Bakhtin, *Problems of Dostoevsky's Poetics*, p. 6.
166. Mehrez, *Egyptian Writers between History and Fiction*, p. 36.
167. Mahfouz, *Before the Throne*, p. 132.
168. Ibid., p. 133.
169. Ramesses II, for instance, tells Nasser, 'what is my affection for you but an extension of my love for myself? For look how much we resemble each other,' while Abnum declares, 'I want to testify that the wretched did not enjoy such security in any age – after my own – as they did in yours.' See Mahfouz, *Before the Throne*, pp. 133 and 134.
170. El-Enany, 'The Novelist as a Political Eye-Witness', p. 73.
171. Shukri, *Naguib Mahfouz: min al-Jammaliyya ila Nobel*, p. 82.
172. Mahfouz, *Before the Throne*, p. 134.
173. Raja' al-Naqqash, *Naguib Mahfouz: Safahat min Mudhakkiratih wa Adwa' Jadida 'ala Adabih wa Hayatih* (Cairo: Markiz al-Ahram li al-Tarjama wa al-Nashr, 1998), p. 193.
174. Mahfouz, *Before the Throne*, p. 136.
175. Al-Naqqash, *Naguib Mahfouz*, p. 198.
176. Mahfouz, *Before the Throne*, p. 136.
177. Muhammad Salmawi, *Fi Hadrat Naguib Mahfouz* (Cairo: Al-Dar al-Misriyya al-Lubnaniyya, 2012), p. 42.
178. Mahfouz, *Before the Throne*, pp. 136–7.
179. Bakhtin, *Problems of Dostoevsky's Poetics*, p. 63.
180. Ibid., p. 59.
181. Ibid., p. 63.
182. Mahfouz, *Before the Throne*, p. 137.
183. Ibid.

3

Nasser in Fiction

In the previous chapter, I discussed the works of Egyptian fiction where Nasser is one of the protagonists. These works are concerned not so much with representing a full biographical account of Nasser as with offering a particular model of engagement with his character. By introducing Nasser as an intellectual, a beast, a martyr, and a defendant, these narratives engage in a process of fictionalisation of the president, whereby Nasser's life is reimagined, altered, distorted, or anachronised. In so doing, the readers of these works are left with multiple Nassers whose representations in the texts, while claiming a link to the historical character that he was, do significantly depart from it. As was mentioned in the previous chapter, however, a larger corpus of Egyptian narratives opts for a different negotiation of Nasser's character. Represented through the actions, dialogues, or monologues of the main characters, Nasser in this category of writings does not emerge as a protagonist. Rather, he is described, debated, glorified, or undermined by protagonists whose lives interact with, or are influenced by, Nasser's. Nowhere in these narratives is Nasser given a voice. Nowhere does he directly speak. Nor, for that matter, do any of these narratives seek to portray portions of Nasser's life. In other words, Nasser emerges as a background, as a major or minor constituent of the history during which the events of these narratives develop.

In this chapter, I shall examine select literary narratives that feature Nasser as part of its discourse. These works, I argue, offer invaluable access to Nasser in the Egyptian imaginary, where the otherwise unknowable subjects of Nasser's Egypt are empowered to speak. As Naomi Sokoloff shows, 'Imaginative writing may penetrate the intimate, never communicated thoughts of someone else and so reveal the hidden side of people, or give voice to those not readily heard by society.'[1] Of all imaginative writing, narratives possess a salient position as a medium in which 'the unspoken thoughts, feelings, perceptions of a person other than the speaker can be portrayed'.[2] These narratives contribute considerably to the process of constructing the image of Nasser in the Egyptian imaginary whereby they are both shaped by, and shaping, the psyche of the nation. Pertinent to this discussion is Benedict Anderson's thesis on the role of the novel in constructing what he famously calls 'imagined communities'.[3] These refractions of the president, who has been one of the major components of Egyptian and, more broadly, Arab nationalism, are informative not only about the character of Nasser but, even more significantly, his impact on ordinary citizens.

As this chapter will demonstrate, these narratives do not share a monolithic discourse on Nasser, nor do they adopt a singular view of him. Rather, he looms as a perfect site of contestation, a contentious character whose multilayered, complicated life can naturally invoke contradictory responses. A Muslim Brother and a communist, for instance, while both sharing prison experience during Nasser's life, at times even languishing in the same cell, may still produce two largely disparate reactions to him. In addition, these narratives do not merely disseminate knowledge about Nasser that exists a priori – they do not, in other words, mirror an already established conception of him. There is no fixed 'Egyptian Imaginary' of Nasser that those works reflect. Instead, he is reproduced whenever a new work which includes him as part of its discourse emerges. If, according to Edward Said, 'nations themselves *are* narration',[4] so too is Nasser – a character that is constantly yet differently born out of the narratives that engage him.

This chapter will consider a thematic approach to the representations of Nasser in Egyptian narratives. Recognising the vast amount of literature, it claims no final word on the topic, still less an inclusive or comprehensive analysis of all the works that are worthy of examination. I argue, however, that the sections below may offer insights into largely unexplored and strikingly overlooked treatments of Nasser in Egyptian narratives. These narratives will therefore be divided into two themes: Nasser and children; and Nasser and women.

Nasser and Children

Children pose a challenge to narrative writers. On the one hand, it is often acknowledged that writers 'utilise childhood as a lucid space through which to criticise the adult world'.[5] Childhood connotes spontaneity, innocence, and beauty. It also signifies a stage where boundaries are often crossed and norms broken. In addition, novelists and autobiographers employ childhood 'as a means of inspecting how the world seemed when it was more settled and their individual lives were "easy under the bow"'.[6] Yet, on the other hand, the voice of the child in narrative may cast doubt on the authenticity of representation for it is a voice that is mediated by an adult author. 'How can any adult writer convincingly represent such an inconsistent and imaginary position with any sense of authority?'[7] asks Susan Honeyman. A solution may lie in the writer's attempt to withdraw from the narration process and let the child narrate only what the latter can see, feel, or perceive. With the author/adult narrator minimising his/her interference, the text will be 'oriented to the child's view, [offering] a simple, unembellished presentation of information available to the boy himself, in a form that often approaches deadpan'.[8]

The problem becomes all the more pressing when one recalls that the essentialist view of childhood has been debated in the last few decades. Following French historian Philippe Aries who, in his influential study *Centuries of Childhood*, shows that there was no concept of childhood in medieval cultures,[9] numerous scholars and intellectuals now maintain that 'in contrast to children, childhood as we know it, or have constructed it, has not existed since the beginning of time'.[10] The notion of the child has been seen as a modern phenomenon, a constructed category that emerged as 'everything the sophisticated adult was not, everything the rational man of the Enlightenment was not'.[11] Perceiving children as muted groups, as subjects who are incapable of representing themselves, modern adults conjured up a sphere of otherness, both elusive and captive, demonic and angelic, that they called childhood.

Having said that, a considerable interest in children, and childhood as a distinct phase in human life, still haunts narrative writers, and Arabic literature is no exception. In fact, Tetz Rooke notes how in recent Arabic autobiographies, for instance, adulthood is completely ignored. Noticing an abundance of texts whose titles bear the word 'childhood', he suggests the existence of 'the autobiography of childhood' as a subcategory of Arabic autobiography.[12] To a much lesser extent, children also feature as protagonists in Arabic novels, most notably in the *Bildungrosman* genre, with the character of Kamal in Naguib Mahfouz's *The Cairo Trilogy*[13] being the most salient example.

Interestingly, a number of Egyptian novels and autobiographies have represented Nasser through the eyes of children who were, in one way or another, directly affected by his personality, decisions, speeches, or ideas. The perspective of children offers these works a rare opportunity to approach Nasser in ways that the world of adults may not. It can indicate the incomprehensibility of the situation in which children find themselves vis-à-vis Nasser. Children's incomplete knowledge of the political context of their lives, these works show, may drive them to adopt different responses towards Nasser from those advanced by their families. As one critic puts it, this assumed unreliability of children's perspective can be seen as 'totally true to their own view of things but unrelated to a "reality" perceived by others. Such viewpoints serve as transparent lenses only for the children's realities.'[14]

More importantly, I argue that these works capture the children's developing awareness of the significance of Nasser at moments of severe familial crises during which their fathers emerge as the most negatively affected ones. In so doing, these works place children in an uncomfortable, unsettling position where 'the father's place . . . loses its unassailable eminence'.[15] The tension is all the more aggravated when the attack on the father at the hand of Nasser's regime is accompanied by the child's growing respect and love for Nasser. As I shall demonstrate below, these works pit biological fathers against Nasser – the figurative father of the nation, children included – and, at times, demand a certain belonging from children. They, in other words, corner children between filiation and affiliation, in Edward Said's articulation of the terms, where the forced absence of the father is juxtaposed with a sudden presence of Nasser in the child's world. Said argues that 'the transition from failed idea or possibility of filiation to a kind of compensatory order that, whether it is a party, an institution, a culture, a set of beliefs, or even a world-vision, provides men and women with a new form of relationship, which I have been calling affiliation'.[16] Similarly, Nasser, though not fully grasped by children, becomes their compensatory order whose very role behind the suffering that befalls their fathers destabilises their understanding of both.

It is worth noting here that Nasser's peculiar relationship with children is not only manifested through Egyptian literature; Egyptian newspapers repeatedly carried pictures of Nasser hugging, shaking hands, or holding children but also of children approaching Nasser, calling him, and finding their ways among the crowds to salute him. Of notable incidents is the picture that was featured on the front page of the Egyptian daily newspaper *al-Gumhuriyya* in the wake of Nasser's first visit to Syria following the declaration of the United Arab Republic in 1958. The picture showed a child approaching Nasser's procession while waving his hands and shouting something. The fact that the newspaper placed the picture, which must have been selected from hundreds that documented the visit, on its front page is indicative of the implied message that *al-Gumhuriyya* meant to deliver. A more recent and perhaps intriguing example is a picture that was widely circulated in the Egyptian virtual sphere in 2014. The picture featured Nasser leaning forward to shake hands with a boy while the latter was saluting him. Tens of Egyptian websites carried the picture, claiming the child shown in it was the then Defence Minister Abdel Fattah al-Sisi. Obviously, the picture was part of an orchestrated media campaign that sought to link al-Sisi to Nasser. While the picture turned out to be real, it was later confirmed that the child was not al-Sisi.[17] These incidents, and many more, testify to a certain pattern in Egyptian history which the fictional narratives below serve to complicate.

In his 1992 debut novel *Inkisar al-Ruh* (Breaking of the Spirit), Egyptian writer Muhammad al-Mansi Qandil (b.1946) portrays a coming-of-age story of the protagonist/narrator Ali against the backdrop of Nasser's and Sadat's Egypt. As the title suggests, the novel is an elegy for the generation of Egyptians who were born and raised during Nasser's regime, inculcated with its ideas, and thoroughly infused with its hopes and ideals, before their dreams were crushed by the 1967 defeat, Nasser's departure, and Sadat's radical change of the country's course. Through a phantom-like, ever-elusive girl named Fatima, who appears and disappears abruptly before Ali's eyes, the novel presents, rather fatalistically, an unfulfilled pursuit of impossible love.[18]

As the narrative unfolds, Ali gets caught up in the unfathomable world of adults. He is the only child of a poor factory worker (Najib) who has leftist leanings. Notwithstanding Ali's repeated announcements that he is 'big enough',[19] the child acknowledges his inability to understand his father's political activities in the factory. The father holds a negative view of the military regime, considering it a continuation of, rather than a rupture from, the previous rulers: 'The workers of this factory are always treated unjustly. The British used to be unfair to them, then the Pashas, and now the Officers are equally unjust to them.'[20] When Ali's mother informs him that his father and the co-workers are calling for a strike, he comments, 'I did not know at the moment what that meant . . . I wondered what was taking place behind the factory's walls. What was my father doing? And why did all workers choose this moment to carry out this thing that they call strike?'[21]

The narrative epitomises Ali's inability to comprehend the events that are taking place at his house with the arrest of his father. In a familiar pattern, perhaps reminiscent of Emir Kusturica's classic film *When Father Was Away on Business*,[22] Ali cannot make sense of what befalls his father. He notices that many soldiers violently break into the house and take the old man with them, descriptively recounting how 'I saw one of the soldiers' big cars waiting for him. I saw them pushing him outside the house door, force him inside the car, and eventually ride in it.'[23] He sees that his father does not return home, yet he never utters the word 'prison' nor, for that matter, does he ask his mother where his father is. In fact, when a few days later the mother informs Ali that they will both visit his father, the child comments, 'I stared at her, surprised . . . My father has a place . . . and we can visit him! Throughout this period, we have avoided speaking about him directly.'[24]

It is against this background that the name of Nasser first arises. Now deprived of his father's wages, Ali cannot afford to pay the nominal fees for school. After proposing a financial support, the history teacher, obviously a Nasserist, tells Ali,

> 'Your father has been too long in prison. These kinds of mistakes occasionally occur. Listen . . . President Nasser will visit the city on the occasion of Labour Day. Why do not you and your mother go and file a complaint?'
> 'Why Nasser? Is it he who imprisoned my father?'
> He rushed to say, seemingly angry,
> 'Never. Your father did not understand that Nasser was on his side. Many people did not understand that. He is not that bad. These are the mistakes of those who are around him.'[25]

Disturbed by the teacher's vague insinuation that his father is to blame, Ali's confused conception of his father vis-à-vis Nasser begins to crystallise. He wonders, 'Was my father really at fault?'[26] The school's principal prepares the kids to greet the president, requiring them to recite numerous national songs upon seeing Nasser's car. Ali, however, refuses to take part in the collective parroting of songs for he is preoccupied with a more personal issue. Worried whether or not he can actually approach Nasser, Ali is nonetheless assured that, if the president hears him, 'he will right away respond'.[27] The narrative leaves unexplained the reason behind Ali's certain belief in Nasser, given his father's repeated attacks on the regime. It seems as though the voice of the adult Ali (or the author) occasionally replaces that of his younger self, as can be recognised when the child sees Nasser and becomes invested in celebratory description of the president's physicality, concluding that 'everything in him was made with a strange touch of sublimity'.[28]

So anticipative of this moment is Ali that he disrupts the conformity of the greeting crowd: 'This is [Nasser] my saviour. I said none of the hymns. I recalled no slogan. I screamed, "give me back my father, O Nasser".'[29] At odds with the principal's attempt to homogenise the linguistic capital of the students in front of Nasser, Ali possesses a discursive agency of his own, functioning as a 'site of resistance to the inflexible, systematizing logic of adult discourse'.[30] The boy believes (or so the narrative suggests) that his scream reaches Nasser who, in turn, exchanges a personal smile with Ali. Unable to enter the stadium where Nasser is supposed to give a speech, Ali hurries home to catch the speech on radio, confident that Nasser 'will talk about my father'.[31] To his surprise, he finds that his father is released from prison but the child, unaware of the political workings of the regime, believes that Nasser has very swiftly responded to his request.

The release of the father places Ali at two concurrent positions. On the one hand, he notices the extent to which his father has physically and spiritually waned: 'He was different. Something in him was missing. What I see before me is the façade of my father, the body of an old man that looks exactly like him, but is not him.'[32] On the other hand, Nasser continues to haunt the child's imagination with speeches that 'give rise to a world of dreams'.[33] The tension grows further as Ali begins to compare the two men, perhaps influenced by the remarks of his history teacher:

> There is something I could not understand. How could my father – the simple worker, whose hands are immersed in grease all year long; whose friends are the poor workers of the factory; who lives in a cramped apartment at a muddy alley – be right, while Nasser, as I saw him in the elegant procession, with people madly and enthusiastically cheering for him, be wrong? Could Abdel Halim, Jahin, and al-Tawil be wrong?[34]

The narrative, however, leaves the tension temporarily unresolved though it repeatedly locates Ali within the world of dreams that is inspired by Nasser. In fact, the novel portrays Ali as rebelling against social norms precisely because he is empowered by Nasser. In a telling scene, Ali accompanies his sweetheart Fatima to her house where he seeks to meet the father so that he can propose. Both just entering secondary school, Fatima's father reprimands them, labelling them as kids, and asks that they both should finish school first, before helplessly commenting, 'I know that my words will go unheeded. This is the time of Nasser: immense misery and big dreams.'[35] Ali shows surprise at the father's comment, wondering to himself, 'Even in love, Nasser exists in one way or another?'[36] Fatima's father turns out to have a nodding acquaintance with Ali's and so asks about his health situation after the prison experience, before adding, 'Poor man. Does he hate Nasser now?'[37] Disturbed again by this juxtaposition, Ali does not know how to answer, uneasily wondering, 'Why do they always pit my father against Nasser?'[38] Fatima's father, however, offers a broader contrast, lamenting Nasser's spell over the children of Egypt: 'Nasser is not ours, not for people in my or your father's age. Nasser is yours. He is the one who implants all these dreams in you.'[39]

It is only when Ali becomes a fresher in medical school that the father/Nasser binary dissolves, with the former having a full disclosure with his son regarding Nasser:

> 'Look at yourself. Who would have thought that the son of a simple worker like me could enter the faculty of medicine? It is a dream, Ali. Nasser empowered us to dream.'
> I looked at him, amazed, unbelieving. He is talking about Nasser in this way! Seeing my look, he exclaimed,
> 'What do you think of me? That I cannot reassess myself? I had not understood Nasser. I was wrong. He did more than what I was expecting.'[40]

The reconciliation did not last long, however, for, as the title had already foreshadowed, it is these dreams that will be aborted. Following the 1967 defeat, Ali grows disenchanted with Nasser, with fathers who hypnotise the younger generation with 'sweet, but extremely false, words'.[41] He criticises people's docility before Nasser and, more importantly, poses as a *revisionist* of his younger self's narratives on the president, questioning, for instance, whether Nasser had actually seen him and listened to his scream on that day. Yet, for all the disillusion that he experiences, Ali, echoing a familiar pattern among many Egyptians, still has an enduring, seemingly illogical love for Nasser:

> This man is really strange. Although he arrested my father, I could not hate him. Nay, even my father loved him when he, thanks to Nasser, was able to send me to medical school . . . Nasser would beat us, and we would resort to him, *would run to Nasser from Nasser*. Even inside the prison, prisoners under torture used to chant his name. They thought that what happened was a kind of bitter misunderstanding.[42]

Against a comparable background of prison experience is the character Nada's growing relationship with Nasser in Radwa Ashour's 2008 novel *Faraj*.[43] Similar to Ali in *Inkisar al-Ruh*, the five-year-old Nada cannot understand the reason behind her father's absence. A university professor, he was arrested in 1959 because, as we learn later, of his political activities. Noticing numerous relatives coming to stay with them following the incident, Nada, the narrator of the novel, is not satisfied with their explanations. She even accuses her French mother of lying to her by hiding the fact that her father has actually died, at which moment the mother feels obliged to simplify the truth as much as she can. The narrative portrays Nada as a 'deceptively innocent inquisitor whose capacity to ask questions exceeds the ability of his elders to provide answers'.[44] Thus, when the mother tells Nada that there are officers who, disagreeing with her father, have put him in prison, Nada protests,

> 'What does a "prison" mean?'
> 'A closed place that one cannot exit.'
> 'Like the lion in the zoo?'
> 'Like the lion in the zoo!'

'And then?'

'I am not telling you a story. I am explaining why papa is not living with us now. He did not die. He will remain there for a while, before they let him return home.'[45]

Nada's father spends five years in prison. On her first visit to the prison, she does not recognise him. Years later, the adult Nada will acknowledge that she actually never knows her father fully, partly because of those years of absence.[46] This period, however, is the temporal space in which Nasser emerges. In a chapter entitled, 'Which of the Two Men Is Better?' Nada narrates how the comparison between Nasser and the father haunts not only her but also other children in her school whose fathers are sent to prison, too. In a blend of fiction and reality, so common in Ashour's writing, Nada speaks about her friend Muna Anis, daughter of renowned Egyptian intellectual Abdel 'Azim Anis, himself a prisoner at that time.[47] Muna tells Nada that one of Nasser's sons is her classmate, to which Nada responds, 'I asked her to introduce me to him so that I could ask him why his father put our fathers in prison. If his father does not know about it, we will ask his son to relay the news to him.'[48] Nada's request to meet Nasser's son is never met but Muna, equally furious that his father is in prison, tells Nada about a confrontation in class:

> I asked the teacher in front of all students, 'who is better: my father or his father?' when the teacher did not answer, I said, 'my father is a PhD holder who teaches at a university. He was teaching at the University of London when Britain attacked Egypt. He led protests there before deciding to return home to help his country. As for his father [Nasser], he is an army officer. True, he participated in the Palestine war and led the revolution, but he does not hold a PhD, nor had he taught at the University of London. My father is more educated and he knows more!'[49]

Unlike Muna's certain favouring of her father, Nada falls prey to conflicting arguments, torn as she is between filial bonds and national belonging. At first, she attempts to create a balance between her father and Nasser, at times leaning towards the former – 'my father has a PhD from the Sorbonne . . . he surely knows more than the officers' – at others sensing that her father may not be 'smarter nor better than Nasser'.[50] In reality, however, the assumed battle between Nasser and the father for influence over Nada is decisively won by the president. This conforms to similar patterns in postcolonial literature where, as Richard Browning observes, 'the idea that biological parents, or even the traditional family structure, are replaceable' is prominent.[51] 'At the absence of the incarcerated father,' Nada hums, 'Nasser's name, voice, and image were reverberating throughout the day.'[52] On top of that, Nada's growing knowledge of Nasser's political stances, including his support for the Algerian revolution and challenge to French imperialism,[53] significantly increases his prestige, inducing Nada to factor them into the ongoing debate over 'who is right: the president who put my father in prison, or my father whose opinions led him to prison and exile from family all these years?'[54]

Notably, Nada's ruminations over the significance of Nasser brings to attention the juxtaposition between what Alicia Otano calls 'the child focaliser against an adult self'.[55] Commenting on how to transmit an experience that is deemed too sophisticated for a child, Otano recognises in a body of Asian-American novels the position of the focaliser who is 'a character within a represented world which is narrated by an older "self" thus giving way to an interplay of a dual perspective'.[56] Central to her remarks is Gerard Genette's famous differentiation between '*who is the character whose point of view orients the narrative perspective?* and *who is the narrator?*'[57] With regard to Nada and Nasser, *Faraj* alternates between the two positions. While the child's remarks and thoughts are occasionally neither denied nor confirmed, thus leaving the reliability of her judgements to the readers' conviction – as when she notices that Nasser may in fact look like her father[58] – the adult Nada at times senses an obligation to intervene, clearly highlighting the difference between what she sees as a child and what she makes of it now (which could be the late 1990s though it is never precisely determined):

> [Nasser] was not a mere leader or president about whom people talked frequently at home, in school, or in the streets. Rather, he was simply flowing in the space in which we grew, as though he was water, air, soil, or rays of light that we embodied to become what we became. Nasser was raising me, though I was proud to belong to my father ... *I do not think any of those thoughts had ever occurred to me at that age.*[59]

Contrary to Ali's later revisionist approach to Nasser in *Inkisar al-Ruh*, the adult Nada never reconsiders her younger self's perception of the president, his seemingly negative impact on her familial bonds notwithstanding. In fact, not only does the absence of the father leave an indelible scar on his relationship with Nada but the somewhat irrational love for Nasser exacerbates the feelings of alienation, detachment, and dissociation that engulf the experience of Nada's mother in Egypt, eventually ending in a divorce. Throughout the narrative, Nada recounts her French mother's frequent struggles to engage in conversations with members of the extended family, with the child occasionally posing as interpreter. The parents' disputes, however, indicate a deeper level of miscommunication, one that exceeds the language barrier to more psychological, emotional, and national levels. The pinnacle, very tellingly, involves Nasser. It is 1967, three years after the father was released from prison. The parents are watching Nasser's resignation speech in the wake of the 1967 defeat. Nada, aged thirteen at the time, describes the reaction of her parents as follows:

> The speech ends. My father wails. Sobs like a child. My mother passes into a sudden hysterical state, screaming, 'I do not understand. I absolutely do not understand. Why are you crying over him? Is he not the fascist officer, the dictator tyrant who unjustly placed you in prison for five years? Is not it . . . Was not it he . . . Did not you say . . . ?' A sequence of words frantically follows, my mother's voice gradually rising. Abruptly, my father said, 'you are blind', then left home. My mother uttered no word, and neither did I.[60]

Years later, the adult Nada comments that this incident, which was shortly followed by the divorce and her mother's return to France, was 'the most tragic example of the problems of translation',[61] perhaps referring to her mother's inability to understand her father's apparent sympathy for the very same man who had inflicted so much pain upon him. It is as though the relationship with Nasser is not only personalised but also Egyptianised, leaving its subtleties inaccessible to a foreign audience. Indeed, the mother's reaction is only a fictional example of a wider puzzlement which, as Nasser historian Robert Stephens puts it, 'reflected partly the continuing failure of Westerners to understand the nature of Nasser's relationship with the Egyptian people, the decisive element of consent mixed with the authoritarianism of his regime and the significance of what he had achieved inside Egypt itself'.[62]

Nada's French mother, however, was not the only case in which the encounter with Nasser would magnify one's estrangement from Egypt. By enunciating Egypt's Arab identity, Nasser's ideology had alienated some sectors of Egyptian society whose identification with pan-Arabism was less than cordial. This constitutes one of the major themes that dominate Leila Ahmed's account of Nasser in her autobiographical work *A Border Passage*.[63] Known for her significant studies on Islam and on women,[64] Ahmed was born in Cairo in 1940 to an upper-class family. Her autobiography offers yet another example of a child's uneasy awareness of Nasser as it sheds light on Ahmed's experience of growing up in a house that was radically hostile to the new 1952 regime and to Nasser personally. Among the many factors that contributed to this unease was the father's own opposition to Nasser. 'A prominent engineer, the father chaired the Nile Water Control Board and the Hydro-Electric Power Commission when he opposed, for ecological reasons, Nasser's project to build the High Dam.'[65] This led to a series of harassments by the government, and the father himself was at times put under house arrest.

Ahmed's book was mainly received as a discourse on identity that complicates 'the metaphorics of boundaries constituting not simply the imperialist discourses Ahmed examines but perhaps more so the anticolonial nationalism epitomised by Gamal Abdel Nasser as the champion of the third world'.[66] Pertinent to our discussion here is the way in which her childhood encounter with Nasser destabilised her notions of Egypt and the Arab world. Ahmed was twelve years old when Nasser assumed power. She had been brought up in an earlier era 'when the words "imperialism" and "the West" had not yet acquired the connotations they have today'.[67] As was the case with many upper-class Egyptians, Ahmed's parents, who adored Western culture, sent their child to an English school where she not only became infatuated with the English language and spoke it much better than she did Arabic – which at the time was not even taught in such schools – but even her own name was anglicised: everyone in school called her 'Lily'.

All this was bound to change after the revolution. First came the Arabic language which became a mandatory subject in all foreign schools in Egypt. While she spoke colloquial Egyptian colloquial, Ahmed was distant from Standard Arabic, and her indifference to the language often provoked her

Arabic teacher, a woman of Palestinian origin. 'Those moments', Ahmed recalls later, 'were in large responsible for the feelings of confusion, anger, and guilt that I've felt all my life in connection with the issues of Arabness, identity, the Arabic language, and the like.'[68] It is her personal encounter with Nasser, however, that will cause the greatest confusion about identity which she ever experiences at that stage. Attending a cinema with a cousin named Muna, Ahmed and the audience are surprised when they find Nasser among them, sitting with some men in the balcony. The two cousins join the scores of people who line up to shake hands with the president:

> As we shook hands, he asked us our names and my cousin readily replied 'Muna', a perfectly good Egyptian Arab name. I, however, was rooted to the spot, unable to speak. I could not say 'Lily', my name at school – not to this man who, I knew, hated the British. How could I, an Egyptian girl, have such a name? How could I confess to such a name? I could not say 'Nana', either. Nana, I suppose, was too personal, a name for family and intimates only.[69]

Ahmed leaves the tension unresolved, offering no more information on how the encounter ends. What matters, however, is that, for her, Nasser becomes an identity marker, a realm with specific associations, the lack of which precludes one from inhabiting it. Whereas Ahmed can in the past be both Lily and Egyptian, she now has to forsake any British manifestations within her, including the nickname. Egypt, henceforward, is exclusively Arab.

Not that the child is fully aware of all the nuances of these identity politics; still less is she initially hampered by them or by Nasser's broader ideology. On the contrary, Ahmed frequently supports Nasser and his project against her family's interests. It is as though the revolutionary and the child are both rebelling against the entrenched rules of society, with Ahmed being 'not yet assimilated into normative societal rules'.[70] Thus, she finds Nasser's ideals about equality and social justice very appealing, 'whatever the family adults were saying'.[71] She even believes that the members of her mother's family, who 'were constantly muttering against Abdel Nasser and his socialism'[72] owing to their loss of considerable property to the government, are just selfish. With less easily accessible situations, the child declares her inability to grasp her family's stance. For instance, she finds it confusing that her family receives the news of the military coup so dispassionately. 'I'd often heard my parents lament the corruption of the king,' she recalls, adding, 'so logically they should be pleased now, I thought.'[73] Perhaps noticing the overwhelming support for Nasser and the new regime among the people that she knows, the child grows distressed as she realises her family's significantly different take on the president. For her, embracing Nasser becomes synonymous with belonging, with finding a space in the society, something that her parents' attitude makes difficult to realise. She even thinks that her family may be the only household that was not euphoric about the nationalisation of the Suez Canal: 'How I wished that we could just for once be like everybody else, that we could be nationalistic and anti-imperialist and just support Abdel Nasser'.[74]

Ahmed is recognised in her family as the only one 'young enough to be significantly shaped by the notion of Egypt that the revolutionary government was in the process of defining'.[75] In fact, the relationship between her generation and the nascent regime is reciprocal, with the latter's leader seeking out children and claiming them. As is the case with other postcolonial leaders, Nasser shows 'great preoccupation with gaining the allegiance of children'.[76] In an interesting anecdote, Ahmed offers an account of such personalised relationships between the president and Egypt's children. Aged thirteen, she is sitting by the radio listening to Nasser:

> He was speaking on an Arabic program called *Children's Hour*. Lunch was being served, and I was called to the table, where my parents and sister and brother . . . had already sat down. 'I'll come in a minute', I called back from the radio room, which opened onto the dining room. 'I have to listen to this. The president is speaking to us.'
> 'Us?' inquired my mother. 'Who's us?'
> 'The children of Egypt,' I replied.
> Everyone found this amusing – that I had so wholly and so unselfconsciously placed myself in the group that the president was addressing.[77]

Ahmed's seemingly unflinching belief in Nasser is put to the test soon after Britain, along with France and Israel, attacked Egypt in 1956. For the sixteen-year-old English school student, the British act is tantamount to betrayal, as she deeply feels hurt the way 'when one had believed in the goodness and uprightness of someone and then discovered that they have after all been deceiving one'. Yet Nasser's fierce rhetoric against the 'enemy' perturbs Ahmed who, after all, knows this very enemy 'all too intimately', unable to 'hate and reject everything English'. Thus, while Nasser and the war contribute to Ahmed's growing nationalistic sentiments, they also teach her how 'complicated things were – politics, justice, truth'.[78] One such complication occurs only a few weeks later when Ahmed's Jewish classmate tells her that her family has decided to leave Egypt. Arguing with her anti-Nasser mother over the soundness of this decision, Ahmed invokes her belief in Nasser: 'But the president said the Jews were welcome to stay'. The mother, however, lacking such faith in Nasser, says that the Jews of Egypt should not trust him, and that he will perhaps change his mind. Not realising that Nasser's words do not make any difference to her mother, Ahmed insists on resorting to the president again: 'But why should he change his mind? . . . He said that they are welcome in Egypt. He *said* that.'[79]

Unlike the ambiguous location of the narrator vis-à-vis his/her younger self in the previous works, Ahmed's narrative is obviously retrospective. The adult narrator leaves no doubt that her 'now' perspective comments on whatever thoughts she had in the past, including her perception of Nasser. For instance, she often inserts disclaimers such as 'at that time' in the context of speaking about Nasser in order to indicate that she no longer shares her younger self's point of view. In addition, she moves from past to present, locating her disagreement with her parents over Nasser in the 1950s before hastily reminding the reader that 'and of course they were right'.[80] It is as though Ahmed believed in Nasser and his ideology only *because* she was a naive child. Her intellectual journey, as recalled in this book, is in a way a rebuttal of the presumably false Nasserite ideals with which she was indoctrinated before where the rejection that she shows of an imposed Arab identity on her becomes a result of 'her abhorrence of Nasser and his aggressive brand of Arab nationalism'.[81] Ahmed's current dismissive views of Nasser and what she sees as his coercive construction of an identity become so intense that any laudatory view of him throws her off. Part of her criticism of Edward Said's *Orientalism*, for instance, is the book's 'resonance to my ears with the perspective and rhetoric of Arab nationalism'. So appalled by Nasser is Ahmed that she cannot emotionally accept Said's different take on the president: 'Nasser, for instance, figures in its pages only fleetingly, but he is there as hero and only as hero'.⁸² One can argue that her relationship with Nasser, both as a child and as an adult, is irrational, reflecting less a thoughtful examination of the president than an inescapable struggle to come to terms with one's past:

> Whether I liked it or not, words like *ishtirakiyya, al-wataniyya al-Arabiyya* – socialism, Arab nationalism – and the Glorious Revolution, became for me redolent of fraud. This was not an analytical reaction and I do not believe I even consciously registered it intellectually. It was merely an emotional, lived perception.⁸³

Nasser and Women

In her critically acclaimed 1997 documentary *Four Women of Egypt*, Tahani Rached (b.1947), a Canadian-based Egyptian film-maker, offers an intimate look into the lives of four female activists and intellectuals who are nevertheless divided by their political ideologies and affiliation and united through their friendship, experience, imprisonment and, more importantly, love for Egypt. Growing up and maturing during Nasser's regime, the four women share their views, admirations, disillusions, and disappointments in the 1952 revolution.⁸⁴ Of all their anecdotes, one in particular invites much consideration. The camera alternates between a recorded interview of Nasser speaking calmly to a British journalist, and the face of Shahinda Maqlid,⁸⁵ her eyes emanating a certain mix of longing, grief, and admonishment. A heated discussion ensues, in which Maqlid and the Nasser-detractor, Safinaz Kazim, a liberal-turned-Islamist writer and intellectual and the former wife of Egyptian vernacular poet, Ahmed Fouad Negm, battle over the legacy of Nasser. As though to reduce the intensity of the exchange, Kazim humorously interrupts Maqlid's argument with a couplet from a famous song by Muhammad Abdel Wahhab (1902–91) that goes, 'I love him despite what I suffered because of him; I love him despite everything people said about him.' Maqlid tries in vain to deny that her defence of the president is based on a personal love for him, as Kazim reveals to the audience that Maqlid had just told her off record, 'I love Nasser, *ya Safi*'. Kazim teasingly comments, 'it is true. She loves him. What can she do?'

Kazim locates what she sees as Maqlid's irrational support for Nasser within a lover's discourse, to borrow Roland Barthes's famous book title.

According to Kazim, Maqlid is a hapless lover, one who is unable to rethink her stance towards the beloved despite the ugly truth that she knows about him. The anecdote is significant, not least because it raises the issue of Nasser as a romantic hero, as a gendered president whose appeal 'would turn politics into a form of romantic popular narrative'.[86] Often missing in his biographies, Nasser's masculine presence can offer an invaluable window on to the imagination of Egyptian and Arab audiences and, more particularly, women. In fact, politics and the political sphere have been a favourite site of masculinity studies, 'whether in identifying the ideological basis of exclusionary practices, or exploring the relationship between civilian and military masculinities, or "gendering" the body politic itself'.[87] In addition, nationalism has often invoked the image of the masculine leader who protects the honour of the nation against its enemies, especially at times of colonial encounters. As feminist intellectual Cynthia Enloe puts it, 'Nationalism typically has sprung from masculinised memory, masculinised humiliation, and masculinised hope. Anger at being "emasculate" – or turned into a "nation of busboys" – has been presumed to be the natural fuel for igniting a nationalist movement.'[88]

It comes as no surprise, then, that Nasser has been seen by many as an embodiment of anti-colonial Egyptian and Arab masculinity. Amy Zalman demonstrates how 'the era of Arab nationalism is often referred to as masculine, dominated by the image of the charismatic Nasser and his muscular rebuttals of Western intervention'.[89] Aside from the position of the presidency which is often related to a certain degree of masculinity,[90] Nasser's military career magnified his masculine identity, as militaries are perfect sites for constructing – and constructed – masculinity.[91] Interestingly, some of Nasser's major interventions in Egypt underlie not-so-subtle sexual innuendoes, whether in his 'taking' land from the rich and distributing it to the poor, or in 'erecting' the phallic Cairo Tower (1956–61), not to mention his lifelong project, the Aswan High Dam, whose first-stage ceremony in 1964 dramatised a climactic moment that was immortalised in documentary films and photos.[92]

Nasser's physicality had certainly added to his sexual appeal. According to Said Aburish, Nasser had inherited the physical attributes of his father: 'Tall, dark, sturdily built, and handsome', and 'improved on them by having piercing black eyes which twinkled'.[93] Though Nasser biographers have thoroughly described the excitement that overtook the Egyptian masses upon seeing him, unfortunately absent is any particular interest in female reaction. Egyptian writer Salwa Bakr, who was a member of the Youth Organization in the 1960s, relayed to me how she and her fellow female members used to prepare themselves whenever Nasser visited them. 'Girls would wear their best dresses and put on make-up,' she said. 'For us, Nasser was not a president. He was like Rushdi Abaza, a heart-throb who would travel with us on a white horse.'[94]

But where history falls short, literature compensates. In a poem that resonates with Bakr's account, lesser-known Egyptian poet Lusi Ya'qub describes her occasional meetings with Nasser. Entitled, 'Do You Remember, Nasser?', the poem deserves attention more for its rare approach to the president than for its literary merit. It begins,

> Do you remember, Nasser
> When I first saw you
> When I met you
> When I touched your hands
> And looked at your eyes?[95]

The poet goes on to describe a visit by Nasser to a factory in Sinai in which she works:

> Eyes embrace you ... hearts beat loudly
> for Nasser, their dear beloved
> Sinai girls and I
> Look at you, like a dashing hope.[96]

Similarly, Egyptian novelist Ibrahim Abdel Meguid (b.1946) offers a vivid account of Nasser's female audience in his acclaimed novel *Tuyur al-'Anbar* (Birds of Amber).[97] Set against the notorious 1954 'Manshiyya Incident', where Nasser faced an assassination attempt,[98] the scene describes a group of Alexandrian women who attended Nasser's speech in Manshiyya. The scene, so uncommon in Egyptian novels, is worth quoting in full:

> The girls had not gone out together for quite some time, not since the day they went to watch Gamal Abdel Nasser give a speech in Manshiyya on the occasion of the English withdrawal from Egypt, which turned out to be a

black day. Someone shot at Gamal and there was such a great commotion they were almost trampled underfoot and indeed might have been had not Abdel Nasser himself exhorted the people to stand steadfast, 'If Gamal died, each of you would be Gamal'. But at the end, after they got away from Manshiyya on their way back home, they were happy that the handsome hero with the resonant voice had not been hurt even though they were still frightened.[99]

In what follows I shall discuss the representations of Nasser in three Egyptian women's autobiographies, paying particular attention to gender and masculinity. I seek to unmask whether a notion of Nasser's sexuality and masculinity – an image of a 'gendered' Nasser – has ever found space in these female imaginary productions and, if so, in what way.

A few months after the eruption of the 2011 Egyptian revolution, Cairo-based publishing house Dar al-Shuruq released *Dhikrayat Maʿahu* (Memories with Him).[100] Written by Nasser's wife, Tahia, the book had been first serialised in two newspapers in Egypt and Lebanon, with the first episode appearing a week before the revolution. Tahia, who died in 1990, wrote these memoirs in 1973 as a commemoration of the third anniversary of Nasser's death but never published any of them. Nor do we know why Nasser's family had suddenly decided to disclose their mother's narrative long after she had died. That it was made available to a wider readership in the form of a book at such a crucial time in Egypt is a double-edged sword. While it may enliven Nasser's memory and reposition him in the limelight as a predecessor of the revolutionaries at Tahrir Square, the political situation in Egypt is so intense and urgent that it can easily overshadow any intellectual production, on Nasser or otherwise. The fact remains, however, that the serialisation of the memoirs in newspapers preceded the revolution, and so the timing question is still valid.[101]

It has been widely acknowledged among Nasser historians that his wife, Tahia, had led a modest, demure, and low-profile life, posing in stark contrast to the model of Egypt's first lady that her later counterparts Jehan Sadat and Suzanne Mubarak would adopt afterwards. Born to a well-off family of Persian origin, she was introduced to Nasser some time in the early 1940s, and the couple got married in 1944.[102] Theirs was said to be a stable, happy marital experience, quite separate from, and almost not affected by, the turbulent events that Nasser was regularly facing outside. Loyalty was a pillar in their life, something that 'may have been a reflection of love and affection, or simply of mutual respect'.[103]

Tahia's book poses a challenge for what is stereotypically seen as a main feature of Arab women's autobiographies where writing becomes a means to break the silence and violate the space that men impose on them. What is often sought after in these intellectual productions, so goes the common argument, is how women can 'transcend or trespass beyond the boundaries and traditions of the cultures they are writing or telling within'.[104] As such, autobiography for Arab women is a way to reclaim a self that is long suppressed, and to reinscribe one's story against the 'metanarratives that write them out of active political presence'.[105] Tahia's narrative does obviously subvert this paradigm. As the title emphatically suggests, Tahia exists in the book only insofar as her life intersects with Nasser's. In fact, the chronological order which the book follows begins with the meeting between Nasser and Tahia in the 1940s and concludes with Nasser's death in 1970 – the narrator is silent about her life before or after.

Equally significant is that Tahia subjects her will to write to Nasser's judgement. Rather than writing against boundaries, Tahia perpetuates them by soliciting Nasser's approval of the act of writing. In the foreword, she explains that her first attempt to write these memoirs goes back to 1959. Despite Nasser's welcoming, however, she decided to forsake it. It is therefore legitimate for Tahia to pursue the project again in 1973, for

> I know very well that the president was sorry that I did not continue to write and got rid of what I had written. I now live as if he is next to me, and will do nothing that he does not like. *Had I known that he did not want me to write, I would have never done it.*[106]

Nowhere in the memoirs does Tahia shy from identifying completely with her husband, declaring her pride at ignoring any quest for 'the completed self' beyond the traditional role of the wife/mother. She even joyfully relates her satisfaction with the distance that Nasser had created between her and the public sphere in which he so immerses himself.

Readers of such political memoirs cannot resist their desire to be illuminated with hidden secrets, surprising confessions, and intimate details about the figures that have often created an unshakable barrier between their private and public lives. The usual outcome, however, as one article in *The Telegraph* had it, is 'so disappointing'.[107] Instead of revealing what is hidden, political memoirs often indulge in didactic, tedious, and terse, self-celebratory anecdotes about the 'self-made' individual. This is why, for many, a political memoir *cannot* be a good memoir. As Rick Shenkman puts it,

> A memoir to be successful must be honest. No president can afford to be truly honest. He can't explain the deals he made, the compromises he accepted, the sacrifices of his principles on the altar of personal ambition. So instead of the truth we get the president *as he would like to be remembered*. This is death to a good memoir. For a person who has spent their life concealing who they are – and all politicians do this to an extent – the memoir is especially unsuited as a literary form to presidents. For the memoir depends on revelation.[108]

Judged by these standards, it is partly true that Tahia's memoir does not offer readers anything profoundly new about Nasser. Rather, it confirms and elaborates on what has been circulated by word of mouth about Nasser's modesty, austerity, devotion to work, intimate relationships with his children, passion for cinema and photography, and the like. A second reading of *Dhikrayat Ma'ahu*, however, shows a text that reworks the details of Nasser's private life in a way that says much by saying almost nothing. Of particular interest to our discussion about the romantic image of Nasser is tracing how Tahia deals with the presumed masculine aspect of her husband. In contrast to the handsome, well-built, sexually appealing, piercingly black-eyed man, I argue that Tahia *desexualises* Nasser, presenting a relationship with him that borders on heterosociality. As such, Nasser emerges less as a passionate lover than as a compassionate friend.

Notably, the book is entirely bereft of any reference to Nasser's physical attributes, with a single exception in the foreword where Tahia mentions 'his voice' among the things she misses the most about him. She does not describe Nasser's appearance nor does she hint at any specific features that may have attracted her to the young officer who proposed to her in 1944. As mentioned earlier, Tahia knew Nasser through family friendships. While theirs was not a love story, they both saw and knew each other before marriage. Yet, in her chapter 'Nasser proposes to Tahia', the would-be Mrs Nasser recounts neutrally, if not dispassionately, how Nasser asked for her hand and how her brother – who was her guardian following her father's death – eventually agreed.[109] Though the narrative testifies to Tahia's ability to capture minute details of the houses and the apartments in which she lived,[110] she nevertheless does not dwell on her wedding party, drawing no pictures of how she and Nasser looked, what they wore, or what the setting was, as well as hiding any indications of how it went. In a rather sparse style, she says only,

> My brother organised the wedding party. After writing down the marriage contract, I went with Gamal to the photographer Arman. It was the first time I went out with him alone. We filled the car with garlands of roses . . . We returned home for the party. At 1 a.m., the guests left, and the wedding was over.[111]

Also absent from the book are details of Nasser's routine activities, particularly those that are related to being male, such as shaving and trimming the moustache, as well as those with sexual connotations, including wearing cologne. While she tells fully of her assiduous care for Nasser's appointments, work, and guests, only once does Tahia disclose something about Nasser and clothes. She mentions how Nasser's secretary used to bring samples of suits to their house, saying 'I will leave them until he [Nasser] finds time to see them and select what he likes'.[112] It seems as though Tahia has no say in Nasser's sartorial preferences: 'I know he likes the cloth that is striped with quiet colours such as light blue, so I used to pick it up on his behalf'.[113] Yet readers encounter no incident of Tahia buttoning Nasser's shirts, combing his hair, or putting a suit jacket on him. Nor do they hear her complimenting her man on his famously elegant style. In fact, Tahia proudly refers only to her own well-dressed appearance, asserting that 'I never forgot to be elegant at home'.[114]

Strikingly, the only time in the narrative in which Tahia mentions kissing is moments after Nasser's death, where 'I entered the room, stood next to the president, kissing him and weeping'.[115] Physical contact between Nasser and Tahia is completely overlooked, with a rare exception relating to the wedding night where, going up to their apartment on the third floor, Tahia relays how 'we climbed the stairs until the second floor, then he carried me to the third'. There, 'Nasser held my hand, leading me to see all the rooms. I liked everything, and was extremely happy.'[116] Throughout the book, all the encounters between Tahia and Nasser, including those that are in their house, are devoid of carnality. Even when the context invites an embrace, a hand touch, or a kiss, the narrative, intentionally or otherwise, ends the scene apparently incompletely, thus ending the readers' expectations for any simple physical manifestations of married life. For instance, when Nasser returns home in 1949 in the wake of the al-Falluja Siege in Palestine, Tahia, who had been terrified during Nasser's absence, merely mentions how 'on 6 March 1949, Gamal came from al-Falluja. I was filled with an indescribable joy.'[117] Similarly, when she delivered her first son, Khalid, Nasser 'entered the room and congratulated me, saying, "Are you happy? It's a boy."'[118]

Nor do verbal displays of affection occupy a important position in the narrative. The text is filled with exchanges between the couple, both personally and through letters that Nasser used to send before the revolution while deployed outside Cairo. So sober are these exchanges, however, that they come across as semi-formal. In all the letters that Tahia includes in the narrative, Nasser, writing from Palestine during the 1948 war, is merely quoted as saying, 'I hope you are well with the dear kids'; 'I am very well, concerned only about you all'; and 'I miss our house very much. I will come soon *inshalla*'.[119] Only during the al-Faluja Siege does Nasser's exchange with Tahia include more sentimentality, as his letter relates:

> I never thought I would leave you that long. Thanks be to God, anyways ... Your deep belief in God should soothe you not to worry or be saddened. We will meet very soon and thank God ... I am well, we will forget everything, and remain together forever, my dear love.[120]

It is striking that the word 'love', or any explicit expression of emotion at appropriate moments, are generally missing. For instance, when Tahia tells of their trip to Alexandria on their eighth wedding anniversary, we read only this: 'We congratulated each other on the anniversary'.[121] Similarly, on the eve of the revolution, Nasser, uncertain whether he would come back alive or not, leaves the house uttering only a goodbye to Tahia.[122]

Subtly, the narrative shows a woman trying to come to terms with the obvious fact that her husband was not entirely hers. On the one hand, she often declares how happy she is and how satisfying her life is, asserting repeatedly that Nasser's extremely busy life outside, even before the revolution, does not bother her. So long as she is assured of 'Nasser's loyalty, nobility, fidelity, and love' for her and her children, she is 'elated, joyful, and unbothered by anything'.[123] On the other hand, there is a creeping sense of unease and hatred of anything that stole Nasser's days, years and, eventually, life from her. This, I argue, can in part explain Tahia's detached and indifferent descriptions of major events during Nasser's tenure, such as the nationalisation of the Suez Canal and the unification and subsequent separation between Egypt and Syria. For Tahia, whatever increases Nasser's responsibilities and concerns is to be dismissed as unwanted, so much so that, on hearing of Nasser's resignation following the 1967 defeat, hers and her children's consolation was that 'dad will have time to rest now'.[124] This inner disquiet concerning a Nasser forever being taken away from her manifests itself finally when he dies when, after she is taken out of the room to be given a sedative, when she returns she finds that the body had already been taken away. In a frank moment, she says, 'Even now, they took him'.[125]

If Nasser's physicality is rather understated in his wife's memoirs, it receives a radically different treatment in famed Egyptian feminist Nawal El Saadawi's (b.1931) autobiography *Walking Through Fire*.[126] With El Saadawi, Nasser's body becomes a signifier, a field of meanings, an independent entity that foretells the nature of the person who inhabits it. It is as though the body, more than anything else, is what makes Nasser who he is – the leader of the revolution.

While it is not her first autobiographical work, *Walking Through Fire* marks El Saadawi's most elaborate approach to Nasser. Its antecedent and much-discussed *Mudhakkirati fi Sijn al-Nisa'* (Memoirs from the Women's Prison) had expectedly little space for Nasser, as it draws heavily, though not exclusively, on the controversial writer's prison experience during the Sadat era.[127] In fact, Sadat's ferociously negative presence in *Mudhakkirati* which, by comparison, can minimise the down sides of any leader who had preceded him, hints at an implicit nostalgia for Nasser. With Sadat, El Saadawi states, 'for the first time, the meaning of "autocracy" is embodied before me. For the first time, dictatorship takes tangible form before my eyes.'[128] This is not to render pre-Sadat Egypt flawless – nothing is further from El Saadawi's judgement. But, even when she critically recalls the 1960s, Nasser himself does not feature as culpable for it is 'the top aides of Nasser',' led by none other than then Vice President Sadat himself, who are the targets of the writer's anger.[129]

The first reference to Nasser in *Walking Through Fire* occurs as the narrator romantically engages in remembering the initial days of the 1952 revolution. Born in 1931, she was studying medicine at Cairo University when the Free Officers overthrew the monarchy. As her narrative on the departure of King Farouk aboard his yacht *al-Mahrusa* unfolds, she begins to identify a few of those new agents in Egypt's political scene: Muhammad Naguib, Zakariya Mohieddin, and Anwar Sadat. As though to address readers' implied question about Nasser, the narrator hurries to say, 'But the lion in this story had not yet appeared openly in the scene'.[130] Following such a powerful epithet, the narrator explains:

> My father spotted the lion standing in the photograph next to [Muhammad Naguib]. He pointed at him and said, 'This man is the real leader of the revolution, Nawal.' At the beginning people used to hail Muhammad Naguib and proclaim his name. No one knew Gamal Abdel Nasser. I asked my father, 'How did you discover that?' He answered, '*From his eyes.*' So I looked at his eyes in the photograph. Big, dark, wide-open eyes looking straight out of the picture from under a broad obstinate forehead. His sharp nose stood out in his face, slightly hooked. His thin lips were pressed together with determination or in anger, an anger that had kept growing since he was a child. *Muhammad Naguib's features next to him looked innocent and naively childish.*[131]

While El Saadawi's attention to Nasser's body is awakened by her father, her detailed description goes well beyond her father's initial remarks about the eyes. By recognising the masculinity in him, El Saadawi deterministically declares Nasser the actual leader of the revolution.

As years go by, those preliminary reflections on Nasser's powerful and manly features yield to a more eroticised perception of him. It will require a meeting in person, however, before El Saadawi fully realises the man in Nasser – pictures cannot capture the whole truth. Ten years after the revolution, she meets Nasser for the first time during the National Congress of

Popular Forces: 'When I looked into Gamal Abdel Nasser's face I found him more attractive than in his pictures. The cameras could not catch the strong glimmer in his big, black eyes.'[132] This was the heyday of Nasser's regime, when 'the revolution was moving forwards, mobilizing to strike down the remaining bastions of feudalism and comprador capitalism and had announced what were called the Socialist Decrees'.[133] But the associations of Nasser's body do not end here. Powerful, angry, and sexual, Nasser's body is also *Egyptian*: 'His skin was brown, the colour of fresh silt brought down by the Nile. He was tall, very tall, with a slight stoop to his shoulders like my grandmother and my father.'[134] As is commonly noted, the body is a site for constructing a native self, an autochthonous essence that 'poses as the carnal representation of identity and existence'.[135] As the 'first native ruler of an independent Egypt since the Persian invaders destroyed the twenty-sixth and last pharaonic dynasty in 525 BC',[136] Nasser is seen by El Saadawi as another pillar of Egyptian identity. Perri Giovannucci notes how El Saadawi's 'description of Nasser develops these two motifs of native identity: the basically familial concept of the Egyptian peasantry and the conception of the Nile, that most ancient signifier of Egypt'.[137]

Wittingly or unwittingly, El Saadawi's fascination with the image of Nasser is present in some of her encounters with men, largely exacerbating her disenchantment with, and revulsion by, them. Lacking what she physically admires in Nasser, together with meagrely sharing his ideals, these men feature as anti-Nasser, unseemly partners for a woman whose feelings towards people are always 'born in a first encounter'.[138] Nasser's features, I argue, become the standards against which these men are measured. El Saawdawi tells the story of Dr Rashad, an assistant professor who taught her in the department of surgery. From the outset, she notices his arrogant, harsh and inattentive treatment of poor children in the hospital, the ones who come from peasant families that share Nasser's and her family's physical features: 'There was a small child in the ward called Mustafa whom I always remember. His features resembled those of my cousin in the village . . . his skin was brown like mine, his eyes like mine, large and black, shining brightly.'[139] After a few unreciprocated gestures, Rashad formally proposes to El Saadawi. For her family, this man is *lu'ta*, a great catch, with his own apartment, clinic, and Chevrolet car. As for El Saadawi, 'never in my life have I rejected a man as I rejected Dr Rashad'.¹⁴⁰ Despite all the possessions that he owns, Rashad's eyes are not appealing. Unlike Nasser, whose eyes El Saadawi never tires of romanticising, repeatedly fixating on their radiant qualities, Rashad's do not shine. When her father disapprovingly asks her why she refuses Rashad, she is at a loss for words: 'How could I say to my father that what attracted me to living creatures was the shine in their eyes?'¹⁴¹ To make matters worse, Rashad assesses Nasser critically during his visit. It was 1957, when Egypt had begun to improve its relationship with the Soviet Union following the 1956 Tripartite Aggression. While El Saadawi's father praises Nasser's role as a national leader, Rashad anxiously questions the president's openness towards what he sees as the communist threat. What is missing in the discussion is El Saadawi who, while supposedly the visit's *raison d'être*, is nevertheless not asked to offer an opinion. Enraged, she blames her father for 'not asking me what I thought of Gamal Abdel Nasser or Dr Rashad himself'.¹⁴²

Unlike her resistance to Rashad, El Saadawi succumbs to society's conditions when she marries a man she does not love. Reasoning that it was only to erase the memory of her first failed marriage, she admits that nothing binds them together except a piece of paper. In an almost exact inversion of her earlier description of Nasser, El Saadawi dispassionately details the physical attributes of her husband:

> When he charged into my room I lifted my head and looked at him. I felt as though I had never seen him before. He had a round face with pink cheeks, the kind of face that I dislike in men. His body was squat and fleshy, the kind of body which I found repugnant even in women. When I looked into his eyes I could not find what I was searching for. His nose was soft and flabby with nothing challenging or proud in it, and when he spoke there was no warmth, no ring in his voice. *He had none of the things I found attractive in a man*, and yet this man was my husband.¹⁴³

If Nasser's eyes, skin, and nose contrast sharply with those of her husband's, so too does his voice which is repeatedly characterised throughout the book as *yudawwi*, or resonant: 'Abdel Nasser's voice echoed loudly from thousands of radios in the houses and on the streets'.¹⁴⁴

Occasionally, the narrative offers unfavourable accounts of Nasser, particularly in relation to freedom of expression and the persecution of dissent.

El Saadawi, for instance, counts Nasser, along with God and sex, as the 'sensitive topics' that writers in Egypt were instructed to avoid.[145] Pertinent to the discussion above is to notice how, in the midst of criticising Nasser, El Saadawi and her female friends regard him as the man of the nation, comparing their physical relationships with their husbands to Egypt's relationship with Nasser. In a scene that deftly reflects the difference between the nation and the woman, Samia, one of El Saadawi's closest friends, whose husband Rifa'a is imprisoned because of his communist views, wonders if Nasser is truly loyal and faithful to Egypt. Against the backdrop of increasing disillusion with the regime among a group of intellectuals who cite the crackdown on communists and the collapse of the United Arab Republic, Samia concludes that 'Nasser cannot possibly be loyal to the country after all that had happened'.[146] Abruptly jumping from the political to the personal, she asks if her husband Rifa'a is faithful to her, before adding, 'Do you think Nasser is faithful, Nawal? Do you think Rifa'a is faithful? Can we separate marital from national faithfulness?'[147]

To the dismay of El Saadawi, disillusion with the regime was fully realised with the humiliating defeat of 1967. Given the nature of the warring parties and the shock of the swift collapse of Egyptian and Arab armies, the defeat would soon acquire symbolic meaning in Egyptian and Arab minds, including a gendered perception of the battle. As is often noted, loss at war leaves a 'profound sense of masculine vulnerability',[148] ushering in a feminisation of the vanquished side. Hence the damage that the 1967 *naksa* has done to the once powerful, masculine image of Nasser. Syrian intellectual Georges Tarabishi argues that the *naksa* was tantamount to an emasculation of Nasser at the hands of Israel whose colonisation of Palestine was also described as *ightisab*, or rape. For Arabs, Tarabishi explains, Israel was seen as a woman, a stepdaughter of colonial powers who nevertheless possesses a phallic image of aggression, usually identified as a 'dagger' in the heart of the Arab world. Passing away before standing up to this 'manly woman', Nasser failed to repair 'the crushed dignity and its symbolic equivalent: amputated manhood'.[149]

Suffocated in a devastated Cairo, El Saadawi volunteered with other Egyptian male physicians to join the Palestinian camps in Jordan. The camps were burgeoning with *fida'iyin*, militants of various origins who were launching attacks against Israeli targets and who, backed by the Jordanian army, had just fought and arguably triumphed in the Battle of Karama in 1968. The Palestinian narrative views the battle as a small but significant victory over the conceited Israeli army, a key incident that helped lift the morale of the entire Arab world after it had so precipitously declined in 1967.[150] It is worth pondering that El Saadawi chose to move temporarily from the realm of a defeated Nasser to that of rising, competent freedom fighters in Jordan. Interestingly, and in perhaps the most powerful scene in the book, she engages in an intimate conversation with Ghassan, a *fida'i* who had lost his limbs during the war. Ghassan deliriously contemplates the meaning of an incomplete body for both a man and a freedom fighter like himself, before surprisingly turning to El Saadawi, asking,

> But you, Dr Nawal, what brought you here to our camp? Are you looking for a hero, for a man on whose shoulder you can rest your head? Our leaders, despite everything, have a certain attraction for women, and the higher up they move in the ranks the greater the attraction they are able to exercise on women looking for some excitement in their lives.[151]

Obviously taken aback by his observation, El Saadawi denies she is looking for a man. She states that she can no longer bear to live in a mourning Cairo. She still perceives Nasser physically, however – only that his masculine features prior to the defeat were no longer there. 'Everybody seemed to be carrying a heavy load, even Abdel Nasser. His face went old, the look in his eyes was no longer defiant, it was defeated, like a badly wounded lion that feels its death is approaching.'[152] Whether or not Ghassan's observation was accurate, it still forces El Saadawi to let out a sigh in nostalgic contemplation of the sexual image that Nasser once had. A leader in defeat is inevitably less lionised and, as defeat dims the shining eyes of Nasser, death draws just a few steps away.

Unlike the previous two books, Zaynab al-Ghazali's (1917–2005) *Ayyam min Hayati* (Days from My Life) reorients the associations of Nasser's masculinity in a totally different direction. A leading female member of the Muslim Brotherhood in Egypt and the founder of the Muslim Women's Association in 1937, al-Ghazali was imprisoned in 1965, along with fellow members of the Brotherhood, on charges of plotting to assassinate Nasser. Marking the second major confrontation between the regime and the Brotherhood since the revolution,[153] the campaign culminated 'on 21 August 1966 in the sentencing by the Supreme State Security Court of seven Brothers to death by hanging and a hundred or so more to prison terms of varying lengths'.[154] Of the seven executed Brothers, Sayyid Qutb was the most prominent one. Al-Ghazali was sentenced to twenty-five years in prison before she was released in 1971 following the death of Nasser. *Ayyam min Hayati* chronicles al-Ghazali's prison experience during these six years, with a few references to earlier incidents.

Published in 1977, al-Ghazali's book belongs to what Fedwa Malti-Douglas calls 'Islamic autobiographical writing', a sub-genre of Arabic autobiography that is 'written from a consciously Islamic perspective'.[155] More specifically, it is a founding text in describing the prison experience in Nasser's Egypt from the perspective of a Muslim Brother. Depicting shocking scenes of torture, beating, and humiliation, the book paved the way for a series of less critically acclaimed chronicles by former Brotherhood prisoners, the most famous and widely circulated of which is Ahmad Ra'if's *Al-Bawwaba al-Sawda'* (The Black Gate). Unlike the prison memoirs of other political groups in Egypt, such as the communists,[156] the Brothers' memoirs do not differentiate between Nasser and the regime. Rather, both are condemned, with Nasser seen as the ultimate pharaoh, the source of ills whose personal role in persecuting the Brothers is a major concern of these memoirs.

It is this kind of bitter relationship with Nasser that permeates almost every page of *Ayyam min Hayati*. More importantly, al-Ghazali conceives of her feud with Nasser in gendered terms, as an ongoing war between a *male* oppressor and an oppressed female, where her prison experience becomes the ultimate testimony to Nasser's hegemonic masculinity. Instead of surrendering to this unequal relationship between a man and a woman, however, and helplessly succumbing to its conditions, I argue that al-Ghazali's narrative often operates to invalidate Nasser's masculinity. By depicting him as personally ordering the torture of al-Ghazali and the violation of her body, the text deprives Nasser of the role of the 'protector of the nation', the hero who defends 'feminine and national virtue'.[157] Equally significant, al-Ghazali seeks emphatically to prove that she not only defies Nasser but triumphs over him. Unable to bend a woman to his will, Nasser emerges as an impotent masculine, a tyrant whose manhood is severely damaged at the hands of an enduring woman.

From its inception, the narrative personalises the otherwise ideological enmity between al-Ghazali and Nasser. Entitled, 'Abdel Nasser Hates me Personally', the first chapter relays the story of a car accident that al-Ghazali had. She soon establishes from the reports surrounding her that the accident is, in fact, not so accidental and that it was orchestrated by Nasser's secret agents to kill her at the behest of the president himself. The last, so al-Ghazali's secretary informs her, 'hates you personally, *hajja* Zaynab. He cannot stand to hear your name pronounced by anyone. Whenever someone mentions you, he gets agitated and furious and ends the meeting.'[158] Interestingly, al-Ghazali receives this news with joy, as though Nasser's hatred for her testifies to the righteous path that she follows.

As soon as al-Ghazali is arrested by 'the men of the *taghut*',[159] the narrative indulges in unceasing, rather repetitive sequences of horrific torture. During these sequences, her 'body becomes the battlefield on which the contest between good and evil is played out,.[160] While al-Ghazali is surrounded by other male inmates who share her ordeal, she tirelessly seeks to affirm her gender as a female prisoner. Flogged and beaten by male jailors for refusing to confess or give the names of those who conspired against Nasser, al-Ghazali celebrates her courage, patience and endurance. If women 'frame their physical violation as evidence of their equality with men',[161] al-Ghazali goes so far as to place herself above many of her male counterparts who allegedly collapse under torture and offer information to the inquisitors. In a telling scene, al-Ghazali contrasts Ali 'Ashmawi, a Brother who could not endure torture and collaborated with Nasser's men, with the unwavering and unbroken Abdel Fattah Ismail. Ashamed of 'Ashmawi's behaviour, al-Ghazali disdainfully describes his appearance following the favourable treatment he now receives from the prison authority, almost de-masculinising him: 'Ali 'Ashmawi came. He was wearing clean, elegant, silk pajamas, his hair combed, and no traces of torture left on him.'[162] Precisely the opposite is Ismail, a leading Brother member whose 'blue prison uniform was torn. The signs of torture on his body bespeak to the amount of suffering he passed through.'[163] Commenting on the two, al-Ghazali states, 'I was comforted. Yes. I was comforted by the glory of manhood that Abdel Fattah Ismail displayed.'[164] It is as though the endurance of physical violence, or the absence thereof, becomes central to the construction of true masculinity.[165]

Aware of her extraordinary capabilities, Nasser grows increasingly determined to break al-Ghazali. The narrative tells of a letter that the prison authority receives from Nasser. It reads, 'By orders of the President of the Republic Gamal Abdel Nasser, Zaynab al-Ghazali is to be tortured more harshly than men.'[166] Nevertheless, al-Ghazali never surrenders, memorialising with each page her fortitude in the face of excruciating agony. Hence the book's excessive iteration of nearly identical torture scenes. Nadja Odeh rightly wonders whether *Ayyam min Hayati* is, in reality, an 'auto-hagiography'.[167] Indeed, al-Ghazali repeatedly refers to the dreams that she sees in which the Prophet appears asking her to withstand her abuse and promising victory over her enemies.[168]

In contrast to El Saadawi, who romanticises her personal meeting with Nasser, focusing on his physical appeal, al-Ghazali refuses a deal through which she can meet the president. Whereas the prison authority offers the meeting as an alluring prize for a few concessions on her part, al-Ghazali dismisses it, conceiving of Nasser's body as implicated in the crimes that are committed against her and her fellow Brothers: 'I want nothing from you. I will never accept to meet with Nasser, nor will I shake the hand that is stained with the blood of Ismail al-Fayyumi, Rif'at Bakr, Muhammad 'Awwad, and others.'[169] Ultimately, al-Ghazali gets to see Nasser, albeit involuntarily. In a rather surreal scene following a torture session, she wakes up to see Nasser in the room, leaning back on Abdel Hakim Amer, and holding black sunglasses in his hand. Upon seeing him, 'I forgot my pain, with a strange sense of awakening creeping into my body.'[170] Contrary to expectations, Nasser remains motionless and silent throughout the meeting, offering the floor to his minister of war, Shams Badran, to interrogate al-Ghazali. Nor does al-Ghazali dwell on describing the appearance of Nasser. In fact, the narrative leaves the reason behind Nasser's alleged attendance an enigma, and the details it offers about this particular interrogation session raises legitimate doubts concerning its authenticity. As Pauline Lewis observes, 'It is difficult to assess the validity of al-Ghazali's claims that Nasser considered her a top threat to his security.'[171] What remains, however, shows al-Ghazali subverting the probable purpose of the meeting. While the presence of Nasser is meant to startle her, al-Ghazali plucks up enough courage to retort to Shams Badran's argumentative questions about the aims of the Muslim Brotherhood. In addition, the meeting serves to underscore Nasser's baseness and villainy by showing him indifferent to a *woman*'s physical suffering at the hands of his men. Despite the flogging and the beating, Nasser is shown to never move a hair. Victorious, al-Ghazali comments, 'I said everything I wanted him [Nasser] to know. And now he did know.'[172]

As mentioned earlier, al-Ghazali is investing fully in gendering her struggle against Nasser. Aside from his given name, he is referred to as a pharaoh, a *taghut*, or a *taghiya*,[173] all of which suggest an oppressive patriarch. In addition, she often calls her jailors and inquisitors *rijal Abdel Nasser*, or *rijal al-taghut*, while mockingly referring to their incompetence and shallowness. During the trial, for instance, she recounts the story of a male judge who, after hearing al-Ghazali's self-defence, including her reference to the Prophet as *'uswa*, or example, shouts hysterically, making a fool of himself: 'Shut up! Shut up! What is she saying? What does *'uswa* mean?'[174] Appalled by his ignorance, al-Ghazali comments, 'At this moment the hall burst out into laughter at that who is assigned as a judge but nevertheless does not understand the word *'uswa*. This is how Nasser chose his men.'[175] Spearheaded by Nasser, these men fail, despite resorting to violence and oppression, to extinguish the Muslim Brotherhood, thanks, first and foremost, to a w*oman*: Zaynab al-Ghazali. Nasser, al-Ghazali believes, has gone mad because a woman has robbed him of the generation that, while born during his regime, was nonetheless 'absorbed in our mission and involved in our ranks'.[176] Thus, Nasser is defeated by a woman.

Nowhere in Egyptian literature does Nasser emerge so demonised, trashed, and desecrated. The largely complicated, multilayered, and turbulent tenure of Nasser is diminished into images of a ruthless, bloodthirsty, oppressive, and secular masculine who does not rule according to Islam. Notably absent from al-Ghazali's narrative is any references to major political events in Egypt. Nor does she offer her own reading of Nasser's main acts, such as the nationalisation of the Suez Canal, unification with Syria, or the construction of the High Dam. Rather, she reduces the narrative of post-1952 Egypt into a struggle against the 'devil, embodied in the Egyptian President Nasser'.[177] The one-sidedness of al-Ghazali's narrative goes so far as to consider Nasser an exceptional, unprecedented case of evil, so much so that 'the Nasser regime has made us forget the immorality of criminals throughout the entire history of mankind'.[178] Such a statement is a striking exaggeration but, for al-Ghazali, the intentionally detailed scenes of torture and humiliation can perhaps pass as a convincing justification.

Conclusion

The presence of Nasser in Egyptian literary narratives takes multiple forms. While he is introduced in certain works as a protagonist, in others he constitutes a part of the historical background in which the narrative takes place. In the latter form, Nasser becomes a reference, a site of contestation where conflicting views over the president and his legacy may battle. Representing Nasser through the perspectives of fictional characters, these works enact a unique source of knowledge about Nasser by creating a world for ordinary citizens whose personal takes on him may otherwise have gone unheard. This knowledge is an essential constituent of the making of Nasser's image in the Egyptian imaginary, both inspired by and inspiring the ongoing debate concerning the meanings of Nasser for Egyptian citizenry.

This chapter paid particular attention to two largely unexplored treatments of Nasser in Egyptian literary narratives. It began with an analysis of the location of Nasser vis-à-vis the child protagonist. Drawing on Edward Said's concepts of filiation and affiliation, it argued that these narratives place the child in a disturbing situation where a growing comparison between Nasser and the father begins to materialise. Concomitant with the child's increasing knowledge about and, more significantly, love for Nasser is his perception of the damage that befalls his father at the hands of Nasser' very regime. These narratives introduce a child grappling with mixed feelings of belonging and loyalty, torn between glorifying Nasser on the one hand and defending his father on the other.

The second part of the chapter explored the image of Nasser as a gendered president, highlighting his masculine identity as it was conceived by his female audience. Analysing three autobiographies that were produced by women with drastically differing relationships with Nasser, the chapter confirmed the absence of a monolithic approach to Nasser's masculinity. While his wife Tahia invests so little in depicting a masculine Nasser, producing what I argued to be a desexualised image of him, Nawal El Saadawi transforms Nasser's body into a field of meanings that connote courage,

rage, and eroticism, largely epitomised by his shining eyes and resounding voice. Still, the masculinity of Nasser acquires an evil dimension in Zaynab al-Ghazali's *Ayyam min Hayati* which approaches the persecution of al-Ghazali in prison as an essentially gendered war between a male oppressor and a female victim.

Notes

1. Naomi Sokoloff, *Imagining the Child in Modern Jewish Fiction* (Baltimore, MD: The Johns Hopkins University Press, 1992), p. 4.
2. Dorrit Cohn, *Transparent Minds: Narrative Modes for Presenting Consciousness in Fiction* (Princeton, NJ: Princeton University Press, 1978), p. 7.
3. See Benedict Anderson, *Imagined Communities: Reflections on the Origins and Spread of Nationalism* (New York and London: Verso, 1991), pp. 24–31.
4. Edward W. Said, *Culture and Imperialism* (New York: Vintage Books, 1994), p. xiii.
5. Susan Honeyman, *Elusive Childhood: Impossible Representations in Modern Fiction* (Columbus, OH: Ohio State University Press, 2005), p. 5.
6. John Hodgson, *The Search for the Self: Childhood in Autobiography and Fiction since 1940* (Sheffield: Sheffield Academic Press, 1993), p. 11.
7. Honeyman, *Elusive Childhood*, p. 4.
8. Naomi Sokoloff, 'Childhood Lost: Children in Holocaust Literature', in *Infant Tongues: The Voice of the Child in Literature*, eds Elizabeth Goodenough et al. (Detroit, MI: Wayne State University Press, 1994), p. 261.
9. See Philippe Aries, *Centuries of Childhood: A Social History of Family Life* (New York: Alfred A. Knopf, 1962). For a discussion of Aries's thesis and a broader overview of the topic, see Gillian Avery, 'The Voice of the Child, Both Godly and Unregenerate, in Early Modern England', in *Infant Tongues*, pp. 16–27, and Richard L. Browning, *Childhood and the Nation in Latin American Literature* (New York: Peter Lang, 2001), pp. 1–11.
10. Ellen Pifer, *Demon or Doll: Images of the Child in Contemporary Writing and Culture* (Charlottesville, VA and London: University Press of Virginia, 2000), p. 17.
11. James Kincaid, *Erotic Innocence: The Culture of Child Molesting* (Durham, NC: Duke University Press, 1998), p. 10.
12. See Tetz Rooke, 'The Arabic Autobiography of Childhood', in *Writing the Self: Autobiographical Writing in Modern Arabic Literature*, eds Robin Ostle et al. (London: Saqi Books, 1998), pp. 100–1.

13. Naguib Mahfouz, *The Cairo Trilogy: Palace Walk, Palace of Desire, Sugar Street*, trans. William Maynard Hutchins et al. (New York: Alfred A. Knopf, 2001).
14. Linda Britt, 'A Transparent Lens? Narrative Technique in Carmen Naranjo's *Nunca Hubo Alguna Vez*', *Monographic Review/Revista Monográphica*, Austin, TX: The University of Texas, No. 4 (1988), p. 129.
15. Edward Said, *The World, the Text, and the Critic* (Cambridge, MA: Harvard University Press, 1983), p. 118.
16. Ibid., p. 19.
17. See <http://www.misr5.com/104205> (last accessed 21 June 2015). For more on the comparison between Nasser and al-Sisi, see the Epilogue, pp. 216–19.
18. Muhammad Bariri offers an interesting reading of this novel in the light of what he argues is its dialogue with Tawfiq al-Hakim's 1933 renowned novel *'Awdat al-Ruh*. See Muhammad Bariri, 'Tawfiq al-Hakim wa al-Mansi Qandil: Bayna 'Awdat al-Ruh wa Inkisariha', *Fusul*, No. 12 (spring 1993), pp. 333–8.
19. Muhammad al-Mansi Qandil, *Inkisar al-Ruh* (Cairo: Dar al-Hilal, 1992), p. 9. This is a recurring theme in the first part of the novel, enunciated whenever the family faces a dilemma. See, for instance, pp. 21–6.
20. Ibid., p. 16.
21. Ibid., p. 18.
22. Awarded the Palme d'Or at the 1985 Cannes Film Festival, this Yugoslav film features a child, Malik, who thinks that his father leaves them to go on a business trip whereas, in fact, the man is arrested by the authorities for a critical comment against Tito's regime. For a discussion of the film, see Goran Gocic, *Notes from the Underground: The Cinema of Emir Kusturica* (London and New York: Wallflower Press, 2001), pp. 23–8.
23. Qandil, *Inkisar al-Ruh*, p. 21.
24. Ibid., p. 23.
25. Ibid., p. 36.
26. Ibid.
27. Ibid., p. 37.
28. Ibid., p. 38.
29. Ibid.
30. Honeyman, *Elusive Childhood*, p. 116.
31. Qandil, *Inkisar al-Ruh*, p. 38.
32. Ibid., p. 39.
33. Ibid., p. 41.

34. Ibid., p. 41. The last sentence refers to the singer Abdel Halim Hafez (1929–77), the vernacular poet Salah Jahin (1930–86), and the composer Kamal al-Tawil (1922–2003) who collaboratively produced some of the most renowned national songs for Nasser. For more on Hafez and Nasser, see Chapter 4, p. 169.
35. Ibid., p. 62.
36. Ibid., p. 63.
37. Ibid.
38. Ibid.
39. Ibid.
40. Ibid., pp. 95–6. The reference here is to free education which was implemented under Nasser's regime.
41. Ibid., p. 127.
42. Ibid., p. 130, emphasis mine. One can hear the author's voice more than Ali's in this part, given that the latter was narrating in 1968, at a time when little was known about prison narratives in Nasser's era. The paragraph above resonates with similar prison tales that were revealed much later, concerning figures such as Shuhdi al-Shafi'i. For more on this, see Chapter 1, pp. 37–43.
43. In Chapter 1 I discussed this novel in the context of writing letters to Nasser. Here I am concerned with Nada's view of Nasser vis-à-vis her father.
44. Mary Jane Hurst, *The Voice of the Child in American Literature: Linguistic Approaches to Fictional Child Language* (Lexington KY: University Press of Kentucky, 1990), pp. 1–2.
45. Ashour, *Faraj*, p. 17.
46. Ibid., p. 122.
47. Anis (1923–2009) was one of the best-known Egyptian Marxists in the past century, noted primarily for his influential 1955 book *Fi al-Thaqafa al-Misriyya*, co-written with his lifelong friend, Mahmud Amin al-'Alim.
48. Ashour, *Faraj*, p. 18.
49. Ibid.
50. Ibid., p. 19.
51. Browning, *Childhood and the Nation in Latin American Literature*, p. 55.
52. Ashour, *Faraj*, p. 19.
53. The knowledge is triggered by another incident that pits Nasser against familial bonds, this time the French mother. Nada, now aged nine, is confronted by a classmate who informs her that her mother's country, France, had, in fact,

attacked Egypt in 1956. Disturbed, Nada demands an answer from her mother who, in turn, explains the political context of the war and, to the child's relief, declares her opposition to her native country's imperial endeavours.

54. Ashour, *Faraj*, p. 23.
55. Alicia Otano, *Speaking the Past: Child Perspective in the Asian American Bildungsroman* (Münster: LIT Verlag, c.2004), p. 15.
56. Ibid.
57. Gerard Genette, *Narrative Discourse: An Essay in Method*, trans. Jane E. Lewin (Ithaca, NY: Cornell University Press, 1980), p. 186, emphasis in the original.
58. Ashour, *Faraj*, pp. 19–20.
59. Ibid., p. 19, emphasis mine.
60. Ibid., p. 52.
61. Ibid.
62. Stephens, *Nasser*, p. 507.
63. Leila Ahmed, *A Border Passage: From Cairo to America – A Woman's Journey* (New York: Farrar, Straus, and Giroux, 1999).
64. Her oft-cited book, *Women and Gender in Islam*, was published in 1992.
65. Waïl S. Hassan, 'Arab-American Autobiography and the Reinvention of Identity: Two Egyptian Negotiations', *Alif: Journal of Comparative Poetics*, No. 22 (2002), p. 17.
66. Bernadette Andrea, 'Passage Through the Harem: Historicizing a Western Obsession in Leila Ahmed's *A Border Passage*', in *Arab Women's Lives Retold: Exploring Identity Through Writing*, ed. Nawar al-Hassan Golley (Syracuse, NY: Syracuse University Press, 2007), p. 3.
67. Ahmed, *A Border Passage*, p. 5.
68. Ibid., p. 148.
69. Ibid., p. 150.
70. Sokoloff, *Imagining the Child in Modern Jewish Fiction*, p. 25.
71. Ahmed, *A Border Passage*, p. 160.
72. Ibid., pp. 160–1.
73. Ibid., p. 164.
74. Ibid., p. 165.
75. Ibid., p. 149.
76. Browning, *Childhood and the Nation*, p. 12.
77. Ahmed, *A Border Passage*, p. 149.
78. Ibid., pp. 170, 171, and 172, respectively.
79. Ibid., pp. 173 and 174, emphasis in the original.

80. Ibid., p. 164.
81. Hassan, 'Arab-American Autobiography', p. 23.
82. Ahmed, *A Border Passage*, p. 240.
83. Ibid., p. 205.
84. The four women are Safinaz Kazim, Widad Mitry, Amina Rashid, and Shahinda Maqlid. For more on the film, see Margot Badron's review 'Speaking Straight: "Four Women of Egypt"', *Al Jadid*, Vol. 4, No. 24 (summer 1998).
85. One of the best-known Egyptian female activists of the last fifty years, remembered especially for her involvement in what is known as the 'Kamshish Affair'. Maqlid lost her husband, Salah Husayn, who was shot by feudalists in the village of Kamshish in 1966. For more on her, see Shirin Abu al-Naga, *Min Awraq Shahinda Maqlid* (Cairo: Mirit, 2006).
86. John Hellman, *The Kennedy Obsession: The American Myth of JFK* (New York: Columbia University Press, 1997), p. 114.
87. John Tosh, 'Hegemonic Masculinity and the History of Gender', in *Masculinities in Politics and War: Gendering Modern History*, eds Stefan Dudink et al. (Manchester: Manchester University Press, 2004), p. 41.
88. Cynthia Enloe, *Bananas, Beaches, & Bases: Making Feminist Sense of International Politics* (Berkeley, CA and Los Angeles, CA: University of California Press, 1990), p. 44. Similarly, George Mosse notes how 'modern masculinity from the very first was co-opted by the new nationalist movements of the nineteenth century'. See *The Image of Man: The Creation of Modern Masculinity* (New York: Oxford University Press, 1996), p. 7.
89. Cited in Samira Aghacy, *Masculine Identity in the Fiction of the Arab East since 1967* (Syracuse, NY: Syracuse University Press, 2009), p. 6. See also Hoda Elsadda, *Gender, Nation, and the Arabic Novel: Egypt, 1892–2008* (Syracuse, NY: Syracuse University Press, 2012), pp. xxx–xxxi, where she contrasts the Arab *naḍa* hero with its nationalist, Nasser-like counterpart.
90. See Frank Rudy Cooper, 'Our First Unisex President? Black Masculinity and Obama's Feminine Side' (Suffolk University: Legal Studies Research Paper Series, 2009), pp. 633-4.
91. It should be noted, however, that, unlike other revolutionary figures of the era, such as Fidel Castro and Che Guevara, Nasser showed little interest in donning the military uniform.
92. The highlight of the ceremony featured Nasser, along with Soviet leader Khrushchev, Iraqi President Arif, and Yemeni President al-Sallal, all pressing a button to blow up a huge sand barrage and divert the River Nile into a canal.

93. Aburish, *Nasser*, p. 8.
94. In discussion with the author in Cairo in October 2011. Sonalla Ibrahim concurs, similarly invoking a comparison with Rushdi Abaza. The reference to Abaza is significant for he, more than any other Egyptian actor, epitomised the 'virile male' on the screen. For more on cinematic masculinities in Egypt during Nasser's era, see Walter Armbrust, 'Farid Shauqi: Tough Guy, Family, Cinema Star', in *Imagined Masculinities: Male Identity and Culture in the Modern Middle East*, ed. Mai Ghoussoub and Emma Sinclair-Webb (London: Saqi Books, 2006), especially pp. 199–200.
95. Lusi Ya'qub, *Nasser Baladi* (Cairo: Maktabat al-Anjlu al-Misriyya, 1971), p. 35. While the collection is published a year after Nasser's death, It is left unmentioned the exact date of the poem above.
96. Ibid., p. 38.
97. For the English translation, see Ibrahim Abdel Meguid, *Birds of Amber*, trans. Farouk Abdel Wahab (Cairo: The American University in Cairo Press, 2005).
98. The attempt is widely debated in Egyptian historiography, with an overwhelming view that the perpetrator was a Muslim Brother. See Gordon, *Nasser's Blessed Movement*, pp. 175–90. Interestingly, Gordon states that the incident marks 'the beginning of Nasser's romance with his people'.
99. Abdel Meguid, *Days of Amber*, p. 120.
100. For the English translation, see Tahia Gamal Abdel Nasser, *Nasser: My Husband*, trans. Shereen Mosaad (Cairo: The American University in Cairo Press, 2013).
101. As'ad AbuKhalil is overstating when he argues, in an article he wrote for the English edition of the Lebanese newspaper *al-Akhbar* (10 February 2011) that 'the life of the Nasser couple, as revealed in her memoirs, was one of many sparks that triggered the Egyptian uprising'. With the first serialised episode appearing a week earlier, the memoirs can hardly be relevant to the uprising.
102. Tahia states in her memoirs that her family and Nasser's were old friends, and that Nasser first saw her when he used to visit them with his uncle. French journalist Jean Lacouture says, however, that it was Abdel Hakim Amer who first introduced Nasser to Tahia. See his *Nasser* (London, 1973), p. 49.
103. P. J. Vatikiotis, *Nasser and His Generation* (London: Croom Helm, 1978), p. 314.
104. Nawar Al-Hassan Golley, *Reading Arab Women's Autobiographies: Shahrazad Tells Her Story* (Austin, TX: University of Texas Press, 2003), p. 80.
105. Miriam Cooke, *Women Claim Islam: Creating Islamic Feminism through Literature* (New York and London: Routlege, 2001), p. xxv.

106. Tahia Gamal Abdel Nasser, *Dhikrayat Ma'ahu* (Cairo: Dar al-Shuruq, 2011), p. 8, emphasis mine.
107. Dominic Sandbrook, 'Why are Political Memoirs so Disappointing?' in *The Telegraph* (15 May 2010).
108. Cited in Nawar al-Hassan Golley and Ahmad al-Issa, 'A Journey of Belonging: A Global(ized) Self Finds Peace', in *Arab Women's Lives Retold*, p. 217.
109. Abdel Nasser, *Dhikrayat Ma'ahu*, pp. 10–12. Tahia mentions that her brother was at first reluctant owing to the fact that she had an older sister who was unmarried.
110. See, for instance, pp. 13, 73, and 74.
111. Ibid., pp. 11–2.
112. Ibid., p. 92.
113. Ibid., p. 93.
114. Ibid., p. 50.
115. Ibid., p. 135.
116. Ibid., p. 13.
117. Ibid., p. 32.
118. Ibid., p. 33.
119. Ibid., pp. 26–7.
120. Ibid., p. 30.
121. Ibid., p. 60.
122. Ibid., p. 65.
123. Ibid., p. 47.
124. Ibid., p. 113. See also Tahia's reaction to the collapse of the United Arab Republic, p. 105.
125. Ibid., p. 136. Tahia's character in Anwar al-Qawadry's film *Gamal Abdel Nasser* expresses something similar when she asks the people who surround the body to leave her with the dead Nasser, saying, 'when he was alive, there was no time for me to sit with him. Now, excuse me, I want to sit with him for a little bit.'
126. Published by London-based Zed Books in 2002, it emerged as a selective translation by Egyptian intellectual and El Saadawi's then husband Sharif Hatata of the second and third volumes of *Awraqi . . . Hayati*, El Saadawi's autobiography which was first published in Arabic in 2000. All references to the autobiography will rely on the English translation.
127. The book was translated into English by Marilyn Booth (Oakland, CA: University of California Press, 1994). For more on it, see Golley, *Reading*

Arab Women's Autobiographies, pp. 148–64, and Fedwa Malti-Douglas, *Men, Women, and God(s): Nawal El Saadawi and Arab Feminist Poetics* (Berkeley, CA: University of California Press, 1995), pp. 159–76.

128. Nawal El Saadawi, *Memoirs from the Women's Prison* (Berkeley, CA: University of California Press, 1986), pp. 134–5.
129. Ibid., pp. 76-8.
130. El Saadawi, *Walking Through Fire*, p. 54.
131. Ibid., pp. 54–5, emphasis mine.
132. Ibid., p. 55.
133. Ibid.
134. Ibid.
135. Perri Giovannucci, *Literature and Development in North Africa: The Modernizing Mission* (New York: Routledge, 2008), p. 194.
136. Stephens, *Nasser*, p. 11.
137. Giovannucci, *Literature and Development in North Africa*, p. 189. For more on the relationship between Nasser and the figure of the *fallah* (the peasant), see Samah Selim, *The Novel and the Rural Imaginary in Egypt*, especially pp. 145–50.
138. El Saadawi, *Walking Through Fire*, p. 59.
139. Ibid., p. 57.
140. Ibid., p. 59.
141. Ibid., p. 64.
142. Ibid.
143. Ibid., p. 165, emphasis mine.
144. Ibid., p. 89. See also pp. 70 and 98.
145. Ibid., p. 120. Arab writers often use the term *al-Thaluth al-Muharram* (The Forbidden Trinity) in reference to politics, sex, and God. Arguably, the term was popularised by Syrian intellectual Bu Ali Yasin whose 1973 book carried the term as its title.
146. Ibid., p. 170.
147. Ibid.
148. Brenton J. Malin, *American Masculinity Under Clinton: Popular Media and the Nineties 'Crisis of Masculinity'* (New York: Peter Lang, 2005), p. 145.
149. Georges Tarabishi, *Al-Muthaqqafun al-'Arab wa al-Turath: al-Tahlil al-Nafsi li 'Usab Jama'i* (London: Riyad al-Rayyis Books, 1991), p. 28.
150. The battle took place in the Jordanian town of Karama whose name, coincidentally, means 'dignity'. For more on the political significance of the battle,

see W. Andrew Terrill, 'The Political Mythology of the Battle of Karama', *Middle East Journal*, Vol. 55, No. 1 (winter, 2001).
151. El Saadawi, *Walking Through Fire*, pp. 229–30.
152. Ibid., p. 230.
153. The first one took place in 1954, and was also related to an assassination attempt on Nasser. See pp. 135–6.
154. Richard P. Mitchell, *The Society of the Muslim Brothers* (London: Oxford University Press, 1969), p. vii.
155. Fedwa Malti-Douglas, 'Postmoderning the Traditional in the Autobiography of Shaykh Kishk', in *Tradition, Modernity, and Postmodernity in Arabic Literature*, ed. Kamal Abdel-Malel and Wael Hallaq (Leiden: Brill, 2000), pp. 389 and 393.
156. For a discussion of Egyptian communists' prison experience during Nasser's regime, see my reading of Shuhdi 'Atiyya al-Shafi'i's letter to Nasser in Chapter 1.
157. Armbrust, 'Farid Shauqi: Tough Guy, Family, Cinema Star', p. 203.
158. Zaynab al-Ghazali, *Ayyam min Hayati* (Cairo: Dar al-Shuruq, 1978), pp. 12–13.
159. Ibid., p. 45. *Taghut,* a word with multiple meanings that is often used now to connote 'tyrant', is the most common reference to Nasser in the text.
160. Miriam Cooke, '*Ayyam min Hayati:* The Prisoner Memoir of a Muslim Sister', in *The Postcolonial Crescent: Islam's Impact on Contemporary Literature*, ed. John C. Hawley (New York: Peter Lang, 1998), p. 127.
161. Julie Peteet, 'Male Gender and Rituals of Resistance in the Palestinian Intifada: A Cultural Politics of Violence', in *Imagined Masculinities*, p. 119.
162. Al-Ghazali, *Ayyam min Hayati*, p. 119.
163. Ibid., p. 120.
164. Ibid., p. 121.
165. See Julie Peteet, 'Male Gender,' pp. 118-9.
166. Al-Ghazali, *Ayyam min Hayati*, p. 87.
167. Nadja Odeh, 'Coded Emotions: The Description of Nature in Arab Women's Autobiographies', in *Writing the Self*, p. 327n.
168. See Al-Ghazali, *Ayyam min Hayati*, pp. 172, 173, 185, and 188.
169. Ibid., p. 140.
170. Ibid., p. 143.
171. Pauline Lewis, 'Zainab al-Ghazali: Pioneer of Islamist Feminism', *Michigan Journal of History* (winter, 2007), p. 24.
172. Al-Ghazali, *Ayyam min Hayati*, p. 145.

173. See, for instance, pp. 18, 19, 45, and 66.
174. Ibid., p. 180.
175. Ibid., emphasis mine.
176. Ibid., p. 190.
177. Cooke, '*Ayyam min Hayati*', p. 127.
178. Al-Ghazali, *Ayyam min Hayati*, p. 69.

4

Nasser on the Screen

Among the surge of serialised television dramas which were sweeping the Arab world during the month of Ramadan 2012, an Egyptian one was highly anticipated. Featuring the first appearance of veteran comedian 'Adil Imam on the small screen in thirty years, *Firqat Naji 'Atallah* (Naji 'Atallah's Team) chronicles the life of an Egyptian diplomat (Imam) who works in the Egyptian embassy in Tel Aviv. Unable to contain his critical and, at times, anti-Semitic comments against Israelis, Imam finds himself dismissed from work. As he prepares to return to Egypt, he stops by the bank to collect his money, only to discover that the bank has placed a hold on his account. The manager attributes the procedure to instructions he received from high officials who suspect that Imam is involved with a terrorist organisation. Dismayed and infuriated, Imam leaves the bank, returns to Egypt, and embarks on an *Ocean's Eleven*-like mission to recruit a team of Egyptian youths to rob the bank.

Naji 'Atallah's Team was largely panned by critics who faulted it for just being an attempt to gather all Imam's now stereotypical cinema characteristics – heroism, nobility, extreme intelligence – into a rather silly plot. Also attacked was the serial's superficial recourse to the Palestinian cause as a way of selling its message to viewers. Imam's first work since the 2011 Egyptian revolution, it was argued, was an effort to divert attention from his reactionary position against the revolution and to present him as a dauntless figure.[1]

It is the way in which the first episode of the series opens that is of interest here, however. A new press attaché arrives in the Egyptian embassy in Tel Aviv. Following a brief meeting with the ambassador, the latter summons Imam to introduce him to his new colleague. The encounter takes place at the ambassador's office, and runs as follows:

AMBASSADOR (addressing Imam, pointing to the attaché) 'I would like to introduce you to the new press attaché in the embassy: Gamal Bey; Gamal Abdel Nasser.'
IMAM 'Who, Your Excellency?!'
AMBASSADOR 'Gamal Abdel Nasser!
IMAM 'Gamal Abdel Nasser is here in Tel Aviv?! What a day! How did he manage to enter? We understood that Sadat could, but now Gamal Abdel Nasser?!'

The irony that the name invokes for Imam (and, presumably, for viewers at home) needs no further explanation. The mere mention of Nasser's name, borne by a regular Egyptian who happens to work in Israel, suffices to connote. It is as though not only Nasser but also his name cannot be imagined to inhabit Tel Aviv. The first few episodes of the serial further introduces this Gamal to the audience: he was born on 23 July 1959 – tellingly the seventh anniversary of Nasser's revolution; his father was killed in the October War in 1973; he shortly proves incapable of handling the fact that he is working in Israel, and consequently resigns and returns to Egypt. The message is then delivered: a *Nasser*, whoever he is, cannot reconcile himself with Israelis. He cannot be part of normalising relationships with Israel.

Nor can Israelis reciprocate. Following their introduction at the embassy, Imam escorts Nasser in his search to find an apartment in Tel Aviv. Upon their success, they sit down with the landlord to sign the lease. The latter asks for the attaché's full name. Once he hears it, the landlord suddenly wears a frown, while Imam whispers in Nasser's ear that 'they [Israelis] lose control when they hear his name'. The attaché is played by a relatively unknown actor (Yasir Ali Mahir) who, while not looking exactly like the person after whom he was named, does have a few of Nasser's physical characteristics, most notably the greying sideboards.

This recent appropriation of Nasser's name reflects a tendency among Egyptian film-makers and producers to capitalise on the popularity that the late president still possesses in people's imagination. As mentioned earlier, Nasser often functions as a site of memory, a plethora of metaphoric references that do not just reproduce the actual characteristics of the historical figure that he once was.[2] This latest employment of Nasser's power, however, conceals a much more complicated story of Nasser on the screen. In fact, and perhaps contrary to expectations, Nasser's immense presence in Egyptian everyday life has hardly approached a commensurate reflection in films. One needs only to remember that the first biographical film on the most important Egyptian politician to emerge from the capital of cinema in the Arab world was made as late as forty-four years after Nasser's revolution and twenty-six years after his death. *Nasser 56*, directed by Muhammad Fadil (b.1938), partly filled a vacuum that had often been negotiated and pondered by scholars and historians. This chapter traces the historical path that Nasser's presence on the screen has taken prior to and after *Nasser 56*. It will discuss how his picture, voice, speeches, and persona have been approached by Egyptian film-makers in feature films. I shall argue that Egyptian cinema has often separated Nasser from the regime that he created. Additionally, Egyptian film-makers have for the most part ignored the complexity of Nasser's character, thus reducing him to a flat sign with a set of attributes that either elevates him to the position of hero or banishes him to the world of ruthless dictators. In other words, rarely has Nasser been introduced as a historical figure on the screen, his deeds and decisions contextualised and thoroughly contemplated. Rather, film-makers have often oversimplified Nasser to evoke in the audience love or hate for him. As this chapter will demonstrate, it is the love that eventually triumphs. Following a brief reflection on Nasser's disproportionately meagre appearance on the screen compared to his influence in reality, the chapter will move on to tackle four major themes: symbolic interpretations of Nasser; the portrait of Nasser; the 'resignation speech'; and, finally, Nasser and biopics.

As mentioned earlier, there is little disagreement among scholars that Nasser has not enjoyed a huge cinematic presence, particularly during his lifetime. Films 'did not encompass Nasser's life details'.[3] In fact, it is acknowledged that Egyptian cinema has often refrained from approaching historical figures, especially contemporary ones. Yet, as Egyptian critic Kamal Ramzi shows, it was puzzling to notice that Nasser's regime did not break away from that tendency.[4] This is even more perplexing because Nasser's photographs and portraits were ubiquitous in Egyptian life. Maria Golia demonstrates how

> the reproduction of his [Nasser's] face became a cottage industry; his photograph was sold in mass-produced, ornately framed portraits, and

reproduced on matchboxes, bric-a-brac and even prayer carpets. Throughout Egypt, civil servants' offices and merchants' shops had a photograph of the president hanging on the wall.[5]

If one agrees with this account, then it is legitimate to wonder why such a powerful image has not made it on to the screen more frequently. It comes as no surprise to find only a few, if any, negative cinematic representations of Nasser during his life. But Nasser rarely appeared, even positively. His portraits 'remain strikingly absent from post-1952 films'.[6] With the exception of a few films, such as *Port Said* and *'Amaliqat al-Bihar* (Giants of the Sea) – both will be discussed below – Joel Gordon reminds us that Nasser's image 'would vanish thereafter from the screen, even as it proliferated throughout city and country, adorning public and private walls, and resonated in the lyrics of revolutionary anthems and school ditties'.[7] And if that was the case for Nasser's portrait, then one can only expect a similar scenario with his voice, not to mention his physical appearance in films through real footage.

There have been various attempts to explain this phenomenon. Raymond William Baker, discussing the relationship between cinema and politics in post-1952 Egypt, traces a broader context that deserves consideration. He argues that 'Egypt has not produced a significant body of official mobilisation films such as one might expect from an ostensibly revolutionary regime'.[8] Among the reasons behind that was the lack of a 'coherent and elaborate ideology'[9] in the newly founded regime, aside from 'inchoate notions of a somehow modernised Egypt'.[10] This view is problematic, however. While it is true that the 1952 revolution and Nasser have not often expressed themselves cinematically, the reasoning that Baker offers is less than convincing. Whether or not Nasser and his regime had a finely defined ideology did not bar them from using the press and the radio as major vehicles for disseminating their message and communicating with the public. The same regime that surely facilitated the ubiquity of Nasser's portrait in Egyptian life could have also transformed it into a cinematic icon.

More tenable is Viola Shafik's assertion that 'the promotion of Nasser's ideas and his image during his lifetime was rather word-oriented'.[11] Words, not images, were Nasser's biggest asset. Indeed, Nasser's relationship with the masses was primarily conceived of as 'a voice with an ear'.[12] Also significant is Shafik's argument that Nasser was rather an iconoclast who 'rejected symbolic deification along with visual representation'.[13] Buttressing this view is the surprising absence of statues of Nasser in a country where far less influential figures were thus materially commemorated. Unlike other authoritarian leaders around the world, Nasser did not highjack the cityscape of Cairo, did not impose his truly larger-than-life figure on the Cairenes of his time. Aside from his portraits, 'there is no designated monument to Egypt's most significant ruler of this century, no stadium, airport, public building, or major thoroughfare that bears his name'.[14] Needless to say, Nasser's physical absence from Egypt's public spaces exponentially intensified following his death, with his pictures replaced by those of Sadat, so much so that even 'at the rarely visited monument to Soviet Egyptian friendship at the Aswan High Dam, Nasser's profile was all but hidden by a superimposed image of the inheritor'.[15] Commonly known as de-Nasserisation, this state-sponsored, yet multilayered and consistent, process of erasing, obliterating, and demonising Nasser, whose manifestations in cinema will be discussed below, did nevertheless fail in consigning him to oblivion.

That Nasser's era was captivated by his voice does, in fact, make even more baffling his under-representation on the screen, for one could legitimately expect to 'hear' more of his speeches in films, especially during his lifetime. As Egyptian historian Sharif Yunus notes, the Free Officers' regime was the most self-expressive one in the history of Egypt, with Nasser's speeches alone numbering 1,359.[16] True, speeches find a warmer vehicle through radio, and Nasser's were no exception. His focus on radio was probably driven by 'the high rate of illiteracy in Egypt and the Arab World'[17] but this could clarify more a distance from the written word than an avoidance of cinema. Moreover, critics have been noting the predominance of the aural over the visual aspect in Egyptian – and Arabic – films. This can be recognised through 'flowing and elongated dialogues to the point of loquacity, as well as the overuse of soundtrack'.[18] This state facilitated the representation of feature films aurally on radio, of which there existed many instances.[19] Still, a few exceptions notwithstanding, Nasser's speeches were rarely used in cinema. From his routine speeches on everyday Egyptian matters to the more significant ones, and, at times, on occasions that made Egyptian history – such as the nationalisation of the Suez Canal and the Tripartite Aggression in 1956, the declaration of the United Arab Republic in 1958, and the inauguration of the High Dam project in 1960 – Nasser's speeches oddly fell short of inspiring Egyptian film-makers in the 1950s and 1960s.

A more direct and conventional view on the cinematic under-representation of Nasser is proposed by Durriyya Sharaf al-Din in her important study on cinema and politics in Egypt. Examining the effect of Nasser's charismatic presence on Egyptian cinema production, she argues that the 1960s witnessed a major cinematic trend that she calls *Cinema al-Khawf* (Cinema of Fear). Driven by the undemocratic nature of the regime, the uncontested leadership of Nasser, and, more importantly, the identification between Nasser and the regime, this cinema 'opted to distance itself from the present time . . . and instead found refuge in the past, as a way to protect and secure itself from the consequences of clashing with the present'.[20] Egyptian film critic 'Isam Zakariyya concurs with Sharaf al-Din, adding that 'Nasser's aura made it implausible to approach him cinematically, even positively'.[21] Therefore, the majority of Salah Abu Seif's (1915–96) and Youssef Chahine's (1926–2008) best works, to mention but notable examples, were either timeless or clearly set in pre-1952 Egypt.

Whatever the reason, the repertoire of the 1950s and 1960s Egyptian cinema was overwhelmingly Nasser-less, whether visually, aurally, or symbolically. The time has come, however, to examine those few exceptions that were alluded to earlier. In what follows I shall consider symbolic cinematic interpretations of Nasser in those decades, films that provoked the Egyptian artistic scene by courageously attempting a negotiation with *el-Rayyis*, albeit indirectly. Needless to say, there is no singular reception of those films, still less a unanimous agreement among critics that their protagonists were accurate representations of Nasser.

Less Fear; a Bit of Fear

Those who are well acquainted with the trajectories of Egyptian cinema may reach two unexpected conclusions. Undemocratic regime though it was, Nasser's Egypt did not ban any film from public screening. Certainly, there were several fierce clashes between film-makers and censors but that did not lead to the disappearance of any film. As Samir Farid recounts:

> Since President Nasser permitted the screening of *Allah Ma'ana*[22] (God Is with Us), personally attending its premiere in 1955 – the same year in which the first post-revolution censorship laws on cinema and theatre were issued – and throughout the 1970s, no Egyptian movie was banned.[23]

More striking is the fact that Egyptian cinema produced the best cinematic allusions to Nasser, both positively and, more importantly, negatively, during his lifetime. Nasser's aura, which was described above, still left room for symbolic takes on him. The 1970s, on the other hand, and despite an open and encouraged criticism of Nasserism, did not create its own Nasser on the screen.

As mentioned earlier, there were very few allegorical representations of Nasser in Egyptian cinema. According to Viola Shafik, 'Nasser's image had only few mythical or, to be more precise, visual symbolic aspects . . . [and] an intersection between him and a legendary figure is only marginally documented'.[24] Arguably, he had a small impact on the image of male heroes in post-1952 films, perhaps better recognised in the so-called '*futuwwa*' or 'tough guy' films. A mix of adventure, love, crime, and physical fights, those were Egypt's film noir, taking place in the dark corners of Cairo. Critics have noted that this quasi-genre experienced a resurrection after 1952 but it lacked a sophisticated treatment to transform it into a child trend of the revolution. It merely expressed a 'desire in Egyptian cinema and its audience to have a strong "hero" who is able to realise his rights by force'.[25]

The image of army officers was another area where the potential influence of Nasser was anticipated. Yet, this again proved an aborted venture, with superficial takes on the revolution abounding, most of which were far from the truth. Instead of digging deeper into the social, political and economical grievances that may have pushed unknown officers to risk a coup, Egyptian cinema was largely content to present the July revolution as a natural product of a society where love between poor men turned army officers and wealthy women was forbidden. Better exemplified in 'Izz al-Din Dhu al-Fiqar's 1957 classic *Rudda Qalbi* (Give me back my Heart), these films depict the July Revolution as an operation orchestrated by some army officers, daughters of feudal families, and members of the political police apparatus prior to 1952. Lacking a conspicuous goal, the revolution, those films maintained, only aimed at realizing happy marriages between girls of aristocratic, feudalist background and low-rank army officers.[26]

In fact, the filmic son of the 1952 revolution was neither an army officer nor a tough *futuwwa* but rather a singer. Unanimously seen as the one 'who rose to prominence in the Nasserite period and is associated with its spirit',[27] the legendary Abdel Halim Hafez brought to cinema a new political dimension. With his short figure, melancholic eyes, and rather effeminate looks, Hafez could certainly be no Nasser. In his films, however, he played constantly the role of the 'orphan in search of love – not only the girl's love but also her family's and, more importantly, her father's'.[28] Many critics have noted the political implication of this pattern, emerging, as it were, in the wake of Nasser's revolution. Hafez's quest for a father echoed Egyptians' dream for a new leader (read: Nasser) who could hold them together. Thus, 'Isam Zakariyya unequivocally asserts that 'the phenomenon of Abdel Halim Hafez, which began after the July revolution, could be politically read as a journey to find the father Gamal Abdel Nasser'.[29] Interestingly, Hafez's last film *Abi Fawqa al-Shajara* (My Father Is Up the Tree), which was produced two years after the defeat of 1967, introduced a modification to the pattern, perhaps necessitated by the blow that was directed at the image of Nasser and, consequently, the father. Instead of searching for the father, Hafez in this film first separates from him. They reunite at the end but after both indulging in an affair with the same woman. 'In a powerfully emotive ending, father and son tearfully confront each other in a cabaret, then walk out arm in arm as the dancer looks on, heartbroken.'[30]

On the other hand, aside from Youssef Chahine's *Al-Nasir Salah al-Din* (Saladin), no ancient Arab or Egyptian hero was cinematically appropriated as a metaphor for Nasser. Arabic poetry and prose abound with heroic figures who were constantly invoked by Arabs, especially in times of crisis. Nabila Ibrahim notes how those heroes were 'recalled and reproduced, both individually and collectively'.[31] For instance, a popular epic tale about 'Antara ibn Shaddad, a great pre-Islamic poet, emerged in Egypt during the Fatimid era.

According to a common view, the hero and the timing combined a metaphor for Egyptians of that era 'to rise against the Fatimid rulers who occupied their land, seized upon their resources, and considered them mere slaves'.[32] Egypt, in particular, was a fertile land for producing and reproducing popular tales and epics on heroes, from Prophet Muhammad's grandson al-Husayn to Taghribat Bani Hilal. Naturally, selecting a historical or mythical figure and presenting it as a metaphor for Nasser is no easy task. A film-maker has to be well versed in Arabic history and popular epics; there has to be an apt figure that could be a metaphor for Nasser; and, more importantly, such a film requires a huge budget, something that was not always within the reach of Egyptian film-makers.

These three factors were present in the case of Chahine's *Saladin*. Produced in 1963, the historical context of this film is in and of itself a clear indication of its contemporary message. The year 1963 is, as Hala Halim notes,

> a year during Nasser's regime; a year that comes after 1948 and 1956 with their harassing and dangerous events; a year, moreover, that follows the unity between Egypt and Syria (1958) and its dissolution (1961). 1963 is, therefore, a year when it is timely – if not imperative – to launch a propagandist film making the statements Saladin makes about a powerful Arab political leader who, by uniting the forces of the Arabs (and Saladin unites Egypt and Syria specifically), manages to achieve a difficult victory over the dangerous colonizing forces of the West in Palestine.[33]

But Saladin himself is the film's most important projection on to contemporary time. No critic who wrote about the film failed to notice Nasser's metaphor in Saladin. The title of the film, itself including Nasser's name in Saladin's nickname (which means 'the victorious'), the fact that Saladin ruled over Egypt, the presence of Palestine, the call for Arab unity, and the Western threat all combine to present an accessible code to decipher. The ironic fact that Saladin himself was not originally an Arab is never mentioned in the film.

A few, however, have noticed the very physical reference to Nasser that the film credits offer. Five minutes into the movie, we see the Arabs of Palestine looking at the horizon, anticipating the arrival of Saladin 'the saviour of *al-'Uruba*', as one of them says. The camera then focuses on an old man who, hearing sounds of horses and drums from afar, begins shouting, pointing his finger to the screen, 'Listen, these are his drums; listen, these are his signs. It is him! It is him!' Credits unfold, with the title of the film first, as if to show to whom the old man is referring. Moments before the credits end, however, Chahine begins to zoom his camera into a face, stopping at the eyes. The eyes very much 'resemble those of Nasser's [sic]'.[34] When the camera zooms out, the audience realises that the eyes are Ahmad Mazhar's, the actor who plays Saladin. Mazhar had by 1963 'turned to a movie career but not yet escaped villainous secondary roles'.[35] Picking him to play such a significant figure in what at the time was 'the most expensive film ever made by the Egyptian film industry'[36] was probably compelled by the fact that he was not only an army officer and a graduate of the military academy but also a classmate of none other than Nasser himself.

The film's audience at the time did act according to these inviting signs. Reportedly, 'Arab audiences would chant "Nasser!" acknowledging the correlation between the twelfth-century battles and Nasser's fight to unite Arab people and liberate Palestine.'[37] Khouri also notes that the film's popularity among Arabs today, almost fifty years after its production, derives not as much from Saladin's status as from 'an enduring nostalgia for Nasser's leadership and a longing for strong, unswerving guidance in the struggle for Arab economic and political independence'.[38]

Chahine was aware he was making a pro-Nasser film (in fact, *the* Nasser film) but he was not only doing that. Defending his project against charges of political propaganda, he clarified his stance towards *Saladin*:

> Let me be clear: perhaps the government back then, among other things, did have this goal in mind [showing support for Nasser's effort to unite the Arab world]. Of course, my feelings about the issue of Arab unity back then were very strong . . . and today they have even become stronger, albeit more studious and substantive. But when I made the film I was simply trying to prove that I could make historical epics and battle scenes without even needing the huge budget that Hollywood uses for the production of such films.[39]

And he did, thanks to the prodigious Shadi Abdel Salam (1930–86) who designed the sets and the costumes. Abdel Salam, whose sole feature film

Al-Mumiya' (The Mummy or The Night of Counting the Years) (1969) tops the list of the best one hundred films in the history of Egyptian cinema, was considered the most important costume and set designer in Egypt, particularly in historical films such as *Saladin*, where he managed to convey the historical setting of the event very intelligently.[40]

Equating Nasser with Saladin, predicated as it was, in the film and beyond, upon dreams of victory and Arab unity that were filling the Egyptian street, became untenable following the 1967 defeat. Rendering the once invincible Nasser a powerless president whose first public response was to step down and leave office, the *naksa* was shattering, a deep wound that Arabs have yet to recover from. Naturally, such an event would leave its scars on Egyptian filmmaking. It belongs elsewhere to discuss the impact of 1967 on Egyptian cinema in detail. What matters here is to trace any changes or developments that the *naksa* brought to the image of Nasser in Egyptian cinema.

With the regime of Nasser weakened and vulnerable, the years 1967 to 1970 'provided directors with a margin of action for criticizing the policies and the abuses of the regime'.[41] Contrary to the 'Cinema of Fear' which dominated the Egyptian production prior to 1967, the *naksa* forced a new trend, that Durriyya Sharaf al-Din calls 'the Green Light'. Initiated by the 'desire of the regime to loosen its iron grip on the freedom of expression in cinema',[42] the trend manifested itself in a group of films that adopted a critical stance towards the regime. Those films varied significantly, however, in the way they situated Nasser within their political agenda. Take *Miramar*, for instance. Kamal El Sheikh's 1969 controversial adaptation of Naguib Mahfouz's 1967 novel is credited for being the first film that 'criticises explicitly, without any resort to symbolism or insinuation'.[43] Yet, for all its directness, *Miramar* leaves Nasser untouched. The closest reference to him comes probably in a passing remark about Saad Zaghlul, made by the former feudalist Tulba Marzuq (played by the legendary Yusuf Wahbi). Marzuq holds Zaghlul responsible for the current situation, despite the fact that the latter died in 1927, long before Nasser's revolution. In a comic scene, Marzuq asserts that Zaghlul is at fault for igniting the spirit of revolution among the masses. Whether Nasser stands as one belonging to the masses or else a Zaghlul-like leader, similarly accountable for agitating the public, is left to the audience.

Three films produced during that period stand out, however. What makes them unique is that all of them resort to abstraction and symbolism, possibly to mask their critical stances, although their symbolism is quite transparent and their reference rather obvious. A year earlier than *Miramar*, Salah Abu Seif made his now classic *Al-Qadiyya 68* (Case 68). Based on a play by leftist writer Lutfi al-Khuli, the film allegorises the shaky and uncertain situation of Egypt through an old building. As 'Isam Zakariyya notes, the theme of collapsing or ruined buildings noticeably reverberated in Egyptian cinema in the wake of 1967, embodying 'the sense of "earthquake" that was caused by the defeat'.[44] Zakariyya also ponders the contrast between this image and the way the July regime attempted to present a strong and firm Egypt, best symbolised by two giant buildings that emerged during Nasser's reign: the Cairo Tower and the High Dam.[45] Along with *Al-Qadiyya 68,* Kamal El Sheikh's 1967 *Al-Mukharribun* (the Vandals) and Sa'id Marzuq's 1972 *Makan li al-Hubb* (A Place for Love) are the most important representatives of this theme. Depending on their take on Nasser, each of these films has a character who owns the building, guards it, or examines the circumstances of its collapse.

The drama of *Al-Qadiyya 68* revolves around 'a local political committee's debate over whether to renovate or raze and rebuild an apartment building that doesn't meet code'.[46] The building's owner, himself the head of the committee, is Munjid (played by Salah Mansur), a good-hearted but weak and indecisive man. The film demonstrates people's love and belief in Munjid whose name tellingly means 'the saviour'. He is surrounded by two groups: the old guards, traditional law-abiding opportunists who seek to maintain the status quo by fixing the building from within, on the one hand, and the idealist, rebellious youths who demand a radical solution to the problem on the other. Amid their heated arguments and counterarguments, the building begins actually to collapse. Consoling Munjid, the youths shout, 'Tear it down, uncle Munjid, and rebuild it anew.'

The film was perceived as a severe attack on the Arab Socialist Union, the only legalised political party in Egypt at the time, whose members in return protested against the screening of *Al-Qadiyya 68*, condemned its director, and physically assaulted him outside Cinema Miami in Cairo.[47] Though the official reception of the film stopped at what they considered a ridicule of Nasser's own entourage, thus ignoring the signification of the Munjid character, numerous critics explicitly affirmed that 'the landlord is Nasser';[48] 'Munjid, according to some, is Nasser';[49] and 'Munjid's name obviously refers to Nasser'.[50]

Also appearing in 1968 was Tawfiq Salih's (1926–2013) controversial film *Al-Mutamarridun* (the Rebels). Unlike *Al-Qadiyya 68*, where reference to Nasser was officially unrecognised (or ignored), the implied message in Salih's film was too obvious to be overlooked. The film revolves around an uprising that takes place in a tuberculosis sanatorium. Enraged by the lack of water and ultimately unable to contain their wrath after a boy is struck and killed by the water bowser, the inmates decide to rebel against the administration. They need, however, leadership, presented in the film through Doctor 'Aziz (played by Shukri Sarhan). Interestingly, 'Aziz belongs to the two warring groups: he is both a patient and part of the medical staff. The uprising succeeds, whereby the inmates take over the sanatorium, expel its director, and replace him with Doctor 'Aziz. With 'Aziz lacking the scientific knowledge needed for good administration, however, and solely relying on words and slogans, the faults of the past are reproduced, eventually restoring the old order, albeit more cruelly. 'Aziz admits his failure, and offers to step down.

Filmed in 1966, *Al-Mutamarridun* was temporarily banned, with the then Minister of Culture, Tharwat 'Ukasha, declaring that he could not 'pass a film which attacked Gamal Abdel Nasser'.[51] Following negotiations, Salih was asked to remove twenty-five minutes from the original print. Moreover, while the film was clearly set in a pre-1952, undefined Egyptian place, Salih was forced to 'shoot a new ending, affirming that the July revolution is the solution'.[52]

But 'Ukasha was not alone in assuming that the doctor in *Al-Mutamarridun* signified Nasser. Decades after its screening, Tawfiq Salih himself acknowledged the relationship, admitting at the same time that unexpected historical events – such as the 1967 defeat – made the film more relevant, if not prescient. He said,

> The 1967 war exploded, and threw us into a debacle. My film took then a dazzling prophetic dimension. I was no longer able to deny that the doctor in *Al-Mutamarridun* is specifically Nasser, especially that he also offers to step down after the defeat.[53]

Clearly, Minister 'Ukasha was not mistaken in reading a Nasser-like character in Doctor 'Aziz. Aside from the stepping-down similarity, 'a scene in which Doctor 'Aziz and his ruling council . . . sit around the director's table immediately after seizing power recalls familiar images of the Free Officers in the early morning hours of July 23'.[54] Moreover, 'Aziz's language plays a significant role in stimulating the audience to follow a symbolic reading. As Raymond Baker puts it,

> Large segments of the doctor's dialogue contain slogans and key phrases lifted directly from speeches by Nasser. At one critical moment during the revolt, he addresses the patients and speaks simply and movingly of the necessity of fighting and even dying for one's dignity: in content, manner of delivery, and effect on those listening, these are unmistakably the words of Gamal Abdel Nasser.[55]

The appropriation of Nasser's character in films escalated significantly after *Al-Mutamarridun*, so much so that the president himself had at times to intervene. The most prominent instance was Husayn Kamal's (1932–2003) *Shay' min al-Khawf* (A Bit of Fear). Produced in 1969, and based on Tharwat Abaza's (1927–2002) novel of the same title, the film features versatile actor Mahmud Mursi playing dual 'Atris roles, the grandfather and the grandson. If Munjid in *Al-Qadiyya 68* is an indecisive head of a committee, and 'Aziz in *Al-Mutamarridun* is a revolutionary turned into an autocrat, then 'Atris is, to put it mildly, a thug. The grandfather leads a gang of aides who assist him in controlling the Dahashna village by force, instilling fear in the hearts of people. As he grows dismissive of his grandson's gentleness, supposedly because he sees him as a potential heir, he exposes him to multiple violent situations, trying to indoctrinate him that only by force does 'Atris survive. Prior to the grandfather's death, the young 'Atris never commits a crime, having avowed to his childhood sweetheart Fu'ada that his hands will never be stained with blood. When a villager shoots the grandfather, however, the latter asks his grandson to avenge him. And he does, instantly.

The concept of fear is reiterated throughout the film. The grandfather declares at the beginning of the film that 'a bit of fear does not harm'. When the grandson, now the leader of the gang, loots and robs the villagers of their harvests, the villagers do not resist because they are afraid. When 'Atris publicly flirts with one of his aides' fiancée, the aide cannot respond because of fear. The only villager able to overcome fear is Fu'ada. Though they clearly love each other, 'Atris, now unwilling to let anything drive him other than force, decides to coerce Fu'ada into marrying him, imposing a fake marriage contract on her father. Legally his wife, Fu'ada goes home with 'Atris, avowing nonetheless that she will not yield herself to him.

The last part of the film sees a major transformation befalling the village. Astonished to know that Fu'ada does not actually give her consent, the villagers, influenced by Shaykh Ibrahim, consider the marriage invalid. In what is perhaps one of the most famous processions in Egyptian cinema, Shaykh Ibrahim leads the villagers to 'Atris's house, shouting, *gawaz 'Atris min Fu'ada batil* (the marriage of 'Atris and Fu'ada is invalid). Eventually, the rebellion succeeds, Fu'ada escapes the house, 'Atris's aides leave him, and he himself perishes by burning to death.

The villagers were not alone in their efforts to conquer their fears. The film also scared the censors who quite easily and quickly got the message: Nasser is 'Atris who has usurped Egypt! To add to the dilemma the film was produced by the Public Film Organisation, funded as it was by the regime itself. Ali Abu Shadi recounts that the story reached Nasser who then asked to watch the film. To people's shock, Nasser passed the film. He asked the censor if he considered his government a gang. The censor said no. Nasser then asked him if he considered him the leader of a gang. The censor repeated his no. Nasser then commented, 'If we were like that we really would deserve to be burnt.'[56]

Nasser's passing of the screening was read as an attempt to show his magnanimity and liberalism compared to his subordinates,[57] or to offer artists and intellectuals an opportunity to release their anger.[58] I would suggest a different reasoning, however. The anecdote with the censor shows Nasser protesting not against the film but rather against the censor's assumption that the film was a reference to Nasser. By passing the screening, Nasser denied any resemblance to 'Atris and imposed another reading of the film that would not relate to him. In so doing, he was fighting back against the film-maker, albeit indirectly. By simply ignoring the otherwise obvious message of the film, Nasser's act was meant to deprive Husayn Kamal of the very courage the latter would claim. Had Nasser banned the film, he would have accepted the fact that not only was he 'Atris but also that some of his people were brave enough to think so.

The Politics of the Portrait

In his well-known reflections on photography, Roland Barthes demonstrates that, by its mere process, the portrait fragments the 'I' that it seeks to capture. Standing in front of the camera, the 'I' of the photographee simultaneously becomes the one he thinks he is, the one he wants others to think he is, the one the photographer thinks he is, and the one the photographer makes use of to display his art.[59] Barthes then proceeds to enunciate the temporal difference between cinema and the photograph:

> In the photograph, something *has posed* in front of the tiny hole and has remained there forever (that is my feeling); but in cinema, something *has passed* in front of this same tiny hole: the pose is swept away and denied by the continuous series of images: it is a different phenomenology, and therefore a different art which begins here, though derived from the first one.[60]

As such, photographs and portraits are not narratives; they do not unfold with the passing of time. They are born complete and, therefore, dead; hence their intrinsic melancholic feature of which Barthes conceives.

With the portrait shown in the film, however, a new life is restored. The portrait is now narrativised through its temporal and spatial presence in the film. Emerging at a specific moment (or moments) in the film, the portrait acquires new connotations that may confirm or contradict the ones that are associated with it outside itself. Cinema has the ability of 'shifting the emphasis of the look',[61] says Laura Mulvey. But whose look are we talking about here? At play in the case of the portrait-in-film are two looks: the protagonists' and the audience's. If photography is 'to appropriate the thing photographed ... putting oneself into a certain relation to the world that feels like knowledge – and therefore power',[62] the portrait-in-film magnifies this appropriation. When Egyptian actress Soad Hosny, for instance, gazes at Nasser's portrait in *Al-Karnak*, the audience in the cinema gazes at both: Hosny and the portrait. It is this complicated status as a doubly seen photograph that adds new meanings to the portrait.

In what follows I shall trace the emergence of Nasser's portrait in Egyptian cinema (or the absence thereof). Guiding my analysis is the assumption that this portrait has, by and large, never appeared in films *superfluously*. That is, it is a signifier; it does not merely occupy the background of the setting where the scene takes place. The politics of showing or hiding Nasser's portrait sheds light on the message the film-maker is seeking to deliver. In other words, Egyptian cinema did not mirror the reality when it showed offices and government buildings during Nasser's life. Though his portrait certainly did occupy those spaces, it was not normally seen in films – except when a message was needed. More informative a case is the cinema of de-Nasserisation which swept Egypt after the death of Nasser. While the absence of Nasser's portrait from the offices of police or intelligence officers during the 1960s was unthought of, the films that sought to condemn the oppression of Nasser's regime did often eliminate it, thus sending a specific message to the audience, as will be shown below.

As mentioned earlier, Egyptian cinema rarely showed Nasser's portrait during his life. When it did, the portrait served a specific purpose within the broader context of the film. A major example of this is patriotic films, particularly those that treated the 1956 Suez War or the emergence of the United Arab Republic in 1958. Also significant is that this context witnessed an unintentional contest between showing Nasser in a military uniform or in civilian dress, the latter normally a suit. The contest began with the 1957 *Port Said*, arguably the first film to show Nasser's portrait. Directed by 'Izz al-Din Dhu al-Fiqar (1919–63), and produced under the auspices of the regime, the film shows the city during the Suez War, with special homage paid to its residents for their courageous resistance and for fighting against the invaders. Featuring an ensemble cast, including Farid Shawqi, Shukri Sarhan, Amina Rizq, and Rushdi Abaza, the film also introduces the actress/singer Huda Sultan performing a song in tribute to Nasser. Entitled, *Ammim Gamal al-Qana* (O' Gamal, Nationalise the Canal), the song is a rare incident in Egyptian cinema in which a singer directs a song at the president.

If *Port Said* shows Nasser only in his military uniform as one might expect, *'Amaliqat al-Bihar* (Giants of the Sea) combines the military and the civilian. Produced in 1960, this rather flat representation of the same war focuses on the contributions of the Egyptian navy, headed in the film by real-life army officer Ahmad Mazhar. Nasser's portrait appears three times in the film but only once in uniform. Another film in the same year, however, *Watani wa Hubbi* (My Homeland, My Love), opts to exclude the military uniform of Nasser once and for all. Featuring actor-director Husayn Sidqi (1917–76) in the role of Wahid, an army officer sent to Syria in the wake of the Egyptian–Syrian unification, the film is historically significant for its representations, albeit sentimentally, of Syrians and Palestinians, a rare occurrence in mainstream Egyptian cinema.

In those three instances of patriotic cinema, Nasser's portrait serves to show both the officers' loyalty to their president and the latter's enormous role in the events around which the films revolve. Interestingly, however, the portrait exclusively appears in official spaces: that is, offices and buildings belonging to the Egyptian army. Nowhere in these films do we see the portrait hung in houses or apartments, nor in public spaces such as clubs, schools, or libraries. The civilian Nasser would triumph over the militant in *Watani wa Hubbi*, and his portrait in cinema would henceforward show the signature shot of Nasser, where 'he was almost always pictured grinning winningly'.[63]

Unlike the former blatantly positive appropriation of the portrait, the 1960s witnessed a few incidents of a more critical approach. Galal al-Sharqawi's 1967 adaptation of Yusuf Idris's *Al-'Ayb* (The Shame) foreshadowed a future trend. The film is a frank condemnation of the corruption and opportunism that were sweeping the bureaucratic apparatuses of Nasser's regime. Contrary to the films of the 'Green Light', where the setting is either timeless or clearly pre-revolution, Joel Gordon notes how, in this film, 'Nasser's portrait, not Farouk's, hangs in the government office where a group of opportunistic bureaucrats sell government permits for LE 75 [75 Egyptian pounds], then attend liquor-splashed parties hosted by the bribe-profferers'.[64] The trend, however, would not find instant followers for, even in the more explicit attack on Nasser's regime that proliferated in Kamal El Sheikh's 1969 *Miramar*, Nasser's portrait remained unseen. Only after Nasser's death was the door opened for a radically different treatment of the portrait.

It is often acknowledged that the so-called Sadat's Corrective Revolution of May 1971 facilitated the emergence of what Durriyya Sharaf al-Din calls 'the most important movement witnessed by Egyptian cinema in the 1970s;

namely, the Cinema of Centers of Power'.⁶⁵ Named after Nasser's influential state security apparatus, particularly the state intelligence service which was dismantled by Sadat, this loosely defined movement took aim not only at the failures of Nasser's regime but, more broadly, at the whole post-1952 experience, reducing it to an era of fear, oppression, and torture. Promoted in this cinematic wave was a pattern that hardly changed which, as Ali Abu Shadi puts it, replaced the traditional evil man of melodramatic Egyptian films with a representative of a centre of power from Nasser's epoch. 'He is either a minister, a director of prison, the intelligence chief, or an army officer,' Abu Shadi recounts, 'who is merciless, has an appalling appearance, finds pleasure in torture, and causes the good girls of Egypt to be raped, transformed into prostitutes, or stolen from their helpless husbands.'⁶⁶

It merits attention, however, that, even after Sadat's deviation from Nasser's road, the latter's portrait still found a warm welcome. A notable example was Saʿid Marzuq's (1940–2014) technically innovative film, *Makan li al-Hubb* (A Place for Love). Produced only a year after the Corrective Revolution, the film revolves around an affair between the photographer, Ahmad (played by Nur al-Sharif), and Suad, a poor girl from Suez (played by Soad Hosny) who loses all of her family members during the 1967 war. Though the political leanings of Ahmad are never explicitly revealed, the pictures which hang on the wall of his room speak to some. While the director's slow camera pans the room, it abruptly lingers over a specific corner, gradually zooming into two large portraits. Not only do we see Nasser's smiling face but we also find it next to none other than Alberto Korda's iconic photograph of Che Guevara (1928–67). The juxtaposition, a unique occurrence in Egyptian cinema, is laden with associations, implicitly referring to a real-life encounter between the two men that occurred during Guevara's visit to Cairo in 1959, a picture of which is also widely circulated.

Ali Badrakhan's notorious 1975 adaptation of Naguib Mahfouz's lukewarmly received novella, *Al-Karnak*, is recognised as the most important representative of 'Cinema of Centers of Power', so much so that critics have also labelled the latter as *al-Karnaka* (Karnakisation) in a reference to other films that followed Badrakhan's suite.⁶⁷ Though the film bears the name of the café where students and regular Cairenes used to meet, it is the intelligence offices, interrogation rooms, and prisons that constitute the major setting of *Al-Karnak*. Filled with images of blood and torture, coupled with a long rape scene that befalls the prisoner Zaynab (Soad Hosny) at the behest of the intelligence chief (ably played by Kamal al-Shinnawi), the film relays the story of innocent students who, despite being advocates of Nasser and his revolution, find themselves taken prisoner by intelligence forces.

A groundbreaking film by all accounts, *Al-Karnak* engages in a careful dialogue with Nasser's portrait. Eight minutes into the film, the camera lingers over posters that combine Nasser with the then Soviet statesman Aleksei Kosygin (1904–80) on an unspecified street in Cairo. Surrounded by the red Russian flag, the juxtaposition is telling of both the Soviet presence in Egypt and the timing of the film – the 1960s. Contrasting with the 'foreign' redness of the poster is the redness of the Egyptian sports club, al-Ahli, whose fans we see cheering in buses immediately after the scene with the poster. In so doing, the film attempts to create a distance between what merits Nasser's attention and what concerns his people. As though to justify Sadat's later break with the Soviet Union, Nasser's portrait with Kosygin is left unnoticed by passers-by and unmentioned by normal Egyptians who have another 'red' passion about which to care.

Also of interest is the politics that orient the appearance of Nasser's portrait in government offices. When the two main protagonists of *Al-Karnak* (Soad Hosny and Nur al-Sharif) are taken at night by the police, their families go to the police station to ask of their whereabouts. As we would expect, Nasser is seen smiling behind the police officer. When the prisoners are transferred to the intelligence office, however, the portrait disappears. The ruthless chief, Khalid Safwan, occupies a huge space in which no portrait of Nasser is hung. Nor do we see the portrait in the dark rooms in which interrogation and torture take place. It reappears only at the office of a kind-hearted member of the parliament whom Hosny and al-Sharif visit to complain about their first arrest.

The manipulation of the portrait in *Al-Karnak* would set the pattern for others to follow. With Nasser unseen in the office of the intelligence chief, the film is partly exonerating him. The ruthless chief shows no association with the president, not even through a picture. Moreover, while the member of the parliament expresses his utter disapproval of what is happening 'behind the sun' – as the title of another film of the movement reads – asserting that the chief of intelligence's acts constitute a serious precedent in the country, the camera lingers on Nasser's image. The final part of the film, however, allows Khalid Safwan to speak. Having been dismissed and jailed following Sadat's Corrective Revolution, Safwan attempts to fight back, refusing to be the scapegoat of the transition. When furious prisoners surround him and beat him, he shouts, 'we all are criminals; we all are victims'.

The epitome of *Al-Karnak's* negotiation with the portrait occurs neither in government offices nor in the streets of Cairo. Rather, it is Hosny's apartment that witnesses 'the most poignant scene in the film'.[68] Terrified by the chief of intelligence and his henchmen after she is raped, Hosny agrees to spy on her circle of friends, including her lover (al-Sharif), in return for her release from prison. Arriving home after a passionate night with al-Sharif, she goes right into her room, sits down at her desk, and begins to write the report. Suddenly, the audience is surprised to see a portrait of Nasser hanging over her desk – a scene that does not appear in Mahfouz's text.[69] Hosny stares briefly at the portrait. It is noteworthy that the film never reveals the presence of the portrait in Hosny's room before this moment. Undoubtedly, Nasser is always there, from the beginning of the film, but only the politics of the portrait can determine the right moment for it to appear. The brief stare at Nasser, as Joel Gordon notes, 'reflect[s] a combination of lingering adoration, disbelief at the ruler's potential complicity, and the intense pain of betrayal'.[70]

Less powerfully, several films would mimic a similar approach to the portrait, particularly its selective presence and absence from police and intelligence offices. Husayn Kamal's 1979 *Ihna Btu' al-Utubis* (We Are the Bus People), teaming 'Adil Imam with another famous Egyptian comedian, Abdel Mun'im Madbuli, follows the tragic fate of two neighbours who are taken to the police station because of a fight with the conductor on a public bus. Seemingly trivial and apolitical, the case coincides with rumours throughout the country about a plot to overthrow the regime. No matter what their charges are, all detainees on that day are indiscriminately implicated with the supposed plotters. A strong man – a centre of power – whose office is adorned with a large picture of Nasser calls the director of the prison, demanding signed confessions from all detainees about their political associations. And torture takes place.

Similar to *Al-Karnak,* the heartless director of the prison possesses no visual relations with Nasser, his office bereft of the president's portrait. The dissociation between Nasser and those who work in his name is further amplified when the prisoners blame their situation explicitly on the president's entourage who convinces the otherwise benign leader that conspiracies against his rule are proliferating, hence the need for an iron fist against suspicious citizens. In fact, the film is keen on demonstrating the prisoners' loyalty to the regime. Upon hearing the news about the outbreak of the 1967 war, for instance, they identify with the very same system that is unjustly punishing them, declaring, as one prisoner says, that 'we are not important. The country is.' Also significant in this context is the two neighbours' disbelief that the higher authorities might know about what is happening to them. They both reiterate their ultimate trust that, once the authorities realise there is a mistake, they will release them. Hence the recurring, unheeded shout in the film, released regularly after each torture session, 'we are the bus people, O brothers'.

With the coming of the 1980s, preceded as it was by Sadat's visit to Israel and the *Infitah* (Open Door) liberal economic policy, a generation of so-called 'neorealist' film-makers was born. Disenchanted with Sadat's promises of a prosperous economy, and experiencing an inner grief over the collapse of the Nasserite dream, those film-makers represented an Egypt where 'the economy let down the simple Egyptian man, whose livelihood was devoured by the *Infitah's* monsters; where a parasite class emerged, whose fortune multiplied enormously'.[71] Khayri Bishara (b.1947), Muhammad Khan (b.1942), 'Atif al-Tayyib (1947–95), and Dawud Abdel Sayyid (b.1946), to mention only the most significant ones, dominated the scene, producing films that were 'sparked off by the *Infitah* or Open Door policy launched by the Sadat government in the 1970s'.[72] Contrary to the 1970s, the 'Cinema of Centers of Power' found no space within these productions. In the films of the new generation of film-makers, Nasser's portrait began to return positively, albeit irregularly, in a process that would ultimately turn it into an icon with fixed and trans-historical associations.

The most eloquent instances of the portrait revisited were made by 'Atif al-Tayyib. A true son of Nasser's regime (born in 1947), al-Tayyib made his directorial debut in 1982 with a rather commercial film, *Al-Ghira al- Qatila* (Fatal Jealousy). It was his second, 1983 film, however, that made him into an important film-maker. *Sawwaq al-Utubis* (The Bus Driver) stars al-Tayyib's favourite actor, Nur al-Sharif, as Hasan, a 1973 war veteran who works as a bus driver in the day and a taxi driver at night. Hasan's father owns a carpentry workshop whose situation deteriorates owing to the negligence of his son-in-law 'Awni who oversees it. Unable to sustain itself, the workshop is shut down, owing thousands of dollars to merchants and customers. To Hasan's dismay, all his family members suggest selling the workshop. Hasan, the last moral person in a decadent environment, refuses, and embarks on a journey to borrow the money required. Where does Nasser fit into this gloomy picture? Nasser's portrait is seen hanging in the workshop, tellingly blurred by the camera. On the other hand, the father's apartment has no portrait of Nasser. The director adeptly exploits this presence/absence of the portrait when he makes Hasan agree to sell the apartment, not the workshop. The workshop/Nasser/father associations function as symbols of a bygone era, one that Hasan is fighting not to lose. Eventually, however, Hasan manages to acquire the money, and hurries home to tell his father the good news, only to find the old man dead. Enraged, Hasan engages in a physical fight with the first person who misbehaves on the bus, shouting, as the credits unfold, '*ya wlad el-Kalb*' (sons of a dog).

But, if *Sawwaq al-Utubis* offers an elegy for an irretrievable past, al-Tayyib's 1986 adaptation of Mahfouz's novella, *Al-Hubb Fawqa Hadabat al-Haram* (Love on the Pyramids' Plateau) condemns a hypocritical present. The film presents a rare, if bleak, treatment of sexual deprivation in Egypt through the protagonist Ali (played masterfully by Ahmad Zaki) who seeks answers from intellectuals, journalists, religious figures, and family members on how he can satisfy his sexual needs. Also rare in this film is the form that Nasser's portrait assumes. Rather than the more common photograph in a frame, it is in *Al-Hubb* a drawing that is located at the centre of a large rectangular tile on a café's wall. The tile is coloured with the red and the black of the Egyptian flag, with Nasser's face replacing the eagle in its middle.

The café is a setting for two brief encounters between Ali and an old journalist called 'Atif Hilal. Ali looks for the journalist in order to confide in him his sexual dilemma, hoping he will offer an answer. Interestingly, they both sit at a table immediately beneath Nasser's portrait, with the Nasser situated in the space between them. In the first meeting, the journalist sits closer to the portrait, sharing the same direction as Nasser's gaze – presumably Ali. After hearing Ali's story, he tells him that it is a common problem, that the entire society must change, and that Ali should work towards realising that goal. When Ali protests that he cannot wait until the whole society is changed, the journalist excuses himself to leave.

In the second meeting, it is Ali who shares Nasser's perspective. After mockingly pretending to have solved his problem because of a lucky acquisition of millions of dollars, Ali's encounter with the journalist ends abruptly and unexpectedly. As the journalist instructs him not to gain the world and lose himself, Ali, his gaze and Nasser's fixed on the journalist, begins shouting, 'Liar, liar'. He becomes hysterical as he accuses the journalist of hypocrisy, of selling words while, in fact, being just an opportunist. Sharing Ali's point of view, Nasser's portrait is obviously there to agree. By situating Ali and the portrait against the journalist, the film condemns the old generation – the 1952 generation – by showing that they betray Nasser's principles. Compared to the first meeting, Nasser, generationally associated with the journalist, is now reclaimed by Ali who has nothing to resort to but a portrait.

The continuing decline of Egypt – politically, socially, and economically – has added to the romantic, nostalgic reception of Nasser's portrait. From the 1990s on, it will be almost exclusively approached through those eyes, thanks to Youssef Chahine's disciples – a group of leftist film-makers who began their careers as assistants to the legendary director, including Radwan al-Kashif (1952–2002), Yousry Nasrallah (b.1952), Khalid al-Hagar (b.1963), and Khalid Yusuf (b.1964). In al-Kashif's 1993 highly acclaimed *Lih ya Banafsig?* (Why, Violets?), the protagonist Ahmad (played by Faruq al-Fishawi), suffering from an impossible, unrequited love, is seen sitting in his room between Nasser's and Abdel Halim Hafez's portraits, two major icons of the aspirations of the 1960s generation, to whom the film is dedicated. Produced in the same year was Nasrallah's *Mercedes* which features al-Nubi, a communist who, after Nasser's death, believes he is personally responsible for bringing about justice, equality, and freedom for people. Those words are uttered while the screen plays footage of Nasser's funeral, his large portraits carried by the grieving mourners.

Khalid Yusuf, a self-declared Nasserist and Chahine's assistant director of ten years, relies frequently on Nasser-related motifs; and, certainly, the portrait. In his 2001 debut, *Al-'Asifa* (The Storm), a film that 'laments the loss of pan-Arab nationalism',[73] a woman named Huda (played by Yusra) recounts how her husband disappears. A war veteran, he returns home injured after the 1973 war, only to see a gradual vanishing of the principles he fought for. Sitting in front of Nasser's portrait that hangs over a television, 'the flashback shows him witnessing Sadat's visit to Israel on television, then images of the Camp David Accords, and later the opening of the Israeli embassy in Cairo with the raising of the Israeli flag'.[74] Unable to contain his rage and shock, he stands, stares at Nasser's portrait, and leaves home forever. Yusuf revisits the portrait again in his 2009 *Dukkan Shihata* (Shihata's Shop). The film chronicles the life of the kind-hearted Shihata whose birth coincides with Sadat's assassination, his relationship with his father, an old man obviously representing Nasser's generation, and his troubled relationship with his two older siblings, apparently standing in for Sadat's era. Nasser's portrait decorates the wall of the father's room. In one scene, the father asks Shihata to move the portrait a little bit so that it 'covers the crack in the wall'. The brothers conspire against Shihata to send him to prison. He is released, years later, only to learn of his father's death. In a scene that is too explicit, Yusuf shows Shihata crying, holding Nasser's portrait, and murmuring, 'Rest in peace, father'.

As has been demonstrated, Nasser's portrait has cinematically travelled through contested narratives and conflicting intentions but eventually emerged as an icon whose mere presence connotes singular nostalgia for an era that no longer exists. In other words, the portrait is no longer historicised, nor is it subjected to neutral reflections on the good and the bad of Nasser's regime. Rather, it is there only to express the dissatisfaction with the present along with hope – not necessarily for a return of the son, to borrow the title of Chahine's famous film, but for a better tomorrow of social justice and freedom. It is no wonder, then, that Nasser was the only Arab leader whose pictures were carried by protestors in Tahrir Square during the 2011 Egyptian revolution.[75] As Egyptian scenarist Mahfuz Abdel Rahman (b. 1941) recounts, in rather flowery fashion,

> And on 25 January, I saw the sun of Nasser . . . True, it is a generation that did not know him, did not probably follow him. But the sun does not need us to know it. We therefore saw Nasser's pictures in the Square. We were

watching the TV, and chant after chant began to rise. I heard an old lady's voice feebly rising, 'Long live, Gamal Abdel Nasser!'[76]

The Resignation Speech

More than any other utterance of Nasser, the 1967 *tanahhi* (resignation) speech occupies, from the 1970s onward, a special place in Egyptian cinema. In fact, the speech is the most featured archival footage in the history of Egyptian cinema, surpassing other seminal moments in modern Egyptian history, such as the funeral of Nasser himself in 1970, the Egyptian crossing of the Suez Canal in the 1973 October War, or Sadat's visit to Jerusalem in 1977.[77] Triggered by the humiliating defeat of 1967, the speech showed a hurt Nasser assuming full responsibility for the *naksa* and consequently announcing he would step down. With the exception of Muhammad Hasanayn Haykal, who reportedly co-wrote the speech,[78] the announcement was surprising news to all Egyptians, including Nasser's own wife Tahia who, in her memoirs, acknowledged that she did not know its contents prior to its delivery.[79]

Apart from its performative and informative aspects, the speech, delivered on 9 June, is remembered remarkably for the reaction it inspired in hundreds of thousands of Egyptians who, hearing of their leader's intention to leave office, poured into the streets of Cairo for two consecutive nights, their sole goal surprisingly 'the return of an Egyptian president who has led the country to its biggest defeat since the "Battle of Tall al-Kabir" in 1882'.[80]

Notwithstanding the length of the speech – it took 23 minutes and 25 seconds to deliver – the single most important part that reverberated through Egyptian films is the one in which Nasser, towards the end, announces his resignation. It runs as follows:[81]

> I have taken a decision with which I need your help. I have decided to withdraw totally and for good from any official post or political role, and to return to the ranks of the masses, performing my duty in their midst, like any other citizen.

The speech was so much identified with this part that it was labelled *khitab al-tanahhi*, or (the resignation speech), arguably in reference to its massive impact on Egyptians. This, however, has led to 'a relative marginalisation of the topic that was supposed to be the cornerstone of the speech, namely, the defeat'.[82] As we shall see, Egyptians' relationship with Nasser was once again personalised through this speech, leaving aside the more factual and informative aspects of it for the purpose of foregrounding the touching, direct appeal to the masses, which the speech brilliantly articulated.

There has emerged a significant number of studies recently that approach the speech, both linguistically and historically. In particular, historian Sharif Yunus and linguist 'Imad Abdel Latif both brilliantly analyse the speech, the latter arguing that 'the rhetorical formulation of the speech did influence the responses that followed it'.[83] Concurring, Yunus shows that the speech addressed the situation in a way that, if it would not necessarily have led to the historic responses that followed, 'it nevertheless was formulated in a way as to strongly encourage it'.[84] Whether or not that formulation was intentionally meant by Nasser is hard to determine but the effects are easily attested. One of the most powerful aspects of the speech was the fact that it was, up to the time it was delivered, the 'only political act in the country'[85] since the beginning of the war four days earlier. Highly anticipated amid conflicting news of victory and defeat, the speech came as the first and last straw thrown to Egyptians who were desperate for a hopeful sign from their leader. As such, the speech, ending as it did with the resignation, was tantamount to leaving the already shattered Egyptians in a state of 'catastrophic orphanhood'.[86]

In addition, the speech appropriated several rhetorical devices to magnify its impact on listeners. For instance, it euphemistically referred to the disastrous defeat as merely a *naksa,* or setback, thus playing down its then unknown consequences. Moreover, unlike 'defeat', the word 'setback' is 'ambiguous and unspecified, and therefore open to interpretations'.[87] On the other hand, 'Imad Abdel Latif argues that, parallel to euphemism, the speech also employed dysphemism in its choice of words to label the war. Instead of referring to the Israeli act as war, invasion, or occupation, it described it as *'udwan,* or aggression. In so doing, the speech avoided representing the situation as a war between two political entities, and opted rather for a term that is laden with connotations of 'taking others by surprise, and assaulting against a peaceful party'.[88]

Ironically, the speech with which Nasser intended to leave office would be his most memorialised and immortalised act, both visually and aurally, in

Egyptian cinema as well as in other media outlets, establishing a 'mnemonic practice'[89] within the Egyptian imaginary. The revolutionary figure – hero of nationalisation, triumphant in the 1956 Tripartite Aggression,[90] builder of the High Dam, and advocate of the peasants and the poor – is predominantly reduced into images of a crushed man, his face sweating, his voice, once powerful, low and quavering. Nowhere in Nasser's life is the tragic quality of his character better manifested than in the 1967 defeat. Even his funeral three years later, attended by unprecedented millions of mourners, would fall short of competing visually with his image delivering the resignation speech. The tragic hero and the dreams he lived by – in fact, the whole era that was associated with him, 'all ceased to exist on 9 June 1967, and the resignation speech was an honest, internal sense of the end'.[91] As his once vice president and later detractor, Anwar Sadat, put it,

> The events of 5 June dealt him [Nasser] a fatal blow. They finished him off. Those who knew Nasser realised that he did not die on 28 September 1970, but on 5 June 1967, exactly one hour after the war broke out.[92]

Doubtless, the speech, coupled with the circumstances that led to it, are laden with implications that would be employed by several film-makers. The persistence of the speech, however, in cinema and elsewhere, equally speaks to the unceasing impact of the 1967 defeat on Egyptian and Arab collective memory. The speech is ubiquitous primarily because it is a historical marker of a wound that is yet to heal. As Georges Tarabishi argues, the trauma of 1967 is still manifested in Arabs' lives – intellectuals or otherwise – through their constant search for a 'father' that could replace the refuge that Nasser had once offered to Arab masses up to the defeat – hence the revival, after 1967, of Islamic movements and the return to the golden *turath*, or heritage.[93] 'The society has not got over the defeat', says Egyptian journalist Wa'il Abdel Fattah. Even though the Egyptian army did restore some of its status with the achievements of the 1973 war, the 1967 scar still 'seems present and fresh'.[94]

Sentimentalising the speech, most of the cinematic appropriations of it focus primarily on the stepping-down part, leaving aside whatever Nasser had to say concerning the actualities of the war. They differ, however, on an essential aspect of the speech – the image of Nasser. For, unlike most of Nasser's previous speeches, this one was televised, with Nasser's appearance magnifying its impact on viewers. As we shall see, film-makers have, in later years, alternated between an 'emotional, televisual viewing experience'[95] of the speech, on the one hand, and an aural representation of it, devoid of images, and where only Nasser's voice is heard, on the other. The contexts of these choices will be illuminated below, along with a discussion of the most prominent instances of the speech in Egyptian cinema.

The first cinematic appropriation of the speech dates back to 1974, with the screening of Youssef Chahine's *Al-'Usfur* (the Sparrow). Centring on what seems to be a criminal case, the film moves from the public interest in an unseen bandit, referred to as 'Abu Khadir', into unearthing the structural corruption of the regime. In so doing, it 'takes a lucid look at the reasons for the 1967 defeat at the hands of Israel, finding them not simply in specific errors by Nasser or weakness in army tactics but in the very structure of Egyptian society'.[96]

Al-'Usfur is set in the few days before, during, and after the 1967 war. In this period, the film maintains, there are 'two Egypts, each moving in a direction opposite the other'.[97] Rather than attributing the defeat to external forces, *Al-'Usfur* shows that the characteristics of the first Egypt – corruption and demoralisation of state apparatuses – are the actual factors behind the catastrophe. The second Egypt, on the other hand, is portrayed by a group of men and women – a journalist, a police officer, a progressive sheikh, and an activist – who are connected through their relationships with Bahiyya, an elderly woman whose house becomes their meeting place and therefore a prominent space in the film. It is in this house that Bahiyya, her friends, and the viewers first watch Nasser's speech.

The speech comes towards the end of the film, breaking the protagonists' uncertainty regarding the outcomes of the war. Sensing a forthcoming disaster, Bahiyya, upon learning of an imminent speech by Nasser, orders the others to stop speculating, commenting, 'Now he will talk, and we will know'. Moments before the speech begins, Chahine pans his camera across the streets of Cairo, showing how they were quiet, and practically deserted. Cutting to Bahiyya's house, we hear Nasser's words before seeing him, with the camera alternating between the president relaying the news on television and the reaction of stunned protagonists who are unable to believe what they hear. The most powerful part of the film emerges right after Nasser utters his intention to step down, when Bahiyya screams, 'No, never, we will fight'. She spontaneously runs into the street, followed by dozens of neighbours, all shouting, 'We will fight. Long live Egypt.' The spontaneity of the crowds is further underscored by a scene in which a seeming state functionary calls his colleagues, wondering, 'Who are those people in the street? If they are not ours, who are they?'

Much has been written about the signification of Bahiyya whose name also features in the legendary duo Ahmed Fouad Negm's (1929–2013) and Sheikh Imam's (1918–95) song with which the film begins and ends. Viola Shafik argues that Bahiyya stands for 'Mother Egypt', the female nation 'that is not just in danger of losing its leader but which finds itself betrayed by the new class of functionaries'.[98] In fact, the metaphor is explicitly established in Negm's and Imam's song whose most famous part is, '*Masr yamma, ya Bahiyya*' (O Egypt, mother beautiful).[99]

In addition, the film is amply engaged with speech and utterances. Throughout the film, Bahiyya states that she suppresses her words and chooses not to share her pain with others. Only when the pain becomes collective is her voice heard, attempting to alleviate people's fear prior to Nasser's speech. When her daughter asks her to stop analysing the situation, she responds, 'You always try to mute me. Now I will not be silent.' In the light of this, Nasser is not the only one who speaks at the end. His low voice, however, is brilliantly juxtaposed with Bahiyya's and people's loud voices in defiance of the enemy, 'indicative of the long repression of the peoples' voice'.[100] Bahiyya subverts the traditional division of roles in Egyptian nationalism where 'the man was the actor, the speaker, the lover; the woman was the acted upon, the listener, the beloved'.[101] Instead, Nasser's helplessness is contrasted with the agency of Bahiyya who does not only 'speak' but also mobilises people into flooding the streets – the act that eventually empowers Nasser and reinstates him as president. In this regard, the relationship between Nasser and Bahiyya in the film can be seen as a reference to the traditional Egyptian epic *Yasin wa Bahiyya* (Yasin and Bahiyya), which itself reproduces the story of Isis and Osiris. In the tale, Yasin is murdered and Bahiyya retrieves his body and gives him a proper burial.

Yet while Chahine's film captures people's allegiance to Nasser following the speech, Ali Badrakhan's *Al-Karnak* mocks that very same reaction.

As mentioned earlier, the film is credited for ushering in the 'Cinema of Centers of Power'. Instead of presenting the speech, the film opts for another approach. It juxtaposes footage of the early Israeli raids against the Egyptian air force on the morning of 5 June with scenes where the imprisoned protagonists in the film are tortured at the hands of prison security. This simultaneous crushing of Egyptians, by both Israel and the oppressive Egyptian regime, serves to show the irrelevance of the protests that follow Nasser's speech. Passing by Karnak café, one customer wonders what those people are saying. 'Nasser. Nasser. We will fight,' another replies. The camera then zooms into the customer's face, who sarcastically comments, 'by the prophet, we are kind people'.

A more critical take on the speech is found in Husayn Kamal's 1979 *Ihna Btu' al-Utubis*. Whereas *Al-Karnak* ridicules people's standing by Nasser despite the defeat, *Ihna Btu' al-Utubis* attacks the speech itself, considering it the epitome of the failures of the regime. Amid joyful scenes of prisoners celebrating the early news of an Egyptian victory over Israel, Nasser's speech, aurally broadcast through the radio, cuts into the scene. Beginning with the resignation part, the speech is responded to by the jailer Abdel Mu'ti who, thus far, believes that the prisoners are true enemies of Egypt. Standing by the speakers, he confoundedly wonders, 'What happened? Why did not we win the war? Why? The prison is full of the bad people we are afraid of. What more do we need?' Nasser's mention in the speech of great sacrifices by Egyptians during the war is further contradicted when the camera cuts to the cells, showing several close-ups of those tortured Egyptians against Nasser's celebratory words. As we would expect, the prisoners show no reaction to the resignation but the defeat, coupled with the death of a poet prisoner following the news, trigger an internal uprising against the director of the prison.

If the earlier appearances of the speech testified to a conscious, highly politicised appropriation, few other films treated the speech as a rather temporal marker. Whether to set up the historical context of the events or to inform about the way the protagonists knew about the defeat, the speech does not occupy an integral part of the films' narrative, emerging only *en passant*. This is true of 'Atif al-Tayyib's 1987 *Abna' wa Qatala* (Sons and Killers) and 1992 *Naji al-Ali* although the latter transfers the reception of the speech to Kuwait where the would-be well-known Palestinian cartoonist

Naji al-Ali (1938–87) (played by Nur al-Sharif) was living in 1967. In both cases, we listen only to Nasser's voice, with the protagonists expressing signs of grief and shock following the resignation news. This is not to suggest, however, that selecting the speech as the marker for the defeat (or even for the late 1960s)[102] is not in and of itself political. On the contrary, the recurring appearance of the speech, even in films in which the narrative does not necessarily require it, adds more to its specificity.

With the screening of Khalid al-Hagar's 1993 highly autobiographical debut, *Ahlam Saghira* (Little Dreams), the cinematic approach to the speech took on a different shape. Rather than reflecting the collective, overtly political reaction to it, the speech is now seen through the eyes of a thirteen-year-old child. Dedicated to the people of Suez, *Ahlam Saghira* narrates the story of Gharib[103] in the few days before and after the war. Also the narrator of the film, Gharib tells us that his father died during the 1956 Suez War when he was only two. Ever since, Gharib has grown up haunted by the feeling of fatherlessness. His situation is further complicated when he is surrounded by two men: Salah, the cruel landlord for whom Gharib works and who constantly flirts with Gharib's mother; and Mahmud, a leader in the popular resistance groups in the city who had fought side by side with Gharib's father in 1956.

In contrast to the harsh treatment that Gharib receives from Salah, Mahmud warmly embraces him, tells him about his father 'the martyr', and cultivates in him love for Egypt and readiness to fight for it. In one of his frequent visits to Mahmud's house, Gharib finds a huge portrait of Nasser in which he is hugging a child Gharib's age. While gazing at the portrait, Gharib listens at the same time to the speech in which Nasser announces he is closing the Gulf of Aqaba to all Israeli shipping. Mahmud explains that there will be war and that everyone must be ready to fight for Egypt.

Gradually, Gharib begins to develop a unique, spiritual relationship with Nasser. Whenever he sees his picture, he pauses, staring at it, his eyes filled with love and admiration. Seeing the father in him, Gharib continuously recalls the image of Nasser hugging the child. In one of the most beautiful scenes of the film, Gharib runs from Salah towards the beach. He lies down, holding Nasser's picture in his arms, imagining. Suddenly, the camera moves to a forest, where Gharib stands facing the spectre of a tall man looking into the distance. The man, who could be Nasser, Gharib's father, or a combination of the two, begins to walk towards Gharib, his face blurred. He taps Gharib on the shoulder, holds his hand, and walks.

Gharib's yearning for a father is partly satisfied through an imagined relationship with Nasser but is also challenged when he realises that his mother has finally surrendered to Salah's tireless requests to marry her. Interestingly, they marry on 5 June, and Salah, the anti-father for Gharib, orders the family to escape the war and go to Cairo. Gharib refuses and, instead, joins Mahmud who assures him of the victory that Nasser promises. When the ominous news of the defeat spreads, Mahmud convinces Gharib that it is all rumour and that Nasser will speak now and tell the truth. They both sit in a café watching, and the speech, televised, confirms the initial, disastrous reports. While the crowds immediately leave the café upon the announcement of the resignation, screaming, 'No. Do not leave us now,' Gharib and Mahmud remain. The child looks at Mahmud and says, 'You are liars. You fooled me. You all are liars.' Whether or not he includes Nasser among those 'liars' is not certain. He runs into the street, however, to join the protestors, only to be killed when hit by a lorry that carries the portrait of none other than Nasser himself.

Nasser's speech is a confirmation of the defeat. For Gharib, however, it is the final absence of a father. Gharib has to die precisely because he realises, following the speech, that Nasser (read: father) is truly dead, hence the extinction of the refuge that empowers him. The voice of Gharib, who is buried next to his father, emerges once again in the final scene of the film, wondering if his half-brother, whom his mother gives birth to after the war, will ever find a father who will protect him.

The relationship between the speech and the absence of the father is also articulated by Osama Fawzi (b.1961) in his 2004 film *Bahib al-Sima* (I Love Cinema). The film caused a huge controversy in Egypt, largely because it 'focuses, in an unprecedented way, on the daily life of a Coptic middle-class family in Shubra'.[104] The plot is centred on Na'im, a Coptic child growing up in Shubra on the eve of the 1967 defeat. But whereas Gharib in *Ahlam Saghira* is shown missing his dead father, Na'im is oppressed by the conservative, patriarchal nature of his father 'Adli who forbids him from watching films because he considers them *haram* (sinful). The film, however, is 'eager to connect its narrative and the problematic of the family to its temporal framework, namely the Nasserist period'.¹⁰⁵ The narrative unfolds with several situations that suggest an atmosphere of fear and oppression spreading in all aspects of Egyptian society, culminating in a powerful scene where ʿAdli, drunk for the first time, establishes a monologue with God, admitting that he fears rather than loves him.

ʿAdli's confession, coupled with his discovery of his heart condition, 'finally brings about a total transformation in his relationship with his family'.¹⁰⁶ The film turns inward towards elucidating the change in the father–son relationship, leaving the developments of Egypt's political situation untouched. It is in the final part of the film, however, that the two worlds are reconnected. Foregoing any reference to the war, the film introduces the speech in a crucial scene. As Samia Mehrez describes it, ʿAdli

> is hit by a stroke as he is peddling his son Naʿim on a bicycle at the seashore with the sun setting on the horizon on the very day that President Nasser delivered his abdication speech (simultaneously played on the soundtrack) after the Egyptian defeat against Israel in June 1967.¹⁰⁷

In the following scene we see ʿAdli dead while performing his morning prayers in his apartment.

Similar to *Ahlam Saghira*, Osama Fawzi's film associates the speech with the death of a father. While in the former, Gharib searches personally for a father before the speech crushes this dream and, literally, the child himself, the latter presents the speech, and ʿAdli's changing attitude, as a welcome withdrawal of the patriarch from Egyptian society.

While in the previous films parts of Nasser's actual speech were introduced, in his 1999 biographical film *Gamal Abdel Nasser*, Syrian-born director Anwar al-Qawadri (b.1953) chooses a different path. Rather than using the footage, the speech is acted out by Khalid al-Sawi, the actor who plays Nasser in the film and who, in a setting reminiscent of the actual one, appears on television in the wake of the defeat, delivering what will be the longest part of the speech ever to appear in cinema. Following that scene, and instead of cutting directly to the crowds protesting against the resignation, the film presents a heated discussion between Nasser and Zakariya Mohieddin whom, in the speech, Nasser announces as his heir. Amid the discussion, in which Mohieddin vehemently refuses the appointment, the two men hear the voices of the crowds demanding the return of Nasser. In an exchange that is never documented in official history, Mohieddin says,

> 'You listen? People know that you are the only one who knows the path.'
> 'Why? Why? Why are they doing this? They should hang us.'
> 'The people are refusing the defeat. Gamal, your resignation means only one thing: the realisation of the political goal of the war.

Nasser, totally surprised and overwhelmed by people's love and loyalty, sits down, murmuring, 'These people are strange. I thought they would erect gallows for me in Tahrir Square. Strange.'

Nasser and Bio Pictures

The emergence of Muhammad Fadil's 1996 film *Nasser 56* ushered in a new era of Egyptian cinema. Not only was it the first biographical film of Nasser; it also 'broke a long-accepted taboo against cinematic depiction of modern political leaders'.[108] Passionately received by Egyptians and Arabs throughout the world, the success of *Nasser 56* empowered other film-makers to follow suit. Interestingly, the three biographical films which followed had, completely or partly, a Nasser dimension. Aside from the aforementioned *Gamal Abdel Nasser* (1999), Muhammad Khan's 2001 *Ayyam al-Sadat* (Days of Sadat) and Sharif 'Arafa's 2006 *Halim* portray, as the titles clearly suggest, two significant figures whose lives thoroughly intersected with Nasser's – Anwar Sadat and Abdel Halim Hafez. As we would expect, therefore, Nasser himself is abundantly referenced in those films, albeit differently.

Aside from Nasser, the other common denominator of all these films, with the exception of al-Qawadri's, is the casting of Ahmad Zaki in the lead role. Arguably Egypt's greatest actor of all time, Zaki astonished millions of film-goers when he effortlessly impersonated the three extraordinary figures. Certainly, Zaki's 'own persona and origin bears [sic] some resemblance to those he embodied in cinema'.[109] His dark skin aside, Zaki originated from Abdel Halim's village in al-Sharqiyya Province, was an orphan like him and, like Nasser, belonged to a middle-class, rural Muslim family. Given his personal role in encouraging (and producing, in the case of *Ayyam al-Sadat*) the making of these films, the nascent biographical era in Egyptian cinema can be equally attributed to him.

Yet the timing of *Nasser 56* requires more explanation than Zaki's contributions. As mentioned earlier, the image of Nasser, both physically and metaphorically, has, since the 1980s, gradually begun to regain its positive associations, following a decade of harsh demonisation. Mubarak's regime, though politically and economically a continuation of Sadat's, has taken a middle-ground position towards Nasser. It 'criticises the wholesale denigration of the revolution, yet also opposes its idealisation'.[110] In addition, while maintaining the historical importance of Nasser, Mubarak's Egypt attempted to deprive him of any exceptionality; instead, contextualising him within a series of 'several leaders who had raised the banner of national struggle, including Omar Makram, Mustafa Kamil, Muhammad Farid, Saad Zaghlul, Mustafa al-Nahhas, and Muhammad Naguib'.[111] Unlike Sadat, Mubarak has not adopted a rival attitude towards Nasser. His temporal remoteness from Nasser, coupled with the fact that millions of his fellow citizens were born after Nasser's death, have probably led to a less complicated relationship with his legacy.

More importantly, the 1990s witnessed a growing nostalgia towards Nasser. With intensification of privatisation and economic liberalism leading to stark inequality and destitution, and coinciding with tides of religious violence and fundamentalism, Nasserism 'has increasingly come to represent an era of hope, unity, national purpose, social stability, and achievement'.[112] In the few years that preceded the production of *Nasser 56*, the memory of Nasser did experience a wave of revival. Egyptian critic 'Isam Zakariyya describes those years as the ones 'where Nasserist newspapers, such as *Al-'Arabi* (the Arab), reached greater numbers of distribution, and where Abdel Halim's patriotic songs for Nasser were widely reprinted and sold'.[113]

It is in this context that *Nasser 56* was born, testifying to Mubarak's double-edged strategy concerning his predecessor. Following George Custen's definition of the biopic as a film that is 'composed of the life, or the portion of a life, of a real person whose real name is used',[114] *Nasser 56* is surely a biographical film. Yet the very portion of Nasser's life that the film selects highlights the regime's orientation. Produced by the state-owned Egyptian Radio and Television Union, the film revolves around probably the least problematic and most heroic phase in Nasser's life – the nationalisation of the Suez Canal in 1956 and the opening of the Tripartite Aggression. As noted in other biographical films in world cinema, such as Roger Donaldson's 2000

Thirteen Days – which centres on John F. Kennedy exclusively during the Cuban Missile Crisis of 1962 – the 'narrow focus . . . facilitates a favourable and ultimately unbalanced treatment'[115] of the biographee. Indeed, *Naser 56* was initially 'intended as one of a series of hour-long dramatic biographies of Egyptian luminaries for television'.[116] Neither the leading star nor the director (nor the scenarist Mahfuz Abdel Rahman) claimed they were offering a critical, neutral approach to Nasser. The result was a celebratory portrayal, an ode to an era of a great man and national pride.

This is not to suggest that *Nasser 56* is entirely restricted to the treatment of that specific incident – nothing could be further from the truth. For, if the film is temporally confined, Nasser's personality is not. With the aim of making Nasser 'a relevant hero for current times',[117] the film lumps all of his positive features – humble, patriotic, uncorrupted, sympathetic to the poor, lover of the family, among others – and presents them as the background against which the critical events of 1956 unfold. In so doing, the film takes dramatic licence to offer anecdotes and situations that are not part of the official history of the Suez Canal. As Joel Gordon notes,

> The most popular – and memorable – scenes are not those in which Nasser plots with his advisers and walks the public stage, but rather those in which he tries to balance private-domestic with national concerns or in which he interacts with common citizen scenes.[118]

One such powerful instance occurs in the first half of the film when Nasser, staying up all night reading about Ferdinand de Lesseps's (1805–94) authorisation to build the canal, receives a phone call. Misdialled, the other party is an old woman, Umm Yasin, who is looking for someone named Haj Madbuli. Having been told by Nasser that she has the wrong number, she hangs up but then rings again. Again Nasser tells her that she has the wrong number. When the phone rings for the third time, the conversation runs as follows:

> 'Hello, Umm Yasin, this is not Haj Madbuli's house. Tell me where your son is and I will send you someone to take you there.'
> 'But who are you, my son?'
> 'I am Gamal Abdel Nasser.'
> 'May God give you victory, my son.'

The huge commercial success of the film was an indication that Nasser's status among Egyptians has survived years of marginalisation. Yet he is not the only one to enjoy similar success in future projects. Anwar al-Qawadri's *Gamal Abdel Nasser*, produced only three years after *Nasser 56*, has surprisingly failed to generate comparable reactions. Unlike his predecessor, al-Qawadri determined to make a biopic that covered, albeit selectively, the whole of his protagonist's career. And it is precisely this survey-like presentation of Nasser that was strongly criticised. Director Khalid Yusuf, for instance, maintains that the film 'fell into the trap of oversimplification and hastiness, offering pale snapshots of the president's life that lacked a strong dramatic thread to hold them together'.[119]

In fact, the dramatic tension in the film lies in the bittersweet, complicated friendship between Nasser and his lifelong comrade and commander-in-chief of the Egyptian army, Abdel Hakim Amer. Obviously, however, the audience did not find the story appealing. The film shows Amer as an anti-Nasser: hedonist, individualistic, and conspiratorial. Even without regard to the historical authenticity of those details, Amer's character appears flat, one-dimensional, and caricature-esque. Contrary to *Nasser 56*, where the president seems natural, his deeds developing against the circumstances that are unfolding before him, the Nasser–Amer tension in al-Qawadri's project subjects the former to a predefined role, extremely positive yet totally predictable and unoriginal. On top of that, Khalid al-Sawi's interpretation of Nasser pales in comparison with Ahmad Zaki's. The newcomer actor at the time does occasionally capture Nasser's interiorities but the comparison, necessitated by the temporal proximity of the two films, has not been in his favour.

Ahmad Zaki's magnificent interpretation of Nasser acquired a lofty status against which any future cinematic appearance of the president would be gauged. The measuring becomes all the more challenging when Nasser is played in a film in which he is not the main protagonist. This is the dilemma that Muhammad Khan attempted to circumvent in *Ayyam al-Sadat*. The result was, as Joel Gordon describes it, truly bizarre: Nasser is rendered faceless, framed either from behind or in profile.[120] By obscuring the very facial expressions of the actor who plays Nasser, Khan sought to avoid the aura that the mere presence of Nasser can inspire, thus underscoring the centrality of Sadat.

Inevitably, however, *Ayyam al-Sadat* has Nasser as a major point of reference throughout the film. The very opening scene establishes 'a positive link between the two presidents . . . with a devastated Sadat after Nasser's untimely death'.[121] Sadat is shown as declaring allegiance to Nasser yet also rectifying the misdeeds of his predecessor. But, if the history of post-1970 Sadat is well known to people, it is his more obscure role under Nasser that the film unconvincingly articulates. In the scenes that combine the two before the revolution, Sadat is often portrayed as possessing a more leading and powerful presence than Nasser, the latter oddly appearing cold and quiet. Even after the revolution, when Nasser's status cannot be contested, the film is keen to bestow a certain particularity to Sadat. He receives a threatening phone call after the assassination attempt on Nasser; he often calls Nasser by his first name, Gamal; and Nasser calls him in the wake of the 1967 defeat to inform him that Abdel Hakim Amer committed suicide.

Following *Ayyam al-Sadat*'s controversial method of impersonating Nasser, Sharif 'Arafa's (b.1960) *Halim* would opt for a completely different approach. Rather than enacting the president's character, the film employs real footages of Nasser whenever the narrative necessitates his presence. Telling the story of Abdel Halim Hafez, the film pursues the singer's life from orphanhood to stardom to death, interspersed with multiple and intricate encounters and relationships with women, friends, and significant figures of the era, including Nasser. Instead of following linear storytelling, the narrative, triggered by an interview that Hafez gives to the Egyptian radio in 1976, alternates between flashbacks and flash forwards, selectively covering the pivotal moments in the life of 'the son of the Revolution'.[122]

The film features footage of Nasser nationalising the Suez Canal, inaugurating the High Dam project, and, more relevant to *Halim*'s subject matter, attending several of the singer's concerts, particularly those in which he performs his most famous patriotic songs, such as *Bil Ahdan* (With Open Arms) and *Sura* (Picture). The privilege that those attendances of Nasser bestow on the singer is exposed through a bitter rivalry between Hafez and Umm Kulthum. Scheduled to sing second to Umm Kulthum in a huge event commemorating the ninth anniversary of the revolution in which Nasser is present, Hafez appears uneasy as *il-Sit* far exceeds her assigned time. Fearing

Nasser will depart soon, Hafez (played in his early years by Ahmad Zaki's son Haytham) archly wonders when he stands on stage whether singing after Umm Kulthum is an honour or a trap.

Lest the singer be characterised as a mere opportunist who sings to whoever assumes power, the film very meticulously differentiates between Nasser as a person and what he symbolises. Halim vehemently rejects in the interview the allegation that he sings for Nasser personally but rather for 'the dreams that Nasser embodies'. Further elaboration on this subject is shown by comparing Hafez's and famed vernacular poet Salah Jahin's positions in the wake of the 1967 defeat. While Jahin, who wrote Hafez's most memorable patriotic songs, holds a unique view of Nasser, and therefore considers the defeat a decisive end to his own dreams, Hafez insists on singing, even for Sadat, so long as the last realises the aspirations of the nation.

The film, however, leaves unmentioned other aspects of Hafez's truly special relationship with Nasser. Confirming this relationship, journalist Yusri al-Fakhrani has recently revealed how Hafez used to refer to Nasser as *baba*, and how Nasser would call the singer and listen to him singing over the phone. Al-Fakhrani goes so far as to compare Hafez's presence to Haykal's, emphatically stating that, in Nasser's era, 'Haykal writes and Abdel Halim Hafez sings'.[123] Produced by Good News, a company whose owners (the Adib family) are close to Mubarak, *Halim* attempts to depersonalise the singer's relationship with Nasser with an implicit message that Hafez's songs were for the country rather than for the president, insinuating, perhaps by extension, that Hafez, who actually sang for Sadat, could have also sung for Mubarak.

Those four films have shown that, unless he is the main protagonist, the enactment of Nasser poses a dilemma to film-makers. His grand stature requires a cinematic treatment – and appearance – that may steal the limelight from the supposedly main character of the film. Yet a settlement such as the one proposed by *Ayyam al-Sadat* is utterly unconvincing. Real footage may be an answer but its frequency can weaken the fictionality of the film. Anticipating future cinematic projects on other significant Egyptian figures (and where Nasser has undoubtedly to be present), one can only ponder potential alternatives that film-makers may bring out.

Conclusion

The space that Nasser occupied in Egyptian cinema in the 1950s and the 1960s is disproportionate to his significance and ubiquity in Egypt. Rarely did any of his speeches, slogans, or pictures make it on to the screen. While it is understandable to find rare negative cinematic approaches to him during his life, Nasser has escaped even laudatory treatment in Egyptian cinema. In stark contrast with other mass media outlets, such as radio and newspapers, films did not constitute a favourite site for glorifying Nasser and disseminating knowledge about him. Following his death, Nasser was subjected to contested cinematic narratives concerning his legacy. While the 1970s largely experienced a gloomy cinematic picture of him, driven perhaps by the state-sponsored process of de-Nasserisation, later decades have witnessed a revival of a romantic view of Nasser. Both treatments, however, lacked a sophisticated analysis of the president. Instead, they viewed Nasser as a site of memory that connoted certain fixed associations which, depending on the film-maker, can be good or evil, noble or ignoble, corrupted or clean.

This chapter has looked at the story of Nasser on the Egyptian screen through numerous entries. First, I discovered that, contrary to expectations, the most significant critical cinematic interpretations of Nasser were produced during his lifetime. Triggered by the catastrophic defeat of 1967, films such as *Al-Qadiyya 68* and *Shay' min al-Khawf* had a main character who was widely seen as a reference to Nasser. Second, I traced the appropriation of Nasser's portrait in Egyptian cinema, arguing that nowhere did it appear in films *superfluously*. Rather, the portrait's presence or absence have constantly served to convey a certain message that film-makers intended to deliver. A relevant case study was the films of de-Nasserisation, with their way of showing or hiding Nasser's portrait at the offices of police officers and intelligence chiefs, thereby establishing a link or a separation between the president and the abuses of his regime. In addition, the chapter showed that, of all Nasser's speeches, his 1967 resignation speech was by far the most inspiring to film-makers. It was as though Nasser was visually and aurally immortalised through the most tragic event in his life, thus leaving aside more triumphant moments such as the nationalisation of the Suez Canal. Finally, Nasser proved to be the linchpin of the biographical films that have increasingly emerged in the last two decades. From *Nasser 56* to *Ayyam al-Sadat* to *Halim,* these films negotiated various approaches to impersonate Nasser on the screen. The chapter concluded that, unless he is the principal character, the re-enactment of Nasser in films will constantly pose a dilemma to film-makers.

Notes

1. See the various features that were published in *al-Hayat* and *al-Quds al-'Arabi* newspapers on 2 August 2012.
2. See the Introduction, pp. 1–2.
3. Bashar Ibrahim and Jum'a Qajah, *Abdel Nasser wa al-Cinema: Bahth fi Ishkaliyyat al-Ru'ya bayna Cinema al-Sira wa Cinema al-Mu'taqal* (Beirut: Dar al-Tariq, 2004), p. 9.
4. Kamal Ramzi, 'Irtibat Nushu' al-Cinema al-'Arabiyya bi Harakat al-Tahrir al-'Arabi', in *Al-Huwiyya al-Qawmiyya fi al-Cinema al-'Arabiyya*, ed. Abdel Mun'im Talima (Beirut: Markiz Dirasat al-Wihda al-'Arabiyya, 1986), p. 43.
5. Maria Golia, *Egypt and Photography* (London: Reaktion Books, 2010), p. 121.
6. Joel Gordon, *Revolutionary Melodrama: Popular Film and Civic Identity in Nasser's Egypt* (Chicago, IL: Middle East Documentation Center, 2002), p. 89.
7. Ibid., p.90.
8. Raymond William Baker, 'Egypt in Shadows: Films and the Political Order', *American Behavioral Scientist*, No. 17 (1974), p. 395.
9. Ibid.
10. Ibid.
11. Viola Shafik, *Popular Egyptian Cinema: Gender, Class, and Nation* (Cairo: The American University in Cairo Press, 2006), p. 104.
12. Tarabishi, *Al-Muthaqqafun al-'Arab wa al- Turath*, p. 25.
13. Shafik, *Popular Egyptian Cinema*, p. 105.
14. Joel Gordon, 'Nasser 56/Cairo 96: Remembering Egypt's Lost Community', in *Mass Mediations: New Approaches to Popular Culture in the Middle East and Beyond*, ed. Walter Armbrust (Berkeley, CA and Los Angeles, CA: University of California Press, 2000), p. 168.
15. Ibid.
16. Sharif Yunus, *Nida' al-Sha'b: Tarikh Naqdi li al-Aydyulujya al-Nasiriyya* (Cairo: Dar al-Shuruq, 2012), p. 11.
17. Durriyya Sharaf al-Din, *Al-Siyasa wa al-Cinema fi Misr* (Cairo: Dar al-Shuruq, 1992), p. 45.

18. 'Adnan Mdanat, 'Al-Cinema'i al-'Arabi wa Qadaya al-Tiknulujya wa al-*Aydyulujya*', in *Al-Huwiyya al-Qawmiyya fi al-Cinema al-'Arabiyya*, p. 146.
19. Ibid.
20. Sharaf al-Din, *Al-Siyasa wa al-Cinema*, p. 46.
21. In discussion with the author in Cairo, October 2011.
22. Directed by Ahmad Badrakhan, *Allah Ma'ana* was one of the most popular Egyptian films to come after Nasser's revolution. Teaming Egypt's leading actress Faten Hamama with her frequent screen partner 'Imad Hamdi, it addressed the turbulent years of the monarchy that precipitated the revolution.
23. Samir Farid, 'Al-Cinema wa al-Dawla fi al-Watan al-'Arabi', in *Al-Huwiyya al-Qawmiyya fi al-Cinema al-'Arabiyya*, pp. 107–8.
24. Shafik, *Popular Egyptian Cinema*, p. 104.
25. Ahmad Yusuf, 'Al-Waqi'iyya wa Suwar al-Waqi' fi al-Cinema al-Misriyya fi al-Marhala al-Klasikiyya, 1952–1970', in *Al-Cinema al-Misriyya: Al-Thawra wa al-Qita' al-'Aam: 1952–1971*, ed. Hashim al-Nahhas (Cairo: Al-Majlis al-A'la li al-Thaqafa, 2010), p. 50.
26. Muhammad Kamil al-Qalyubi, 'Al-Cinema al-Misriyya wa Thawrat Yulyu: Sira' al-Ihtiwa' bayna al-Cinema wa al-Thawra', in *Al-Cinema al-Misriyya: al-Thawra wa al-Qita' al-'Aam*, pp. 26–7.
27. Walter Armbrust, *Mass Culture and Modernism in Egypt* (Cambridge: Cambridge University Press, 1996), p. 73.
28. 'Isam Zakariyya, *Atyaf al-Hadatha: Suwar Misr al-Ijtima'iyya fi al-Cinema* (Cairo: Al-Majlis al-A'la li al-Thaqafa, 2009), p. 43.
29. Ibid., p. 69.
30. Gordon, *Revolutionary Melodrama*, p. 124.
31. Nabila Ibrahim, *Al-Butulat al-'Arabiyya wa al-Dhakira al-Tarikhiyya* (Cairo: Al-Maktaba al-Akadimiyya, 1995), p. 19.
32. Muhammad Jibril, *Al-Batal fi al-Wijdan al-Sha'bi* (Cairo: Maktabat al-Dirasat al-Sha'biyya, 2000), p. 55.
33. Hala Halim, 'The Signs of *Saladin:* A Modern Cinematic Rendition of Medieval Heroism', *Alif: Journal of Comparative Poetics*, No. 12 (1992), p. 78.
34. Majdi Abdel Rahman, 'Al-Tahawwulat fi 'Imarat al-Manzar wa Tasmim al-Malbas al-Cinema'i wa murfulujiyyat al-Mujtama' al-Misri ba'da 1952', in *Al-Cinema al-Misriyya: al-Thawra wa al-Qita' al-'Aam*, p. 387.
35. Gordon, *Revolutionary Melodrama*, p. 79.
36. George Sadoul, *The Cinema in the Arab Countries* (Beirut: Interarab Centre of Cinema and Television, 1966), p. 309.

37. Malek Khouri, *The Arab National Project in Youssef Chahine's Cinema* (Cairo: the American University in Cairo Press, 2010), p. 48.
38. Ibid., p. 49.
39. Samir Farid, *Adwa' 'ala Cinema Youssef Chahine* (Cairo: Al-Hay'a al-Misriyya al-'Amma li al-Kitab, 1997), p. 126.
40. Abdel Rahman, 'Al-Tahawwulat,' p. 386.
41. Ali Abu Shadi, 'Genres in Egyptian Cinema', in *Screens of Life: Critical Film Writing from the Arab World*, ed. Alia Arasoughly (Quebec: World Heritage Press, Vol. 1, 1996), p. 111.
42. Sharaf al-Din, *Al-Siyasa wa al-Cinema*, p. 126.
43. Ali Abu Shadi, *Al-Cinema wa al-Siyasa* (Cairo: Dar Sharqiyyat, 1998), p. 18.
44. Zakariyya, *Atyaf al-Hadatha*, p. 81.
45. Ibid.
46. Gordon, *Revolutionary Melodrama*, p. 220.
47. Abu Shadi, *Al-Cinema wa al-Siyasa*, p. 14.
48. Sharaf al-Din, *Al-Siyasa wa al-Cinema*, p. 126.
49. Abu Shadi, *Al-Cinema wa al-Siyasa*, p. 14.
50. Zakariyya, *Atyaf al-Hadatha*, p. 82.
51. Baker, 'Egypt in Shadows', p. 415.
52. Zakariyya, *Atyaf al-Hadatha*, p. 84.
53. Abu Shadi, *Al-Cinema wa al-Siyasa*, p. 13.
54. Gordon, *Revolutionary Melodrama*, p. 218.
55. Baker, 'Egypt in Shadows', p. 415.
56. Abu Shadi, *Al-Cinema wa al-Siyasa*, p. 170.
57. Shafik, *Popular Egyptian Cinema*, p. 109.
58. Zakariyya, *Atyaf al-Hadatha*, p. 91.
59. Roland Barthes, *Camera Lucida: Reflections on Photography*, trans. Richard Howard (New York: Hill And Wang, 1981), p. 13.
60. Ibid., p. 78, emphasis in the original.
61. Laura Mulvey, *Visual and Other Pleasures* (Basingstoke: Macmillan, 1989), p. 25.
62. Susan Sontag, *On Photography* (New York: Farrar, Straus, and Giroux, 1977), p. 4.
63. Golia, *Photography and Egypt*, p. 118.
64. Gordon, *Revolutionary Melodrama*, p. 212.
65. Sharaf al-Din, *Al-Siyasa wa al-Cinema*, p. 132.
66. Abu Shadi, *Al-Cinema wa al-Siyasa*, pp. 20–1.

67. Ibid., p. 22.
68. Gordon, *Revolutionary Melodrama*, p. 240.
69. The politics of adding or deleting references to Nasser in cinematic adaptations of Egyptian literature reveals as much about the political inclinations of the film-maker/producer as the temporal circumstances of the production. The case of *Al-Karnak* reflects an atmosphere where criticism of Nasser was welcomed and encouraged. An opposite context, however, may lead to a different treatment. For instance, the scene in Alaa al-Aswani's bestselling novel *'Imarat Ya'qubyan* (The Yacoubian Building), in which Zaki al-Disuqi embarks on a rant against Nasser and the Free Officers, is completely absent from Marwan Hamid's adaptation. See Alaa al- Aswani, *'Imarat Ya'qubyan* (Cairo: Miret, 2002), pp. 228–9.
70. Gordon, *Revolutionary Melodrama*, p. 240.
71. Abu Shadi, *Al-Cinema wa al-Siyasa*, p. 109.
72. Shafik, *Popular Egyptian Cinema*, p. 214.
73. Lina Khatib, *Filming the Modern Middle East: Politics in the Cinemas of Hollywood and the Arab World* (London and New York: I. B. Tauris, 2006), p. 147.
74. Ibid.
75. For more on Nasser's presence following the 2011 revolution, see the Epilogue.
76. Mahfuz Abdel Rahman, Abdel Nasser wa Ana,' *Al-Yawm al-Sabi'* (20 January 2012), p. 17.
77. Zakariyya, *Atyaf al-Hadatha*, p. 88.
78. Sharif Yunus, *Al-Zahf al-Muqaddas: Muzaharat al-Tanahhi wa Tashakkul 'Ibadat Nasser* (Cairo: Miret, 2005), p. 181.
79. Tahia Gamal Abdel Nasser, *Dhikrayat Ma'ahu*, p. 113.
80. Yunus, *Al-Zahf al-Muqaddas*, p. 7.
81. For a full Arabic script of the speech, see the Bibliotheca Alexandrina website, available at <http://nasser.bibalex.org/Speeches/browser.aspx?SID=1221&lang=en> (last accessed 30 June 2015).
82. 'Imad Abdel Latif, 'Bayan al-Tanahhi wa Dhakirat al-Hazima: Madkhal Balaghi li Tahlil al-Khitab al-Siyasi', *Alif*, No. 30 (2010), p. 146.
83. Ibid.
84. Yunus, *Al-Zahf al-Muqaddas*, p. 182.
85. Ibid., p. 181.
86. Yasin al-Hafiz, *Al-Hazima wa al-Aydyulujya al-Mahzuma* (Damascus: Dar al-Hasad, 1997), p. 43.

87. Abdel Latif, 'Bayan al-Tanahhi wa Dhakirat al-Hazima', p. 153.
88. Ibid., p. 154.
89. Jeffrey Olick and Joyce Robbins, 'Social Memory Studies: From "Collective Memory" to the Historical Sociology of Mnemonic Practices', *Annual Review of Sociology*, Vol. 24, 1998, p. 112.
90. An earlier incident of employing dysphemism in the context of referring to wars, the 'Tripartite Aggression', was the Nasser regime's favourite reference to the Suez Crisis.
91. Shukri, *Mudhakkirat Thaqafa Tahtadir*, p. 399.
92. Anwar Sadat, *In Search of an Identity: an Autobiography* (New York: Harper and Row, Publishers, 1977), pp. 179–80.
93. Tarabishi, *Al-Muthaqqafun al-'Arab wa al-Turath*, pp. 26–30.
94. Wa'il Abdel Fattah, 'Fi Intizar Munqidh, *al-Akhbar*, Beirut, No. 1782 (13 August 2012). Interestingly, Egyptian cinema critic 'Isam Zakariyya argues in the aforementioned interview that the first real recovery from the 1967 war came with the Egyptian revolution of January 2011. One can only wait to see if the joyous scenes of Egyptians in Tahrir Square will visually replace the resignation speech.
95. Karen Beckman, *Crash: Cinema and the Politics of Speed and Stasis* (Durham, NC and London: Duke University Press, 2010), p. 152.
96. Roy Armes, *Third World Film Making and the West* (Berkeley, CA, Los Angeles, CA and London: University of California Press, 1987), p. 249.
97. Kamal Ramzi, 'Irtibat Nushu' al-Cinema al-'Arabiyya bi Harakat al-Tahrir al-'Arabi', p. 71.
98. Shafik, *Popular Egyptian Cinema*, p. 98.
99. The word 'Bahiyya' is a pun, for it is a female name that also means 'beautiful'.
100. Khouri, *The Arab National Project in Youssef Chahine's Cinema*, p. 102.
101. Beth Baron, 'Nationalist Iconography: Egypt as a Woman', in *Rethinking Nationalism in the Arab Middle East*, eds James Jankowski and Israel Gershoni (New York: Columbia University Press, 1997), p. 121.
102. In Sa'd Hindawi's 2009 thriller *Al-Saffah* (the Assassin), we hear the speech as the credits unfold, indicating the era in which the protagonist grew up.
103. The name means 'stranger'.
104. Samia Mehrez, *Egypt's Culture Wars: Politics and Practice* (London and New York: Routledge, 2008), p. 194.
105. Shafik, *Popular Egyptian Cinema*, p. 63.
106. Mehrez, *Egypt's Culture Wars*, pp. 195–9.

107. Ibid., p. 199.
108. Joel Gordon, 'Film, Fame, and Public Memory: Egyptian Biopics from Mustafa Kamil to Nasser 56', *International Journal of Middle East Studies*, Vol. 31, No. 1 (February 1999), p. 61.
109. Shafik, *Popular Egyptian Cinema*, p. 101.
110. Meir Hatina, 'History, Politics, and Collective Memory: The Nasserist Legacy in Mubarak's Egypt', *Rethinking Nasserism: Revolution and Historical Memory in Modern Egypt*, eds Elie Podeh and Onn Winckler (Orlando, FL: University Press of Florida, 2004), p. 117.
111. Ibid., p. 116.
112. Gordon, 'Nasser 56/Cairo 96: Remembering Egypt's Lost Community', p. 171.
113. In discussion with the author, October 2011.
114. George F. Custen, *Bio/Pics: How Hollywood Constructed Public History* (New Brunswick, NJ: Rutgers University Press, 1992), p. 6.
115. Mark White, '*Thirteen Days* and the Burnishing of an Image', in *Presidents in the Movies: American History and Politics on Screen*, ed. Iwan W. Morgan (New York: Palgrave Macmillan, 2011), p. 140.
116. Gordon, 'Nasser 56/Cairo 96: Remembering Egypt's Lost Community', p. 162.
117. Mark Wheeler, 'Darryl F. Zanuck's Wilson', in *Presidents in the Movies*, p. 88.
118. Gordon, 'Film, Fame, and Public Memory', p. 74.
119. In discussion with the author, October 2011.
120. Joel Gordon, 'Days of Anxiety/Days of Sadat: Impersonating Egypt's Flawed Hero on the Egyptian Screen', *Journal of Film and Video*, Vol. 54, No. 2/3 (summer/autumn 2002), p. 36.
121. Khatib, *Filming the Modern Middle East*, p. 138.
122. See p. 169.
123. See Yusri al-Fakhrani, *Abdel Halim . . . Abdel Nasser: Sirri Jiddan* (Cairo: Al-Fursan li al-Nashr, 2002), pp. 39 and 109, respectively. See also Joel Gordon's 'The Nightingale and the Ra'is: Abdel Halim Hafez and Nasserist Longings' and Gabriel M. Rosenbaum's 'Nasser and Nasserism as Perceived in Modern Egyptian Literature through Allusions to Songs', both in *Rethinking Nasserism*, pp. 307–23 and 324–42, respectively.

Epilogue: Prospects of a Post-2011 Nasser

More than forty years after his death, Nasser is still present in the Egyptian imaginary. His character is widely invoked, his legacy debated, his pictures raised, and his speeches circulated. Of all the Arab leaders of the past century, few had a lasting impact that extended to other Arab countries as had Nasser. His unparalleled position, still felt to this day, transforms him from history to memory, from the realms of political scientists to the works of writers and artists – in short, from a real figure to a metaphor. Whether glorified or demonised, elevated or debased, hailed as a symbol of freedom, anti-colonialism and social justice, or tarnished as a ruthless dictator who cultivated a personality cult and popularised the authoritarian model of regimes among Arabs, Nasser is an emotional and divisive subject, an agglomeration of meanings that transcend the direct outcomes of his rule to dwell deeply in the psyche of generations of Egyptians and Arabs, becoming a site on to which they project their dreams and aspirations, defeats and disappointments.

In his recent attempt to analyse the Nasserite ideology, Egyptian historian Sharif Yunus concludes by arguing that detractors of Nasser as well as his panegyrists testify to the perennial omnipresence of the president in Egyptian life. For Yunus, Nasser is the ultimate materialisation of the notion of the 'saviour', the dream that is so ingrained in the Egyptian imaginary. Why cannot even those who realise the falsity of this concept 'leave Nasser in his tomb and transcend him?'[1] asks Yunus. His argument is that Egyptians have yet to produce an alternative political model that can replace Nasser's. Those who no longer believe in the 'individual hero' are liberated from a grand delusion but they still cannot fill the vacuum that is left by Nasser, the supreme representative of that model.[2] In other words, for Egyptians to cease invoking Nasser and his associations and consider him part of a distant past, a drastic change must occur to the way they conceive of themselves vis-à-vis their reality, history, and nation state – a transformation of their social imaginary.[3]

This book has sought to identify the exact space that Nasser has occupied in the Egyptian imaginary, its histories, trajectories, forms, particularities, and vicissitudes. It has tried to show that the image of Nasser has not taken a smooth, uninterrupted, singular path of glory or disrepute. Rather, it passed through multiple junctures and turning points, and was produced by several contesting narratives, divergent opinions, and conflicting sensibilities. The largely positive, romantic view of Nasser that has proliferated in Egyptian literature and film in the last two decades hides behind it a much more complicated and multilayered tale of rise and fall. In fact, the survival of Nasser as a site of nostalgia for many Egyptians is in itself indicative of the peculiar position in which he was placed, given the disgracing blow that he received in 1967 and the intense campaign of de-Nasserisation that was launched by his successor.

This book has included writers and film-makers as they were grappling to come to terms with the meanings of Nasser. Enigmatic and ever elusive, however, Nasser has no fixed and determined explanation, nor were those writers left with masses of detail that could explain the various ambiguities and contradictions in his life. Consequently, by seeking to interpret Nasser, each writer has, in fact, produced his/her own Nasser, reimagining, adding, or altering episodes in his life. Thus, as the second chapter of this book demonstrated, Nasser has been seen as an intellectual, a beast, a martyr, and a defendant.

Aside from presenting Nasser as a character, Egyptian literary narratives are invaluable sources for understanding how ordinary Egyptian citizens perceive their relationship with the president. Nasser was largely credited, even among his enemies, for his efforts to appeal to, empower and assist the masses. While his endeavours are minutely recorded by the historians of the era, it is the manifestations of his personal impact on these masses that is often missing. Egyptian literature features characters responding heterogeneously to this personalised relationship with Nasser. Whether by writing letters and turning him into an audience, by conceiving him as a potential replacement of the father and a destabiliser of familial bonds, or by negotiating his masculine identity, those characters have each appropriated Nasser into their own realms, locating him within broader contexts that are largely unrelated to his official position.

The visual representations of Nasser open up other possibilities to examine his status in the Egyptian imaginary. This book found certain politics that oriented the appearance or disappearance of Nasser's portrait in Egyptian cinema. The portrait was transformed from just a picture of the president into a medium through which film-makers sought to deliver specific political messages to their audiences. In addition, one striking aspect about Nasser in Egyptian cinema is the appropriation of his 1967 'resignation speech'. By far his most immortalised speech in Egyptian cinema – in fact, its most frequently recurring archival footage ever – the presence of the speech serves to define the year 1967 as a timeless moment, a lasting wound that Egyptians still cannot mentally overcome.

A major contribution of this book lies in unearthing the ways in which many Egyptians separate Nasser from his regime. While the latter can be seen as oppressive, unjust, and even brutal, Nasser is often detached from its excesses and therefore exonerated as either unknowing or necessarily disapproving of these measures. Egyptian literature and film abound with characters that claim Nasser to their sides and invoke him against his very regime, empowered by a certain belief in his exceptionality. One of the remarkable outcomes of this tendency is that, even among the films that belonged to the de-Nasserisation phase, Nasser himself was hardly criticised, and his portrait, for that matter, rarely appeared in the rooms where interrogation and torture took place.

This study has explored less the actual history of Nasser than the images of that history as represented, reproduced, and reimagined by writers and film-makers. Maintaining that the imaginary has a history of its own, it has sought to identify the major shifts, transformations, and contradictions that surrounded the literary and cinematic representations of Nasser. By attempting to delineate 'plots' that informed these representations, one could speak of a periodisation of Nasser's images from 1952 onwards, resulting in certain stages each of which was marked by a dominant approach towards Nasser. Whereas the four years that preceded the 1956 Suez War saw writers producing mild criticism of Nasser and showing anxiety about the repressive measures that were initiated by him – while, at the same time, acknowledging his good intentions and sincere efforts to improve the country[4] – the period between 1956 and 1967 largely witnessed a Nasser glorified, a symbol declared hero of independence, anti-colonialism, and social justice who, if presiding over a regime in which torture, corruption, and persecution may have taken place, can nonetheless be separated from those misdeeds and claimed by the people. This long period of belief in Nasser was interrupted by the 1967 *naksa*, which caused a rift among writers and film-makers regarding Nasser's own culpability for the disastrous defeat. Thus came three years of disenchantment with Nasser that were interspersed with harsh allegorical cinematic and literary treatments of him, some of which questioned the previous separation between Nasser and the regime, culminating with Husayn Kamal's movie *Shay' min al-Khawf* in 1969.

The negative representations of Nasser reached their acme during Sadat's regime (1970–81), with a systematic attack on his legacy that sought to reduce it to scenes of torture, fear, and oppression. This attack was meant to establish a contrast between Nasser and Sadat and, therefore, to bestow legitimacy over the radical changes that Sadat introduced in the economic, political, and social directions of Egypt. A close examination of this period shows, however, that these representations were found mainly in films, and that most literary narratives (with a notable exception in Mahfouz's *Al-Karnak*) remained silent towards a reappraisal of the image of Nasser in the 1970s. Whereas the majority of writers shared Nasser's class orientations and his ideals of social justice and equality, films came largely out of the private sector and ruled by its values and its stance towards Nasser. Unlike writers who witnessed a collapse of the Nasserite project at the hands of Sadat, a sizeable number of film producers found in this decade a golden opportunity to release the enmity that they had been harbouring over the years towards Nasser and his socialist policies.

Yet the deterioration in the economic and social situation that was felt strongly in the last years of Sadat, and persisted throughout President Hosni Mubarak's Egypt, initiated a positive comeback of Nasser's image that began in the early 1980s and dominated the ensuing years. Interestingly, this favourable return of Nasser nearly eliminated the divergence that was recognised in the previous decade between writers and film-makers and united them both in invoking Nasser against a sinking reality. Thus Nasser became a martyr in Gamal al-Ghitani's *Al-Tajalliyat* and a resort to the poor Zeinat in Salwa Bakr's *Zeinat fi Janazat al-Ra'is*, while a group of young, politically progressive film-makers began to revisit the image of Nasser cinematically and to dismiss the sensational treatment of their 1970s predecessors.[5]

The resurgence of a predominantly nostalgic view of Nasser in the last two decades is more informative about the situations surrounding this resurgence in Egypt than about the president. That many Egyptians still yearn for the same ideals, dreams, and aspirations that Nasser had striven to realise very much indicates that Egypt has experienced a post-Nasser era only temporally. Poverty, social injustice and foreign hegemony have so much permeated the country that they became stable components of Egyptian life. Still worse, the waves of Islamic extremism, sectarian clashes, and migration of major intellectuals, from which Nasser's Egypt was largely free, were only a few of the symptoms of a decaying reality. In addition, the untimely death of Nasser in 1970 befell a nation still traumatised by an unprecedented demeaning defeat whose images and memories never cease to haunt the Egyptian imaginary. Only when Egyptians are truly awakened from that nightmare can 1967 lose part of its damaging associations and become a distant moment in a bygone era. The achievements of the Egyptian army during the 1973 October War presented a potential remedy that was soon aborted by Sadat's political and economic policies. Strikingly, the October War has yet to be warmly embraced and represented by Egyptian writers and film-makers.

This book was conceived almost a year before the 2011 Egyptian revolution, and all the works that the previous chapters discuss predate it. Naturally, it is still too early to offer a definitive answer to whatever impact the recent tumultuous events in Egypt will have on the image of Nasser and his meanings for Egyptians. In fact, the revolution itself, continuing as it is, is still scarcely portrayed in written or visual narratives. Ahdaf Soueif (b.1950) offers an analysis of this situation in an article that is tellingly titled, 'In Times of Crisis, Fiction Has to Take a Back Seat'. Published in August 2012, the article argues that the time has not yet come to produce a mature fictional account of the revolution. If Egyptian novelists 'produced texts of critique, of dystopia, of nightmare' before the revolution, it seems as though they all 'have given up – for the moment – on fiction'. The 2011 revolution is not *fictionalisable* yet because 'the immediate truth is too glaring to allow a more subtle truth to take form. For reality has to take time to be processed, to transform into fiction.' Another reason may lie in the fact that writing a novel necessitates a time of withdrawal from the real world and turning inwards, isolating oneself far from the crowds that are occupying the streets. And it is here that Soueif, herself both a prominent novelist and a participant in the revolution, favours political activism over fictional production, or the citizen over the novelist: 'You, the citizen, need[s] to be present, there, on the ground, marching, supporting, talking, instigating, articulating'.[6] Though written more than three years ago, Soueif's insights have proved to be largely true; seldom has any major literary figure in Egypt produced a significant work concerning the 2011 revolution and its consequences.

That Nasser has been present in the 2011 revolution, however, is abundantly documented. I began the Introduction with an actual incident that speaks of the continuing relevance of Nasser in Egyptians' lives. The images from Tahrir Square which were circulated around the world included groups of Egyptians carrying pictures of Nasser, while live testimonies told of the existence of several booths at Tahrir that broadcast his speeches and well-known songs that were dedicated to him. Since 2011, one can speak of three major phases that have underscored the pertinence of Nasser to current events in Egypt. The first phase ushered in vibrant debates concerning the position that Nasser held vis-à-vis the 2011 revolution. The main question which dominated these debates centred on whether the 2011 revolution signified a rupture with the thirty years of Mubarak, with Sadat's Egypt, or with the entire July 1952 regime – whether, that is, the contemporary Egyptian revolutionaries were a continuity or a discontinuity with Nasser. Egyptian journalist Nagla' Bidir, for instance, warned at the time when Egypt was ruled by the Supreme Council of the Armed Forces (SCAF), against homogenising the Egyptian military and perceiving it as a single entity since Nasser, arguing that the last is not part of the 'the rule of the military'[7] against which revolutionaries were protesting. Egyptian film-maker Khalid Yusuf speculated that the positive image of Nasser would gain new momentum in Egyptian cinema following the revolution, while Sonallah Ibrahim, Ibrahim Abdel Meguid, and Gamal al-Ghitani unanimously declared the revolution as a major incident against *Nizam Yulyu* (the July Regime).[8] In addition, an exhibition which opened a few days before Nasser's first post-revolution birthday had attracted wide attention and underscored a public divide with regard to the memory of the president. Entitled 'Nasser, the Dream', the exhibition, whose opening was attended by none other than Nasser's family,[9] featured old and new paintings, including a few that were created after the 2011 revolution, but all demonstrating 'the bright side of the picture', as the title of one critical review put it. Published in *al-Ahram Weekly*, the review criticised the organisers for attempting to link Nasser to the 2011 revolution, wondering,

> If Nasser should be the symbol of dreams of justice, freedom, and equality among people both rich and poor, then why on earth are we still suffering from injustice and lack of freedom in Egyptian society? And if the principles of the 1952 Revolution have failed to survive, then why are *we still celebrating the dream*? The dream, in other words, that turned out to be a nightmare.[10]

Similarly, Nasser featured in two of the early literary responses to the 2011 revolution. The Marquezian title *Mi'at Khatwa min al-Thawra* (One Hundred Steps of the Revolution) introduces a diary that adopts an ambivalent stance towards the relationship between Nasser and Tahrir's revolutionaries. The writer, who chronicles his personal observations of the eighteen days of protest leading to the fall of President Mubarak, oscillates between portraying the masses in Tahrir as 'chanting from their wounded dignity against thirty years of the dictator's rule'[11] and unequivocally announcing 'the regime of the July revolution is 62 years old . . . This revolution is a total rupture with it.'[12] Far more significant was the comparison between Nasser's resignation speech in the wake of the 1967 defeat and Mubarak's second speech on 1 February 2011, which occurred between a mother and her son Khalid in Hisham al-Khishin's (b.1964) novel *7 Ayyam fi al-Tahrir* (7 Days at Tahrir). Known for its powerful, emotional impact on a large number of Egyptians during the revolution, creating a division between those who believed in Mubarak's concessions and the promises he made and those who did not, the speech convinced Khalid and his friends to leave Tahrir and give Mubarak the interim he requested. Khalid's mother, however, reminds her son of what she sees as a manipulation of Egyptians similar to that practised by Nasser, thus establishing continuity between the two presidents:

> Your enthusiasm, Khalid, reminds me of the days when Nasser resigned. One speech made these kind people fill the streets, begging him who led them to defeat and disgrace to stay. All of the Egyptian leaders understand the emotional nature of the Egyptian public, and they seek to exploit it for their interests.[13]

The second phase coincided with the astounding rise of Hamdin Sabahi, which has undeniably reinvigorated questions concerning the place of the charismatic leader in post-2011 Egypt. A lifelong Nasserist, Sabahi was the dark-horse candidate of the 2012 Egyptian presidential election, surprisingly finishing third by a narrow margin behind the Muslim Brother and eventual winner Muhammad Morsi and the Mubarak-era prime minister Ahmad Shafiq. Described by many observers as a politician in the style of Nasser, Sabahi did not hide his political inclinations, building as he did on his hero's appeal towards the masses. He sought to maintain his own vision of presidency, however, attempting to avoid what he perceived as the pitfalls of Nasser: 'I would uphold Nasser's principles on social justice while pushing for a completely democratic system that clearly defines and limits the role of the president, which Nasser did not do'.[14] The phenomenon of Hamdin Sabahi cannot be attributed solely to Egyptians' yearning for a Nasser-like leader – the fear of the Muslim Brotherhood and the *ancien régime* had certainly driven many voters to search for a third way. Yet his presence served as an initial, if not foreshadowing, reminder of the image of Nasser and its unceasing allure for ordinary Egyptians.

Nowhere can the relevance of Nasser and the power of his image be better recognised, however, than with the rise to power of the former minister of defence Abdel Fattah al-Sisi. In the very well-known episode, the Egyptian army intervened yet again in the political sphere, following days of massive protests against President Muhammad Morsi. On 3 July 2013, al-Sisi, then the chief general of the army, removed Morsi from power in what came to be disputed as either a coup or a second revolution. Almost a year later, al-Sisi, rescinding his initial decision not to run for president, has unsurprisingly won the presidential election against none other than Sabahi himself, this time, however, with a much bigger margin (96.91 per cent). With the emergence of al-Sisi and the inauguration of what Juan Cole described as 'Sisi-mania',[15] Nasser resurfaced in Egyptian life, perhaps unprecedented in the last decade. News channels have broadcast images of thousands of Egyptians carrying posters that featured both Nasser and al-Sisi; some of the country's leading intellectuals, such as Sonallah Ibrahim[16] and Gamal al-Ghitani,[17] have praised al-Sisi and labelled him as a continuation of Nasser; and al-Sisi himself, in various situations and interviews, has capitalised on this comparison and appeared rather flattered and humbled by it.[18] Any Google search on the comparison between the two men will result in tens of hits, both in Arabic and English, covering a wide range of media, from songs to videos to newspaper op-eds and features, hotly engaging in a debate concerning the falsity or authenticity of this comparison.

This recent al-Sisi–Nasser phenomenon, though unfinished and still unfolding, does nevertheless compel us to reflect on the prospects of the location of Nasser in the Egyptian imaginary. First, the strong resurrection of Nasser and his legacy in the past two years tells more about Egyptians than about al-Sisi himself. Up to his intervention in July 2013, al-Sisi was almost unknown to ordinary Egyptians. Situating his photographs next to Nasser's within a few months of his rise to power is a form of wishful thinking, undoubtedly speaking to Egyptians' longing for a Nasser-like figure on whom they could rely and in whom they might find solutions to the many difficult circumstances engulfing them. As mentioned earlier, the initial months following the 2011 revolution had left Egyptians pondering the possibility of transcending the need for a strong leader and fashioning a new social contract whereby the military would enjoy a very limited role in public life. Sisi-mania, however, offered a more definitive answer to this. No matter how much it was orchestrated by Egypt's official media outlets and personalities, it was still undeniable that the al-Sisi–Nasser comparison touched upon certain nostalgic feelings among Egyptians. The associations that Nasser evoked in ordinary Egyptians proved yet again to be a decisive factor which his successors could continue to appropriate, falsely or otherwise.

Second, it is telling to note the way in which Nasser was claimed and appropriated by official Egyptian media, businessmen, and al-Sisi's entourage. Largely consisting of figures whose social, political and economic orientations are antagonistic to Nasser's, this influential segment of Egyptian society was nonetheless capable of selecting a few aspects of Nasser through which they could announce al-Sisi to be his true inheritor – the most important of which was, undoubtedly, both men's crushing of the Muslim Brotherhood. As many observers have noted, 'the upper class and upper middle class that are currently calling al-Sisi as the new Nasser and cheering for him will not tolerate to accept Nasser's social and economic policies once again in Egypt'.[19] Interestingly, Nasser became a floating signifier, a confusion of references whose determinate signification relies not so much on what he did exactly and called for as it did on the power of those who capitalise on his image. This is not to homogenise the entire sector of Egyptian society who adopted this view of al-Sisi as a new Nasser and render them essentially anti-Nasser – a sizeable number of those included renowned leftist intellectuals and activists in Egypt – it included members of Nasser's own family.[20] Rather, it is to note how Nasser can be fragmented into multiple Nassers, each serving the needs of different sectors of Egyptian society.

Third, the 2014 presidential election in Egypt was yet another manifestation of Nasser's relevance in today's Egypt and the apex of claiming Nasser as a way to appeal to ordinary Egyptians. If the 2012 election had pitted the self-declared Nasserist Hamdin Sabahi against a Muslim Brother and a Mubarak-era figure, its 2014 counterpart witnessed Sabahi running against al-Sisi or, as one could perhaps put it, Nasser against Nasser. While the two candidates sought Nasser and his legacy as a way to bestow legitimacy on their projects and blueprints, backed, if disproportionately, by legions of media outlets and personalities, they both opted for the Nasser that suited their interests the most. Eventually, and rather to be expected, the strong, militant Muslim Brotherhood's enemy, Nasser, as exemplified by al-Sisi, triumphed over the socialist version of Nasser that was promoted by Sabahi.

Fourth, although the dominant narrative among the Muslim Brotherhood, both in Egypt and outside, was to view their plight at the hands of al-Sisi as a reincarnation of their bloody conflict with Nasser in the 1950s and 1960s,[21] a few voices within the Brotherhood sought to shatter the comparison between Nasser and al-Sisi, considering it a fake attempt to legitimise an otherwise illegitimate usurper of power. Tellingly, Nasser, a historic enemy of the Brotherhood, was partly redeemed, not so much in order to revisit the Brotherhood's perspective on him as it was to further condemn al-Sisi and single him out as a ruthless tyrant unprecedented in Egyptian history. Thus,

Yasir Abu Hilala, current director general of *Al Jazeera*, established in an op-ed published in 2014 what he believed were nine differences between Nasser and al-Sisi, arguing that the only thing the two men had in common was the military uniform.[22]

As mentioned earlier, the dramatic comeback of Nasser since 2013 attests to his powerful image and its ability to haunt the Egyptian imaginary at such a critical moment in Egyptian history. Whether al-Sisi's performance will have an impact on Egyptians' remembering of Nasser is left to speculation. While al-Sisi's failures, easily noted by now, may lead ordinary Egyptians to abandon the notion of the saviour and dissociate it from their aspirations for a better future, it could nonetheless add more to the exceptionality of Nasser, elevating him to an unparalleled position that neither al-Sisi nor any other political figure could attain. It could prove, yet again, that, for many Egyptians, Nasser is not only a historical figure – a leader who ruled over Egypt at a certain time in their distant past, succeeding occasionally and stumbling at many other times – but rather an idea, a synonym for social justice, dignity and equality. Will these associations run their course and eventually lose their spark in Egypt? Possibly. But until then, Nasser, as the previous chapters have made clear, continues to be an essential component of the Egyptian imaginary.

Notes

1. Yunus, *Nida' al-Sha'b*, p. 738.
2. Ibid., p. 739.
3. See the excellent two-part article that 'Amr 'Adly published in *Jadaliyya* concerning the location of Nasser and Nasserism in current Egypt. His argument is that the only social contract that is imagined by today's Egyptians is inherited from the Nasserite state. Available at <http://www.jadaliyya.com/pages/index/16944> (last accessed 28 May 2015).
4. This approach can be best recognised in Ruz al-Yusuf's letter and Yahya Haqqi's novel *Sah al-Nawm*, discussed in Chapters 1 and 2 of this book, respectively.
5. For more on this new generation of film-makers, see pp. 183–7.
6. Available at <http://www.theguardian.com/books/2012/aug/17/ahdaf-soueif-politics-fiction> (last accessed 1 May 2015).
7. Nagla' Bidir, 'Ayyam Su' al-Tafahum', *al-Tahrir*, No. 81 (21 September 2011). See also Abdel Halim Qandil's 'Al-Hanin ila Abdel Nasser', *al-Quds al-'Arabi*

(7 October 2012) and Iman Ali's 'Zil Abdel Nasser: Fikra Tahkum al-Tarikh al-Muʿasir fi Misr', *al-Hayat* (10 October 2012).

8. In discussion with the author in Cairo, October to November 2011. Sonallah Ibrahim emphasised that the 2011 revolution is 'fatherless', denying the possibility that a certain nostalgia for Nasser might arise afterwards.

9. His two sons, Abdel Hakim and Abdel Hamid, and his two daughters, Huda and Muna.

10. Available at <http://weekly.ahram.org.eg/2011/1068/entertain.htm> (last accessed 20 May 2015).

11. Ahmad Zaghlul al-Shayti, *Mi'at Khatwa min al-Thawra: Yawmiyyat min Maydan al-Tahrir* (Cairo: Mirit, 2011), p. 32.

12. Ibid., p. 117.

13. Hisham al-Khishin, *7 Ayyam fi Al-Tahrir* (Cairo: Al-Dar al-Misriyya al-Lubnaniyya, 2011), p. 92.

14. Available at <http://weekly.ahram.org.eg/2012/1096/eg3.htm> (last accessed 23 May 2015).

15. Available at <http://www.juancole.com/2014/04/raybans-portrait-underwear.html> (last accessed 23 May 2015).

16. Available at <http://www.youm7.com/story/0000/0/0/-/1218467> (last accessed 24 May 2015). See also Ibrahim's interview with Ursula Lindsey, published by Mada Masr, available at <http://www.madamasr.com/sections/culture/voice-dissent-joins-nationalist-chorus> (last accessed 24 May 2015).

17. Available at <http://www.dostor.org/400954> (last accessed 24 May 2015). For more on al-Ghitani's views of al-Sisi, see <http://muftah.org/sisi-nasser-the-great-egyptian-novel/> (last accessed 24 May 2015).

18. See al-Sisi's first television interview in Egypt, aired on private stations CBC and ONTV on 4 May 2014 and conducted by Lamis al-Hadidi and Ibrahim 'Isa, two of the most popular Egyptian television personalities, during the 2014 presidential campaign. The particular part in which al-Sisi was directly asked about Nasser can be found here <https://www.youtube.com/watch?v=aOxf_i2-ubY> (last accessed 10 June 2015).

19. Available at <http://egyptianchronicles.blogspot.com/2013/07/reviving-nasser-in-egypt.html> (last accessed 9 June 2015).

20. See the letter that Huda, Nasser's eldest daughter, wrote to al-Sisi, requesting that he would run for president, available at <http://www.almasryalyoum.com/news/details/199119> (last accessed 5 June 2015).

21. See, for instance, the report that was broadcast on *Al Jazeera* on 6 September 2013, where the channel, a clear supporter of the Brotherhood, drew compari-

son between the ousting of Muhammad Naguib in 1954 and Morsi in 2013. Available at <https://www.youtube.com/watch?v=BWZaNcoAHLM> (last accessed 2 June 2015).

22. Available at <http://www.alghad.com/articles/523208> (last accessed 2 June 2015).

Bibliography

Print Sources

Abdel Ghani, Mustafa, *Al-Muthaqqafun wa Abdel Nasser* (Kuwait: Dar Su'ad al-Sabah, 1993).

Abdel Ghani, Mustafa, *Abdel Rahman al-Sharqawi: al-Dalala wa al-Shahada* (Cairo: Al-Majlis al-A'la li al-Thaqafa, 2010).

Abdel Hakim, Tahir, *Al-Aqdam al-'Ariya: al-Shuyu'iyyun al-Misriyyun, Khams Sanawat fi al- Sujun wa Mu'askarat al-Ta'dhib* (Beirut: Dar Ibn Khaldun, 1974).

Abdel Latif, 'Imad, 'Bayan al-Tanahhi wa Dhakirat al-Hazima: Madkhal Balaghi li Tahlil al-Khitab al-Siyasi', *Alif: Journal of Comparative Politics*, No. 30, 2010, pp. 146–75.

Abdel-Malek, Anouar, *Egypt: Military Society, the Army Regime, the Left, and Social Change under Nasser*, trans. Charles Lam Markmann (New York: Random House, 1968).

Abdel Meguid, Ibrahim, *Days of Amber*, trans. Farouk Abdel Wahab (Cairo: The American University in Cairo Press, 2005).

Abdel Nasser, Gamal, 'Al-Khayt al-Rafi' bayna al-Hurriyya wa al-Fawda', *Majallat Ruz al-Yusuf*, No. 1301, 18 May 1953.

Abdel Qadir, Faruq, *Al-Bahth 'an al-Yaqin al-Murawigh* (Cairo: Dar al-Hilal, 1998).

Abdel Quddous, Ihsan, 'Hal Qara'a Abdel Nasser Hadhihi al-Risala?', in Ihsan Abdel Quddous, *Asif Lam A'ud Astati'* (Cairo: Muntasir, 1980), pp. 6–15.

Abdel Quddous, Muhammad, *Hikayat Ihsan Abdel Quddous* (Cairo: Al-Hay'a al-Misriyya al-'Amma li al-Kitab, 2011).

Abdel Rahman, Mahfuz, 'Abdel Nasser wa Ana', *Al-Yawm al-Sabi'*, 20 January 2012.

Abdu, Ibrahim, *Ruz al-Yusuf: Sira wa Sahifah* (Cairo: Mu'assasat Sijill al-'Arab, 1961).

Abu 'Awf, Abdel Rahman, *Yusuf Idris wa 'Alamuhu fi al-Qissa al-Qasira wa al-Riwaya* (Cairo: Maktabat al-Usra, 2001).

Abu 'Awf, Abdel Rahman, *Ihsan Abdel Quddous bayna al-Sahafa wa al-Riwaya* (Cairo: Al-Majlis al-A'la li al-Thaqafa, 2006).

Abu al-Futuh, Amirah, *Ihsan Abdel Quddous Yatadhakkar* (Cairo: Al-Hay'a al-Misriyya al-'Amma li al-Kitab, 1982).

Abu-Lughod, Lila and Ahmad H. Sa'di, 'Introduction: The Claims of Memory', in Lila Abu-Lughod and Ahmad Sa'di (eds), *Nakba: Palestine, 1948, and the Claims of Memory* (New York: Columbia University Press, 2007), pp. 1–24.

Abu al-Naga, Shirin, *Min Awraq Shahinda Maqlid* (Cairo: Mirit, 2006).

Aburish, Said K, *Nasser: The Last Arab* (New York: Thomas Dunne Books, 2004).

Abu Shadi, Ali, 'Genres in Egyptian Cinema', in Alia Arasoughly (ed.), *Screens of Life: Critical Film Writing from the Arab World* (Quebec: World Heritage Press, Vol. 1, 1996), pp. 84–129.

Abu Shadi, Ali, *Al-Cinema wa al-Siyasa* (Cairo: Dar Sharqiyyat, 1998).

Aghacy, Samira, *Masculine Identity in the Fiction of the Arab East since 1967* (Syracuse, NY: Syracuse University Press, 2009).

Ahmed, Leila, *A Border Passage: From Cairo to America – A Woman's Journey* (New York: Farrar, Straus, and Giroux, 1999).

Al-'Alim, Mahmud Amin, 'Misr Abdel Nasser', in *23 Yulyu: Khamsat Ab'ad* (Beirut: Dar al-Quds, 1974).

Allen, Roger, 'Yusuf Idris' Short Stories: Themes and Techniques', in Roger Allen (ed.), *Critical Perspectives on Yusuf Idris* (Washington, DC: Three Continents Press, 1994), pp. 15–30.

Altman, Janet Gurkin, *Epistolarity: Approaches to a Form* (Columbus, OH: Ohio State University Press, 1982).

Amin, Shahid, 'Gandhi as Mahatma: Gorakhpur District, Eastern UP, 1921–2', in Ranajit Guha and Gayatri Chakravorti Spivak (eds), *Selected Subaltern Studies* (Oxford: Oxford University Press, 1988), pp. 288–348.

Anderson, Benedict, *Imagined Communities: Reflections on the Origins and Spread of Nationalism* (New York and London: Verso, 1991).

Andrea, Bernadette, 'Passage Through the Harem: Historicizing a Western Obsession in Leila Ahmed's *A Border Passage*', in Nawar al-Hassan Golley (ed.), *Arab Women's Lives Retold: Exploring Identity Through Writing* (Syracuse, NY: Syracuse University Press, 2007), pp. 3–15.

Al-Ansari, Muhammad Jabir, *Al-Nasiriyya bi Manzur Naqdi: Ayy Durus li al-Mustaqbal?* (Beirut: Al-Mu'assasa al-'Arabiyya li al-Dirasat wa al-Nashr, 2002).

Appadurai, Arjun, *Modernity at Large: Cultural Dimensions of Globalisations* (Minneapolis, MN and London: University of Minnesota Press, 1996).

Aries, Philippe, *Centuries of Childhood: A Social History of Family Life* (New York: Alfred A. Knopf, 1962).

Aristotle, *Poetics*, translated and introduced by John Warrington (London: Alibris, 1963).

Armbrust, Walter, *Mass Culture and Modernism in Egypt* (Cambridge: Cambridge University Press, 1996).

Armbrust, Walter, 'Farid Shauqi: Tough Guy, Family, Cinema Star', in Mai Ghoussoub and Emma Sinclair-Webb (eds), *Imagined Masculinities: Male Identity and Culture in the Modern Middle East* (London: Saqi Books, 2006), pp. 199–226.

Armes, Roy, *Third World Film Making and the West* (Berkeley, CA, Los Angeles, CA and London: University of California Press, 1987).

'Asfur, Gabir, 'Hal Yamut Hadha al-Zammar?!', *Ibda'*, Vol. 9, No. 9, 1991.

'Asfur, Gabir, 'Naguib Mahfouz's Critics', trans. Ayman A. el-Desouky, in Michael Beard and Adnan Haydar (eds), *Naguib Mahfouz: From Regional Fame to Global Recognition* (Syracuse, NY: Syracuse University Press, 1993).

Ashour, Radwa, Ferial Ghazoul and Reda-Mekdashi, Hasna (eds), *Arab Women Writers: A Critical Reference Guide, 1873–1999* (Cairo and New York: The American University in Cairo Press, 2008).

Ashour, Radwa, *Faraj* (Cairo: Dar al-Shuruq, 2008).

'Atiyya, Na'im, *Yahya Haqqi wa 'Alamuhu al-Qasasi* (Cairo: Maktabat al-Anjlu al-Misriyya, 1978).

'Awad, Luis, *Aqni'at al-Nasiriyya al-Sab'a* (Beirut: Dar al-Qadaya, 1975).

Avery, Gillian, 'The Voice of the Child, Both Godly and Unregenerate, in Early Modern England', in Elizabeth Goodenough, Mark A. Heberle, and Naomi Sokoloff (eds), *.Infant Tongues: The Voice of the Child in Literature* (Detroit, MI: Wayne State University Press, 1994), pp. 16–27.

Ayoub, Mahmud, *Redemptive Suffering in Islam: A Study of the Devotional Aspects of 'Ashura in Tewlver Shi'ism* (The Hague: Mouton, 1978).

'Azab, Khalid (ed.), *Ruz al-Yusuf: 80 Sanah Sihafa* (Alexandria: Maktabat al-Iskandariyyah, 2006).

'Aziz, Khayri, 'Abdel Nasser wa al-Ittihad al- Suvyati', in Anis al-Sayigh (ed.), *Abdel Nasser wa Ma Ba'd* (Beirut: Al-Mu'assasa al-'Arabiyya li al-Dirasat wa al-Nashr, 1980).

Al-Azmeh, Aziz, *Muslim Kingship: Power and the Sacred in Muslim, Christian and Pagan Polities* (London and New York: I. B. Tauris, 1997).

Baker, Raymond William, 'Egypt in Shadows: Films and the Political Order', *American Behavioral Scientist*, No. 17, 1974, pp. 393–423.

Bakhtin, Mikhail, *Problems of Dostoevsky's Poetics*, trans. Caryl Emerson (Minneapolis, MN: University of Minnesota Press, 1984).

Bakr, Salwa, *Such a Beautiful Voice, and other stories*, trans. Hoda Elsadda (New Delhi: Kali for Women, 1994).

Bariri, Muhammad, 'Tawfiq al-Hakim wa al-Mansi Qandil: Bayna 'Awdat al-Ruh wa Inkisariha', *Fusul*, No. 12, spring 1993.

Baron, Beth, 'Nationalist Iconography: Egypt as a Woman', in James Jankowski and Israel Gershoni (eds), *Rethinking Nationalism in the Arab Middle East* (New York: Columbia University Press, 1997), pp. 105–26.

Barthes, Roland, *Camera Lucida: Reflections on Photography*, trans. Richard Howard (New York: Hill and Wang, 1981).

Beckman, Karen, *Crash: Cinema and the Politics of Speed and Stasis* (Durham, NC and London: Duke University Press, 2010).

Berthoff, Warner, 'Fiction, History, Myth: Notes Towards the Discrimination of Narrative Forms', in Morton W. Bloomfield (ed.), *The Interpretation of Narrative: Theory and Practice* (Cambridge, MA: Harvard University Press, 1970), pp. 263–87.

Bin Jum'a, Bushusha, *Al-Qass wa al-Tahawwul* (Lattakia: Dar al-Hiwar, 1998).

Bodnar, John, *Remaking America: Public Memory, Commemoration, and Patriotism in the Twentieth Century* (Princeton, NJ: Princeton University Press, 1992).

Borges, Jorge Luis, *Ficciones* (New York: Grove Press, 1962).

Britt, Linda, 'A Transparent Lens? Narrative Technique in Carmen Naranjo's *Nunca Hubo Alguna Vez*', *Monographic Review/Revista Monographia*, No. 4, 1988, pp. 127–35.

Brown, Daniel, 'Martyrdom in Sunni Revivalist Thought', in Margaret Cormack (ed.), *Sacrificing the Self: Perspectives on Martyrdom and Religion* (Oxford and New York: Oxford University Press, 2001), pp. 107–17.

Browning, Richard L., *Childhood and the Nation in Latin American Literature* (New York: Peter Lang, 2001).

Castoriadis, Cornelius, *The Imaginary Institution of Society* (Cambridge, MA: The MIT Press, 1987).

Cohen-Mor, Dalya, *Yusuf Idris: Changing Visions* (Potomac, MD: Sheba Press, 1992).

Cohn, Dorrit, *Transparent Minds: Narrative Modes for Presenting Consciousness in Fiction* (Princeton NJ: Princeton University Press, 1978).

Cook, David, *Martyrdom in Islam* (Cambridge: Cambridge University Press, 2007).

Cooke, Miriam, *Yahya Haqqi: the Anatomy of an Egyptian Intellectual* (Washington, DC: Three Continents Press, 1984).

Cooke, Miriam, '*Ayyam min Hayati:* The Prisoner Memoir of a Muslim Sister' in John C. Hawley (ed.), *The Postcolonial Crescent: Islam's Impact on Contemporary Literature* (New York: Peter Lang, 1998), pp. 121–39.

Cooke, Miriam, *Women Claim Islam: Creating Islamic Feminism through Literature* (New York and London: Routlege, 2001).

Cooper, Frank Rudy, 'Our First Unisex President? Black Masculinity and Obama's Feminine Side', in *Legal Studies Research Paper Series*, January 2009, pp. 632–61.

Corm, Georges, *Infijar al-Mashriq al-'Arabi: min Ta'mim Qanat al-Suwis ila Ijtiyah Lubnan* (Beirut: Dar al-Tali'a, 1987).

Custen, George F, *Bio/Pics: How Hollywood Constructed Public History* (New Brunswick, NJ: Rutgers University Press, 1992).

Al-Damiri, Kamal al-Din Muhammad ibn Musa, *Hayat al-Hayawan*, trans. A. S. G. Jaykar (London: 1906).

Danielson, Virginia, *The Voice of Egypt: Umm Kulthum, Arabic Song, and Egyptian Society in the Twentieth Century* (Chicago, IL: University of Chicago Press, 1997).

Davies, Lloyd Hughes, *Projections of Peronism in Argentine Autobiography, Biography, and Fiction* (Cardiff: University of Wales Press, 2007).

De Certeau, Michel, *The Writing of History*, trans. Tom Conley (New York: Columbia University Press, 1988).

Dekmejian, R. Hrair, *Egypt Under Nasser: A Study in Political Dynamics* (Albany, NY: State University of New York Press, 1971).

Droge, A. J., *The Qur'an: A New Annotated Translation* (Bristol: Equinox Publishing, 2013).

Elad, Ami, *The Village Novel in Modern Egyptian Literature* (Berlin: Klaus Schwarz Verlag, 1994).

El-Enany, Rasheed, 'The Novelist as a Political Eye-Witness: A View of Najib Mahfuz's Evaluation of Nasser and Sadat Eras', *Journal of Arabic Literature*, Vol. 21, No. 1, March 1990, pp. 72–86.

El-Enany, Rasheed, *Naguib Mahfouz: The Pursuit of Meaning* (London and New York: Routledge, 1993).

El-Enany, Rasheed, *Arab Representations of the Occident: East-West Encounters in Arabic Fiction* (London: Routledge, 2006).

Elsadda, Hoda, *Gender, Nation, and the Arabic Novel: Egypt, 1892–2008* (Syracuse, NY: Syracuse University Press, 2012).

Enloe, Cynthia, *Bananas, Beaches, & Bases: Making Feminist Sense of International Politics*. (Berkeley, CA and Los Angeles, CA: University of California Press, 1990).

Al-Fakhrani, Yusri, *Abdel Halim . . . Abdel Nasser: Sirri Jiddan* (Cairo: al-Fursan li al-Nashr, 2002).

Farid, Samir, 'Al-Cinema wa al-Dawla fi al-Watan al-'Arabi', in Abdel Mun'im Talima (ed.), *Al-Huwiyya al-Qawmiyya fi al-Cinema al-'Arabiyya* (Beirut: Markiz Dirasat al-Wihda al-'Arabiyya, 1986), pp. 95–128.

Farid, Samir, *Adwa' 'ala Cinema Youssef Chahine* (Cairo: Al-Hay'a al-Misriyya al-'Amma li al-Kitab, 1997).

Fischer, Michael, *Iran: From Religious Dispute to Revolution* (Madison, WI: University of Wisconsin Press, 2003).

Gamal Abdel Nasser, Tahia, *Dhikrayat Ma'ahu* (Cairo: Dar al-Shuruq, 2011).

Gaonkar, Dilip Parameshwar, 'Towards New Imaginaries: An Introduction', *Public Culture*, Vol. 14, No. 1, winter 2002, pp. 1–19.

Gasiorowska, Xenia, *The Image of Peter the Great in Russian Fiction* (Madison, WI: University of Wisconsin Press, 1979).

Genette, Gerard, *Narrative Discourse: An Essay in Method*, trans. Jane E. Lewin (Ithaca, NY: Cornell University Press, 1980).

Gerber, David A., 'Epistolary Masquerades: Acts of Deceiving and Withholding in Immigrant Letters', in Bruce S. Elliott, David A. Gerber, and Suzanne M. Sinke (eds), *Letters across Borders: The Epistolary Practices of International Migrants* (New York: Palgrave Macmillan, 2006), pp. 141–57.

Al-Ghazali, Zaynab, *Ayyam min Hayati* (Cairo: Dar al-Shuruq, 1978).

Ghazoul, Ferial, 'Balaghat al-Ghalaba', in *al-Fikr al-'Arabi al-Mu'asir wa al-Mar'a* (Cairo: Dar Tadamun al-Mar'a al-'Arabiyya, 1988).

Al-Ghitani, Gamal, *Kitab al-Tajalliyat: Al-Asfar al-Thalatha* (Cairo: al-Hay'a al-Misriyya al-'Amma li al-Kitab, 1997).

Giovannucci, Perri, *Literature and Development in North Africa: The Modernizing Mission* (New York: Routledge, 2008).

Gocic, Goran, *Notes from the Underground: The Cinema of Emir Kusturica* (London and New York: Wallflower Press, 2001).

Goldberg, Ann, 'Reading and Writing across the Borders of Dictatorship: Self-Censorship and Emigrant Experience in Nazi and Stalinist Europe', in Bruce S. Elliott, David A. Gerber, and Suzanne M. Sinke (eds), *Letters across Borders: The Epistolary Practices of International Migrants* (New York: Palgrave Macmillan, 2006), pp. 158–72.

Golia, Maria, *Egypt and Photography* (London: Reaktion Books, 2010).

Golley, Nawar Al-Hassan, *Reading Arab Women's Autobiographies: Shahrazad Tells Her Story*. (Austin, TX: University of Texas Press, 2003).
Golley, Nawar al-Hassan and Ahmad al-Issa, 'A Journey of Belonging: A Global(ized) Self Finds Peace', in Nawar al-Hassan Golley (ed.), *Arab Women's Lives Retold: Exploring Identity Through Writing* (Syracuse, NY: Syracuse University Press, 2007), pp. 201–21.
Gordon, Joel, *Nasser's Blessed Movement* (New York: Oxford University Press, 1992).
Gordon, Joel, 'Film, Fame, and Public Memory: Egyptian Biopics from *Mustafa Kamil* to *Nasser 56*', *International Journal of Middle East Studies*, Vol. 31, No. 1, February, 1999, pp. 61–79.
Gordon, Joel, 'Nasser 56/Cairo 96: Remembering Egypt's Lost Community', in Walter Armbrust (ed.), *Mass Mediations: New Approaches to Popular Culture in the Middle East and Beyond* (Berkeley, CA and Los Angeles, CA: University of California Press, 2000), pp. 161–81.
Gordon, Joel, *Revolutionary Melodrama: Popular Film and Civic Identity in Nasser's Egypt* (Chicago, IL: Middle East Documentation Center, 2002).
Gordon, Joel, 'Days of Anxiety/Days of Sadat: Impersonating Egypt's Flawed Hero on the Egyptian Screen', *Journal of Film and Video*, Vol. 54, No. 2/3, summer/autumn 2002, pp. 27–42.
Habermas, Jürgen, *The Structural Transformation of the Public Sphere: an Inquiry into a Category of Bourgeois Society*, trans. Thomas Burger (Cambridge, MA: MIT Press, 1991).
Haddad, Fu'ad, *Istishhad Gamal Abdel Nasser: Misr wa Gamal*, in Amin and Hasan Haddad (eds), *Fu'ad Haddad: al-A'mal al-Kamila*, Vol. 2 (Cairo: Al-Hay'a al-'Amma li Qusur al-Thaqafa, 2006).
Hafez, Sabry, 'The Egyptian Novel in the Sixties', in Issa Boullata (ed.), *Critical Perspectives on Modern Arabic Literature* (Washington, DC: Three Continents Press, 1980), pp. 171–90.
Al-Hafiz, Yasin, *Al-Hazima wa al-Aydyulujya al-Mahzuma* (Damascus: Dar al-Hasad, 1997).
Al-Hakim, Tawfiq, *'Awdat al-Wa'i* (Egypt: Dar al-Shuruq, 1974).
Halim, Hala, 'The Signs of Saladin: A Modern Cinematic Rendition of Medieval Heroism', *Alif: Journal of Comparative Poetics*, No. 12, 1992, pp. 78–94.
Hammuda, 'Adil, *Azmat al-Muthaqqafin wa Thawrat Yulyu* (Cairo: Maktabat Madbuli, 1985).
Haqqi, Yahya, *Khatawat fi al-Naqd* (Egypt: Maktabat Dar al-'Uruba, 1961).

Haqqi, Yahya, *Good Morning*, in *Good Morning and other stories*, trans. Miriam Cooke (Washington, DC: Three Continents Press, 1987), pp. 43–112.

Hassan, Waïl S, 'Arab-American Autobiography and the Reinvention of Identity: Two Egyptian Negotiations', *Alif: Journal of Comparative Poetics*, No. 22, 2002, pp. 7–35.

Hassan, Waïl S, 'Teaching a Seminar on Mahfouz', in Waïl Hassan and Susan Muaddi Darraj (eds), *Approaches to Teaching the Works of Naguib Mahfouz* (New York: The Modern Language Association of America, 2012), pp. 25–40.

Hatina, Meir, 'History, Politics, and Collective Memory: The Nasserist Legacy in Mubarak's Egypt', in Elie Podeh and Onn Winckler (eds), *Rethinking Nasserism: Revolution and Historical Memory in Modern Egypt* (Orlando, FL: University Press of Florida, 2004), pp. 100–24.

Haykal, Muhammad Hasanayn, *Li Misr, la li Abdel Nasser* (Cairo: Tawzi' al-Akhbar, 1976).

Hellman, John, *The Kennedy Obsession: The American Myth of JFK* (New York: Columbia University Press, 1997).

Al-Hisni, 'Afifa, *Shahid al-Tadhiyat* (Cairo: Matabi' al-Nashir al-'Arabi, 1970).

Hodgson, John, *The Search for the Self: Childhood in Autobiography and Fiction since 1940* (London: Sheffield Academic Press, 1993).

Holton, Robert, *Jarring Witnesses: Modern Fiction and the Representation of History* (London: Harvester Wheatsheaf, 1994).

Honeyman, Susan, *Elusive Childhood: Impossible Representations in Modern Fiction* (Columbus, OH: Ohio State University Press, 2005).

Hurst, Mary Jane, *The Voice of the Child in American Literature: Linguistic Approaches to Fictional Child Language* (Lexington, KY: University Press of Kentucky, 1990).

Hussein, Taha, *Naqd wa Islah* (Beirut: Dar al-'Ilm li al-Malayin, 1977).

Huyssen, Andreas, *Present Pasts: Urban Palimpsests and the Politics of Memory* (Redwood City, CA: Stanford University Press, 2003).

Huyssen, Andreas, *Twilight Memories: Marking Time in a Culture of Amnesia* (New York, London: Routledge, 1995).

Ibn Arabi, Muhyiddin, *Al-Futuhat al-Makkiyya* (Cairo: Maktabat al-Thaqafa al-Diniyya).

Ibrahim, Bashar and Jum'a Qajah, *Abdel Nasser wa al-Cinema: Bahth fi Ishkaliyyat al-Ru'ya bayna Cinema al-Sira wa Cinema al-Mu'taqal* (Beirut: Dar al-Tariq, 2004).

Ibrahim, Nabila, *Al-Butulat al-'Arabiyya wa al-Dhakira al-Tarikhiyya* (Cairo: Al-Maktaba al-Akadimiyya, 1995).

Ibrahim, Sonallah, *Yawmiyyat al-Wahat* (Cairo: Dar al-Mustaqbal al-'Arabi, 2004).
Idris, Yusuf, 'Delusion', in Ceza Kassem and Malak Hashem (eds), *Flights of Fantasy: Arabic Short Stories* (Cairo: Elias Modern Publishing House, 1985), pp. 27–32.
Idris, Samah, *Al-Muthaqqaf al-'Arabi wa al-Sulta: Bahth fi Riwayat al-Tajriba al-Nasiriyya* (Beirut: Dar al-Adab, 1992).
Irwin, Robert, *Camel* (London: Reaktion Books, 2010).
'Isa, Salah, *Muthaqqafun wa 'Askar* (Cairo: Maktabat Madbuli, 1986).
Iser, Wolfgang, *Prospecting: From Reader Response to Literary Anthropology* (Baltimore, MD and London: The Johns Hopkins University Press, 1989).
Jameson, Fredric, *The Political Unconscious: Narrative as a Socially Symbolic Act* (Ithaca, NY: Cornell University Press, 1981).
Jibril, Muhammad, *Al-Batal fi al-Wijdan al-Sha'bi* (Cairo: Maktabat al-Dirasat al-Sha'biyya, 2000).
Johnson-Davies, Denys (ed.), *The Essential Yusuf Idris: Masterpieces of the Egyptian Short Story* (Cairo: The American University of Cairo Press, 2009).
Kauffman, Linda S, *Discourses of Desire: Gender, Genre, and Epistolary Fictions* (Ithaca, NY and London: Cornell University Press, 1986).
Kauffman, Linda S, *Special Delivery: Epistolary Modes in Modern Fiction* (Chicago, IL and London: University of Chicago Press, 1992).
Kerr, Malcolm H., *The Arab Cold War: Gamal 'Abd al-Nasir and His Rivals, 1958–1970* (London and New York: Oxford University Press, 1971).
Khaldi, Boutheina, 'Epistolarity in a "Nahda" Climate: The Role of Mayy Ziyadah's Letter Writing', *Journal of Arabic Literature*, Vol. 40, No. 1, 2009, pp. 1–36.
Khatib, Lina, *Filming the Modern Middle East: Politics in the Cinemas of Hollywood and the Arab World* (London and New York: I. B. Tauris, 2006).
Al-Khishin, Hisham, *7 Ayyam fi al-Tahrir* (Cairo: Al-Dar al-Misriyya al-Lubnaniyya, 2011).
Khouri, Malek, *The Arab National Project in Youssef Chahine's Cinema* (Cairo: American University in Cairo Press, 2010).
Kincaid, James, *Erotic Innocence: The Culture of Child Molesting* (Durham, NC: Duke University Press, 1998).
Kohlberg, Etan, *Medieval Muslim Views on Martyrdom* (Amsterdam: Koninklijke Nederlandse Akademie van Wetenschappen, 1997).
Kukushkin, Vadim, 'To His Excellency the Sovereign of all Russian Subjects in Canada: Emigrant Correspondence with Russian Consulates in Montreal, Vancouver, and Halifax, 1899–1922', in Bruce S. Elliott, David A. Gerber,

and Suzanne M. Sinke (eds), *Letters across Borders: The Epistolary Practices of International Migrants* (New York: Palgrave Macmillan, 2006), pp. 291–305.

Kurpershoek, P. M., 'The Later Stories', in Roger Allen (ed.), *Critical Perspectives on Yusuf Idris* (Washington, DC: Three Continents Press, 1994), pp. 31–44.

Lewinstein, Keith, 'The Reevaluation of Martyrdom in Early Islam', in Margaret Cormack (ed.), *Sacrificing the Self: Perspectives on Martyrdom and Religion* (New York: Oxford University Press, 2001), pp. 78–91.

Lewis, Pauline, 'Zainab al-Ghazali: Pioneer of Islamist Feminism', *Michigan Journal of History*, No. 6, winter, 2007, pp. 23–70.

Litvin, Margarit, *Hamlet's Arab Journey: Shakespeare's Prince and Nasser's Ghost* (Princeton, NJ and Oxford: Princeton University Press, 2011).

Lukács, Georg, *The Historical Novel*, trans. H. and S. Mitchell (London: Merlin Press, 1962).

MacLean, Gerald, 'Re-sitting the Subject', in Amanda Gilory and W. M. Verhoeven (eds), *Epistolary Histories: Letters, Fiction, Culture* (Charlottesville, VA and London: University Press of Virginia, 2000), pp. 176–97.

Magnusson, Lynne, 'Widowhood and Linguistic Capital: The Rhetoric and Reception of Anne Bacon's Epistolary Advice', *English Literary Renaissance*, 31, No. 1, 2001, pp. 3–33.

Mahfouz, Naguib, *Before the Throne*, trans. Raymond Stock (Cairo: The American University in Cairo Press, 2009).

Malin, Brenton J., *American Masculinity Under Clinton: Popular Media and the Nineties 'Crisis of Masculinity'* (New York: Peter Lang, 2005).

Malti-Douglas, Fedwa, 'Postmoderning the Traditional in the Autobiography of Shaykh Kishk', in Kamal Abdel-Malek and Wael Hallaq (eds), *Tradition, Modernity, and Postmodernity in Arabic Literature* (Leiden: Brill, 2000), pp. 389–410.

El Marraghi, Maha, *Gamal al-Ghitani's Kitab al-Tajalliyat (The Book of Theophanies): A Deconstructive Discourse* (MA thesis: Institute of Islamic Studies, McGill University, Montreal, 1992).

Massad, Joseph, *Desiring Arabs* (Chicago, IL and London: University of Chicago Press, 2007).

Matar, Fu'ad, *Bi Saraha 'an Abdel Nasser: Hiwar ma' Muhammad Hasanayn Haykal* (Beirut: Dar al-Qadaya, 1975).

Mehrez, Samia, *Egyptian Writers Between History and Fiction* (Cairo: The American University in Cairo Press, 1994).

Mehrez, Samia, *Egypt's Culture Wars: Politics and Practice* (London and New York: Routledge, 2008).

Menton, Seymour, *Latin America's New Historical Novel* (Austin, TX: University of Texas Press, 1993).
Milson, Menahem, *Najib Mahfuz: The Novelist-Philosopher of Cairo* (New York: St. Martin's Press, 1998).
Misba'i, Muhammad, *Surat al-Mar'a fi Riwayat Ihsan Abdel Quddous* (Algeria: Dar al-Qasabah li al-Nashr, 2000).
Mitchell, Richard P., *The Society of the Muslim Brothers* (London: Oxford University Press, 1969).
Mojsov, Bojana, *Osiris: Death and Afterlife of a God* (Malden, MA: Blackwell Publishing, 2005).
Mosse, George, *The Image of Man: The Creation of Modern Masculinity* (New York: Oxford University Press, 1996).
Mulvey, Laura, *Visual and Other Pleasures* (Basingstoke: Macmillan, 1989).
Murad, Mahmud, *I'tirafat Ihsan Abdel Quddous: Al-Hurriyya . . . al-Jins* (Cairo: Al-'Arabi li al-Nashr wa al-Tawzi', 1980).
Mylne, Vivienne, *The Eighteenth-Century French Novel: Techniques of Illusion* (Cambridge and New York: Cambridge University Press, 1981).
Najib, Naji, *Al-Hulm wa al-Haya: Fi Suhbat Yusuf Idris* (Cairo: Dar al-Hilal, 1985).
Najib, Naji, *Yahya Haqqi wa Jil al-Hanin al-Hadari* (Cairo: Al-Hay'a al-Misriyya al-'Amma li al-Kitab, 1998).
Al-Naqqash, Raja', *Naguib Mahfouz: Safahat min Mudhakkiratih wa Adwa' Jadida 'ala Adabih wa Hayatih* (Cairo: Markiz al-Ahram li al-Tarjama wa al-Nashr, 1998).
Nietzsche, Friedrich, *The Birth of Tragedy,* in *Basic Writings of Nietzsche*, trans. Walter Kaufmann (New York: The Modern Library, 2000).
Noorani, Yaseen, *Culture and Hegemony in the Colonial Middle East* (New York: Palgrave Macmillan, 2010).
Nora, Pierre, 'Between Memory and History: Les Lieux de Memoire', *Representations*, No 26, spring 1989.
Odeh, Nadja, 'Coded Emotions: The Description of Nature in Arab Women's Autobiographies', in Robin Ostle, Ed de Moor and Stefan Wild (eds), *Writing the Self: Autobiographical Writing in Modern Arabic Literature* (London: Saqi Books, 1998), pp. 263–71.
Olick, Jeffrey and Joyce Robbins, 'Social Memory Studies: From "Collective Memory" to the Historical Sociology of Mnemonic Practices', *Annual Review of Sociology*, Vol. 24, 1998, pp. 105–40
Otano, Alicia, *Speaking the Past: Child Perspective in the Asian American Bildungsroman* (Münster: LIT Verlag, c.2004).

Pannewick, Friederike, 'Passion and Rebellion: Shi'ti Visions of Redemptive Martyrdom', in Friederike Pannewick (ed.), *Martyrdom in Literature: Visions of Death and Meaningful Suffering in Europe and the Middle East from Antiquity to Modernity* (Wiesbaden: Reichert, 2004), pp. 47–62.

Peteet, Julie, 'Male Gender and Rituals of Resistance in the Palestinian Intifada: A Cultural Politics of Violence', in Mai Ghoussoub and Emma Sinclair-Webb (eds), *Imagined Masculinities: Male Identity and Culture in the Modern Middle East* (London: Saqi Books, 2006), pp. 103–26.

Pifer, Ellen, *Demon or Doll: Images of the Child in Contemporary Writing and Culture* (Charlottesville, VA and London: University Press of Virginia, 2000).

Qabbani, Nizar, 'Buka'iyya li Gamal Abdel Nasser', in Muhammad Huwwar, *Buka' Ramz: Gamal Abdel Nasser fi Marathi al-Shu'ara'* (Beirut: Al-Mu'assasa al-'Arabiyya li al-Dirasat wa al-Nashr, 1997).

Al-Qaid, Yusuf, *Muhammad Hasanayn Haykal Yatadhakkar: Abdel Nasser wa al-Muthaqqafun wa al-Thaqafa* (Egypt: Dar al-Shuruq, 2003).

Al-Qalyubi, Muhammad Kamil, 'Al-Cinema al-Misriyya wa Thawrat Yulyu: Sira' al-Ihtiwa' bayna al-Cinema wa al-Thawra', in Hashim al-Nahhas (ed.), *Al-Cinema al-Misriyya: Al-Thawra wa al-Qita' al-'Aam: 1952–1971* (Cairo: Al-Majlis al-A'la li al-Thaqafa, 2010), pp. 15–40.

Qandil, Muhammad al-Mansi, *Inkisar al-Ruh* (Cairo: Dar al-Hilal, 1992).

Al-Qumri, Bashir, *Shi'riyyat al-Nas al-Riwa'i: Qira'a Tanassiyya fi Kitab al-Tajalliyat* (Rabat: Al-Bayadir li al-Nashr wa al-Tawzi', 1991).

Al-Qut, Abdel Hamid, *Bina' al-Riwaya fi al-Adab al-'Arabi* (Cairo: Dar al-Ma'arif, 1982).

Radwan, Noha, 'A Place for Fiction in the Historical Archive', *Critique: Critical Middle Eastern Studies*, 17, No. 1, 2008.

Ramzi, Kamal, 'Irtibat Nushu' al-Cinema al-'Arabiyya bi Harakat al-Tahrir al-'Arabi', in Abdel Mun'im Talima (ed.), *Al-Huwiyya al-Qawmiyya fi al-Cinema al-'Arabiyya* (Beirut: Markiz Dirasat al-Wihda al-'Arabiyya, 1986), pp. 13–87.

Romberg, Bertil, *Studies in the Narrative Technique of the First-Person Novel* (Folcroft, PA: Folcroft Library Editions, 1974).

Rooke, Tetz, 'The Arabic Autobiography of Childhood', in Robin Ostle, Ed de Moor and Stefan Wild (eds), *Writing the Self: Autobiographical Writing in Modern Arabic Literature* (London: Saqi Books, 1998), pp. 100–14.

Rushdie, Salman, 'Imaginary Homelands', in *Imaginary Homelands: Essays and Criticism 1981–1991* (London: Penguin Books, 1992), pp. 9–36.

Ryan, Karen L, *Stalin in Russian Satire: 1971–1991* (Madison, WI: University of Wisconsin Press, 2009).

El Saadawi, Nawal, *Memoirs from the Women's Prison*, trans. Marilyn Booth (Berkeley, CA: University of California Press, 1986).

El Saadawi, Nawal, *Walking Through Fire*, trans. Sharif Hatata (London: Zed Books, 2002).

Al-Sa'dani, Mahmud, *Al-Tariq ila Zimsh* (Cairo: Dar Akhbar al-Yawm, 1993).

Sadat, Anwar, *In Search of an Identity: an Autobiography* (New York: Harper and Row, 1977).

Sadoul, George, *The Cinema in the Arab Countries* (Beirut: Interarab Centre of Cinema and Television, 1966).

Said, Edward, *Orientalism* (New York: Vintage Books, 1979).

Said, Edward, *The World, the Text, and the Critic* (Cambridge, MA: Harvard University Press, 1983).

Said, Edward, *Culture and Imperialism* (New York: Vintage Books, 1994).

Al-Salimi, Habib, *Al-Uqsusa al-'Arabiyya wa Matlab al-Khususiyya: Majmu'at Bayt min Lahm li Yusuf Idris Namudhajan* (Qayrawan: Matba'at al-Nasr, 2006).

Salmawi, Muhammad, *Fi Hadrat Naguib Mahfouz* (Cairo: al-Dar al-Misriyya al-Lubnaniyya, 2012).

Selim, Samah, *The Novel and the Rural Imaginary in Egypt, 1880–1985* (New York and London: Routledge Curzon, 2004).

Seymour-Jorn, Caroline, *Cultural Criticism in Egyptian Women's Writing* (Syracuse, NY: Syracuse University Press, 2011).

Shafik, Viola, *Popular Egyptian Cinema: Gender, Class, and Nation* (Cairo: the American University in Cairo Press, 2006).

Sharaf al-Din, Durriyya, *Al-Siyasa wa al-Cinema fi Misr* (Cairo: Dar al-Shuruq, 1992).

Al-Sharqwi, Abdel Rahman, *Al-Fallah* (Tunis: Mu'assasat Ibn Abdellah, 1975).

Al-Shayti, Ahmad Zaghlul, *Mi'at Khatwa min al-Thawra: Yawmiyyat min Maydan al-Tahrir* (Cairo: Mirit, 2011).

Shukri, Ghali, *Mudhakkirat Thaqafa Tahtadir* (Beirut: Dar al-Tali'a, 1970).

Shukri, Ghali, *Naguib Mahfouz: Min al-Jammaliyya ila Nobel* (Cairo: Al-Hay'a al-'Amma li al-Isti'lamat, 1988).

Shukri, Ghali, *Yusuf Idris: Farfur Kharij al-Sur* (Cairo: Al-Hay'a al-'Amma li al-Isti'lamat, 1992).

Siddiq, Muhammad, *Arab Culture and the Novel: Genre, Identity and Agency in Egyptian Fiction* (New York: Routledge, 2007).

Silverman, David P., 'Divinity and Deities in Ancient Egypt', in Byron E. Shafer (ed.), *Religion in Ancient Egypt: Gods, Myths, and Personal Practice* (Ithaca, NY and London: Cornell University Press, 1991), pp. 7–87.

Sokoloff, Naomi, *Imagining the Child in Modern Jewish Fiction* (Baltimore, MD: The Johns Hopkins University Press, 1992).

Sokoloff, Naomi, 'Childhood Lost: Children in Holocaust Literature', in Elizabeth Goodenough, Mark A. Heberle, and Naomi Sokoloff (eds), *Infant Tongues: The Voice of the Child in Literature* (Detroit, MI: Wayne State University Press, 1994), pp. 259–74.

Sontag, Susan, *On Photography* (New York: Farrar, Straus, and Giroux, 1977).

Sperl, Stefan, 'Islamic Kingship and Arabic Panegyric Poetry in the Early 9th Century', *Journal of Arabic Literature*, Vol. 8, 1977, pp. 20–35.

Stagh, Marina, *The Limits of Freedom of Speech: Prose Literature and Prose Writers in Egypt Under Nasser and Sadat* (Stockholm: Almqvist & Wiksell International, 1993).

Stephens, Robert, *Nasser: A Political Biography* (New York: Simon and Schuster, 1971).

Stetkevych, Suzanne, *The Poetics of Islamic Legitimacy: Myth, Gender, and Ceremony in the Classical Arabic Ode* (Bloomington, IN: Indiana University Press, 2002).

Stock, Raymond T, *A Mummy Awakens: The Pharaonic Fiction of Naguib Mahfouz* (PhD dissertations: University of Pennsylvania, 2008).

Suleiman, Susan, *Crises of Memory and the Second World War* (Cambridge, MA and London: Harvard University Press, 2006).

Talal Asad, *On Suicide Bombing* (New York: Columbia University Press, 2007).

Tarabishi, Georges, *Al-Muthaqqafun al-'Arab wa al-Turath: al-Tahlil al-Nafsi li 'Usab Jama'i* (London: Riyad el-Rayyes Books, 1991).

Taylor, Charles, *Modern Social Imaginary* (Durham, NC and London: Duke University Press, 2004).

Todorov, Tzvetan, *The Conquest of America: The Question of the Other* (New York: Harper and Row, 1982).

Tosh, John, 'Hegemonic Masculinity and the History of Gender', in Stefan Dudink, Karen Hagemann, and John Tosh (eds), *Masculinities in Politics and War: Gendering Modern History* (Manchester: Manchester University Press, 2004), pp. 41–60.

Turner, Joseph W, 'The Kinds of Historical Fiction: An Essay in Definition and Methodology', *Genre*, autumn 1979.

'Urabi, Muhammad Ghazi, *Al-Nusus fi Mustalahat al-Mutasawwifa* (Damascus: Dar Qutayba, 1985).

'Uways, Sayyid, *Min Malamih al-Mujtama' al-Misri al-Mu'asir: Zahirat Irsal al-Rasa'il ila Darih al-Imam al-Shafi'i* (Cairo: Al-Markiz al-Qawmi li al-Buhuth al-Ijtima'iyya wa al-Jina'iyya, 1965).

'Uways, Sayyid, *Hadith 'an al-Thaqafa: Ba'd al-Haqa'iq al-'Ilmiyya al-Mu'asira* (Cairo: Maktabat al-Anjlu al-Misriyya, 1970).

'Uways, Sayyid, *Al-Khulud fi Hayat al-Misriyyin al-Mu'asirin* (Cairo: Al-Hay'a al-Misriyya al-'Amma li al-Kitab, 1972).

Vatikiotis, P. J., *Nasser and His Generation* (London: Croom Helm, 1978).

Warner, Michael, *Publics and Counterpublics* (New York: Zone Books, 2002).

Wheeler, Mark, 'Darryl F. Zanuck's Wilson', in Iwan W. Morgan (ed.), *Presidents in the Movies: American History and Politics on Screen* (New York: Palgrave Macmillan, 2011), pp. 87–108.

White, Hayden, *Tropics of Discourse: Essays in Cultural Criticism* (Baltimore, MD and London: The Johns Hopkins University Press, 1978).

White, Mark, 'The Cinematic Kennedy: *Thirteen Days* and the Burnishing of an Image', in Iwan W. Morgan (ed.), *Presidents in the Movies: American History and Politics on Screen* (New York: Palgrave Macmillan, 2011), pp. 131–50.

Ya'qub, Lusi, *Nasser Baladi* (Cairo: Maktabat al-Anjlu al-Misriyya, 1971).

Yunus, Sharif, *Al-Zahf al-Muqaddas: Muzaharat al-Tanahhi wa Tashakkul 'Ibadat Nasser* (Cairo: Miret, 2005).

Yunus, Sharif, *Nida' al-Sha'b: Tarikh Naqdi li al-Aydyulujya al-Nasiriyya* (Cairo: Dar al-Shuruq, 2012).

Yusuf, Ahmad, 'Al-Waqi'iyya wa Suwar al-Waqi' fi al-Cinema al-Misriyya fi al-Marhala al-Klasikiyya, 1952–1970', in Hashim al-Nahhas (ed.), *Al-Cinema al-Misriyya: Al-Thawra wa al Qita' al-'Aam: 1952-1971* (Cairo: al-Majlis al-A'la li al-Thaqafa, 2010), pp. 41–67.

Al-Yusuf, Ruz, 'Khitab Maftuh ila Gamal Abdel Nasser', *Majallat Ruz al-Yusuf*, No. 1300, 11 May 1953.

Zakariyya, 'Isam, *Atyaf al-Hadatha: Suwar Misr al-Ijtima'iyya fi al-Cinema* (Cairo: Al-Majlis al-A'la li al-Thaqafa, 2009).

Online Sources

Abdel-Baqui, Mohamed (2012), 'In the Footsteps of Nasser', *al-Ahram Weekly*, 3–9 May, <http://weekly.ahram.org.eg/2012/1096/eg3.htm> (last accessed 23 May 2015).

Abdel Nasser, Huda Gamal (2013), 'Risala Maftuha ila al-Fariq Awwal Abdel Fattah al-Sisi', *al-Masri al-Yawm*, 6 August, <http://www.almasryalyoum.com/news/details/199119> (last accessed 5 June 2015).

Abu Hilala, Yasir (2014), 'Tis'at Furuq Bayna Abdel Nasser wa al-Sisi', *al-Ghad*, 9 January, <http://www.alghad.com/articles/523208> (last accessed 2 June 2015).

'Adly, 'Amr (2014), 'Ma Ba'd al-Nasiriyya', *Jadaliyya*, 18 March, <http://www.jadaliyya.com/pages/index/16944> (last accessed 28 May 2015).

Cole, Juan (2014), 'From Raybans to Portrait Underwear: Sisi-Mania Floods Egypt with Kitsch', *Informed Comment*, 29 April, <http://www.juancole.com/2014/04/raybans-portrait-underwear.html> (last accessed 23 May 2015).

Egyptian Chronicles (2013), 'Reviving # Nasser in # Egypt', *Egyptian Chronicles*, 23 July, <http://egyptianchronicles.blogspot.com/2013/07/reviving-nasser-in-egypt.html> (last accessed 9 June 2015).

Khallad, Rania (2011), 'The Bright Side of the Picture', *al-Ahram Weekly*, 13–19 October, <http://weekly.ahram.org.eg/2011/1068/entertain.htm> (last accessed 20 May 2015).

Lindsey, Ursula (2013), 'A Voice of Dissent Joins the Nationalist Chorus', *Mada Masr*, 6 October, <http://www.madamasr.com/sections/culture/voice-dissent-joins-nationalist-chorus> (last accessed 24 May 2015).

Mansur, Ahmad (2013), 'Interview with Sonallah Ibrahim', *al-Yawm Al-Sabi'*, 24 August, <http://www.youm7.com/story/0000/0/0/-/1218467> (last accessed 24 May 2015).

Mukhtar, Hajar and Muhammad Haykal (2014), 'Gamal al-Ghitani', *al-Dustur*, 30 May, <http://www.dostor.org/400954> (last accessed 24 May 2015).

El Shamsy, Ahmed (2013), 'Sisi, Nasser, & the Great Egyptian Novel', *Muftah*, 15 October, <http://muftah.org/sisi-nasser-the-great-egyptian-novel/> (last accessed 24 May 2015).

Soueif, Ahdaf (2012), 'In Times of Crisis, Fiction Has to Take a Back Seat', *The Guardian*, 17 August, <http://www.theguardian.com/books/2012/aug/17/ahdaf-soueif-politics-fiction> (last accessed 1 May 2015).

Films

Abi Fawqa al-Shajara, directed by Husayn Kamal. Egypt: Aflam Sawt al-Fan, 1969.
Abna' wa Qatala, directed by 'Atif al-Tayyib. Egypt: Shadha Film, 1987.
Ahlam Saghira, directed by Khalid al-Hagar. Egypt: Aflam Misr al-'Alamiyya, 1993.
Allah Ma'ana, directed by Ahmad Badrakhan. Egypt: 1955.
'Amaliqat al-Bihar, directed by Al-Sayyid Bidir. Egypt: Abbas Hilmi, 1960.
Al-'Asifa, directed by Khalid Yusuf. Egypt: Aflam Misr al-'Alamiyya, 2001.
Al-'Ayb, directed by Galal al-Sharqawi. Egypt: Sharikat al-Qahira li al-Intaj al-Sinima'i, 1967.
Ayyam al-Sadat, directed by Muhammad Khan. Egypt: Ahmad Zaki, 2001.

Bahib al-Sima, directed by Osama Fawzi. Egypt: Hani Girgis Fawzi, 2004.
Dukkan Shihata, directed by Khalid Yusuf. Egypt: Misr li al-Cinima, 2009.
Four Women of Egypt, directed by Tahani Rached. Canada/Egypt: National Film Board of Canada, 1997.
Gamal Abdel Nasser, directed by Anwar al-Qawadri. Egypt/Syria: 'Adil al-Mihi, 1999.
Halim, directed by Sharif 'Arafa. Egypt: Good News Group, 2006.
Al-Hubb Fawqa Hadabat al-Haram, directed by 'Atif al-Tayyib. Egypt: Abdel 'Azim al-Zughbi, 1986.
Ihna Btu' al-Utubis, directed by Husayn Kamal. Egypt: Cairo Film, 1979.
Al-Karnak, directed by Ali Badrakhan. Egypt: Aflam al-Laythi, 1975.
Lih ya Banafsig, directed by Radwan al-Kashif. Egypt: Dana li al-Intaj wa al-Tawzi', 1993.
Makan li al-Hubb, directed by Sa'id Marzuq. Egypt: Ramsis Naguib, 1972.
Mercedes, directed by Yousry Nasrallah. Egypt: Aflam Misr al-'Alamiyya, 1993.
Miramar, directed by Kamal El Sheikh. Egypt: Al-Mu'assasa al-Misriyya al-'Amma li al-Cinema, 1969.
Al-Mutamarridun, directed by Tawfiq Salih. Egypt: Sharikat al-Qahira li al-Intaj al-Sinima'i, 1968.
Naji al-Ali, directed by 'Atif al-Tayyib. Egypt: 1992.
Al-Nasir Salah al-Din, directed by Youssef Chahine. Egypt: Assia Dagher, 1963.
Nasser 56, directed by Muhammad Fadil. Egypt: Egyptian Radio and Television Union, 1996.
Port Said, directed by 'Izz al-Din Dhu al-Fiqar. Egypt: Aflam al-'Ahd al-Jadid, 1957.
Al-Qadiyya 68, directed by Salah Abu Seif. Egypt: Al-Mu'assasa al-Misriyya al-'Amma li al-Cinema, 1968.
Rudda Qalbi, directed by 'Izz al-Din Dhu al-Fiqar. Egypt: Assia Dagher, 1957.
Sawwaq al-Utubis, directed by 'Atif al-Tayyib. Egypt: Hadirama, 1983.
Shay' min al-Khawf, directed by Husayn Kamal. Egypt: Al-Mu'assasa al-Misriyya al-'Amma li al-Cinema, 1969.
Al-'Usfur, directed by Youssef Chahine. Egypt: Aflam Misr al-'Alamiyya, 1972.
Watani wa Hubbi, directed by Husayn Sidqi. Egypt: Aflam Misr al-Haditha, 1960.
When Father Was Away on Business, directed by Emir Kusturica. Yugoslavia: Center Film Forum Sarajevo, 1985.

Index

Notes: Personal names with the prefix al- are filed under the second element of the name, for example Ruz al-Yusuf is filed as Yusuf, Ruz al-. Page numbers accompanied by 'n' refer to notes.

Abdel Fattah, Wa'il, 189
Abdel Latif, 'Imad, 188
Abdel Meguid, Ibrahim, 135–6, 214–15
Abdel Quddous, Ihsan, 25, 31–7, 42
Abdel Rahman, Mahfuz, 186–7
Abdel Salam, Shadi, 171–2
Abdel Sayyid, Dawud, 183
Abdel Wahhab, Muhammad, 133
'Abdu, Ibrahim, 25
Abi Fawqa al-Shajara (film), 169
Abna' wa Qatala (film), 192
abstraction, 173
Abu al-Rijal (Idris), 73
Abu Hilala, Yasir, 219
Abu Seif, Salah, 167, 173
Abu Shadi, Ali, 176, 180
Aburish, Said, 134
agency, 43, 53, 91, 123, 191
Ahlam Saghira (film), 193–5
Ahmed, Leila, 129–33
al-Ahram (newspaper), 41, 86, 92, 215
Al-Ard (Sharqawi), 45
Al-'Asifa (film), 186
al-Atlal (song), 70–1
Al-'Ayb (film), 179
Al-Banat wa al-Sayf (Abdel Quddous), 32, 35
Al-Fallah (al-Sharqawi), 44–9
Al-Ghira al-Qatila (film), 183
al-Gumhuriyya (newspaper), 121
Al-Hubb Fawqa Hadabat al-Haram (film), 184–5
Al-Karnak (film), 15, 177, 180–1, 191–2
'Al-Khayt al-Rafi' bayna al-Hurriyya wa al-Fawda' (letter, Nasser), 29–31
al-Khud'a (Idris), 86–93
Al-Mukharribun (film), 173
Al-Mumiya (film), 171–2
Al-Mutamarridun (film), 174–5

Al-Nasir Salah al-Din (film), 169–72
Al-Qadiyya 68 (film), 173–4, 202
al-Rihla (Idris), 86
Al-Tali'a (magazine), 37
Al-'Usfur (film), 190–1
al-Zayni Barakat (Ghitani), 73
al-Zuhur Tatafattah (Ghitani), 73
Allah, 36, 41, 47, 96
Allah Ma'ana (film), 168
allegiance, 37–43
Altman, Janet Gurkin, 13, 21, 22, 31
'Amaliqat al-Bihar (film), 165, 178–9
Amam al-'Arsh (Mahfouz), 101–7
Amer, Abdel Hakim, 149 199–200
Anderson, Benedict, 118
animals in symbolism, 85–93
Ansari, Muhammad Jabir al-, 6–7
Arab Socialist Union, 173
Arabi, Ibn, 96
'Arafa, Sharif, 196, 200–1
Aries, Philippe, 119
Aristotle, 7
Asad, Talal, 95
'Asfur, Gabir, 72
Ashour, Radwa, 54–8, 125–9
'Asif Lam A'ud Astati' (Abdel Quddous), 31–7
'Atiyya, Na'im, 79
'Awad, Luis, 72
'Awdat al-Wa'i (Hakim), 72
Awlad Haratina (Mahfouz), 72
Ayyam al-Sadat (film), 196, 199–200, 201
Ayyam fi al-Tahrir (Khishin), 215–16
Ayyam min Hayati (Ghazali), 146–51
Azmeh, Aziz al-, 4–5

Badrakhan, Ali, 15, 177, 180–2, 191–2
Bahib al-Sima (film), 194–5
Baker, Raymond William, 165, 175

Bakhtin, Mikhail, 14, 106–7
Bakr, Salwa, 49–54, 135, 213
Barthes, Roland, 177
Bayt min Lahm (Idris), 86
Berthoff, Warner, 8
Bidir, Nagla', 214
Bishara, Khayri, 183
Black September, 93, 95
Bodnar, John, 11
Border Passage, A (Ahmed), 129–33
Browning, Richard, 127

camels, in symbolism, 86–92
Castoriadis, Cornelius, 2–3
censorship, 27–8, 30, 52, 167–8, 174, 175–7
Centuries of Childhood (Aries), 119
Chahine, Youssef, 167, 169, 170–2, 190–2
children
 Border Passage, A (Ahmed), 129–33
 Faraj (Ashour), 125–9
 Inkisar al-Ruh (Qandil), 121–5
 Nasser and children in fiction, 14, 119–33
cinema *see* film, cinema and television
Cohen-Mor, Dalya, 89
Cole, Juan, 217
communism, 37–43
confidentiality, 21
Cooke, Miriam, 75, 76, 78
Corm, Georges, 20
Custen, George, 197

Danielson, Virginia, 71
de-Nasserisation, 11, 15, 73, 166, 178, 202
Dhikrayat Ma'ahu (Kazem), 136–41
Dhu al-Fiqar, 'Izz al-Din, 168–9, 178
'Do You Remember, Nasser' (poem, Ya'qub), 135
Donaldson, Roger, 197–8
drinking, 76
Dukkan Shihata (film), 186
dysphemism, 188

El-Enany, Rasheed, 102
El Saadawi, Nawal, 141–6
El Sheikh, Kamal, 33, 172, 173, 179
Elsadda, Hoda, 51
Enloe, Cynthia, 134

Fadil, Muhammad, 164, 196, 197–9
Fakhrani, Yusri al-, 201
Faraj (Ashour), 54–8, 125–9
Farazdaq, al- (poet), 100
Farid, Samir, 168
fathers, 120, 169
 Faraj (Ashour), 125–9
 Inkisar al-Ruh (Qandil), 121–5

Fawzi, Osama, 194–5
fiction
 fictional letters, 31–7, 44–58
 and history, 7–9
 Nasser as fiction, 13–14, 68–116; *al-Khud'a* (Idris), 86–93; *Amam al-'Arsh* (Mahfouz), 101–7; fictional resurrection of Nasser, 99–101; fragmentation into multiple Nassers, 69–70, 117; *Istishhad Gamal Abdel Nasser* (Haddad), 94–5; *Kitab al-Tajalliyat* (Ghitani), 96–101; Nasser as a defendant, 101–7; Nasser as a protagonist of the text, 69, 70–4, 107–8; Nasser as an intellectual, 74–85; portrayal of Nasser as a martyr, 93–101; *Qindil Umm Hashim* (Haqqi), 74; representation of Nasser as a beast, 85–93; *Sah al-Nawm* (Haqqi), 75–85, 89; separation of Nasser from misdeeds, 82–3; *Shahid al-Tadhiyat* (Hisni), 94; *Tharthara Fawqa al-Nil* (Mahfouz), 71
 Nasser in fiction, 14, 117–61; Arab identity issues, 129–33; *Ayyam min Hayati* (Ghazali), 146–51; *Border Passage, A* (Ahmed), 129–33; *Dhikrayat Ma'ahu* (Kazem), 136–41; 'Do You Remember, Nasser' (poem, Ya'qub), 135; *Faraj* (Ashour), 125–9; imagined communities, 118; *Inkisar al-Ruh* (Qandil), 121–5; Nasser and children, 119–33; Nasser and women in fiction, 133–51; Nasser as a romantic hero, 133–4; Nasser as an embodiment of masculinity, 134–6, 138, 142–3, 145, 147, 151–2; *Tuyur al-'Anbar* (Abdel Meguid), 135–6; *Walking Through Fire* (El Saadawi), 141–6
fida'iyin, 145–6
film, cinema and television, 5, 14–15, 162–208
 Abi Fawqa al-Shajara (film), 169
 Abna' wa Qatala (film), 192
 Ahlam Saghira (film), 193–5
 Al-'Asifa (film), 186
 Al-'Ayb (film), 179
 Al-Ghira al-Qatila (film), 183
 Al-Hubb Fawqa Hadabat al-Haram (film), 184–5
 Al-Karnak (film), 15, 177, 180–2, 191–2
 Al-Mukharribun (film), 173
 Al-Mutamarridun (film), 174–5
 Al-Nasir Salah al-Din (film), 169–72
 Al-Qadiyya 68 (film), 173–4, 202
 Al-'Usfur (film), 190–1
 'Amaliqat al-Bihar (film), 165, 178–9
 army officers, image of, 168–9
 Ayyam al-Sadat (film), 196, 199–200, 201
 Bahib al-Sima (film), 194–5

biopictures, 196–201
censorship, 167–8, 174, 175–7
Cinema al-Khawf, 167
Cinema of Centers of Power movement, 179–83, 192
Dukkan Shihata (film), 186
fear, concepts of, 167–77
Firqat Naji 'Atallah (drama), 162–3
futuwwa, 168
Gamal Abdel Nasser (film), 195–6, 199
'green light' trend, 172–5
Halim (film), 196, 200–1
heroes as a metaphor for Nasser, 169–72
Ihna Btu' al-Utubis (film), 182–3, 192
leftist film-makers, 185–7
Lih ya Banafsig? (film), 185
Makan li al-Hubb (film), 173, 180
Mercedes (film), 185
Miramar (film), 172, 179
Naji al Ali (film), 192–3
Nasser 56 (film), 164, 196, 197–9
Nasser's cinematic presence, lack of, 164–7, 168
Nasser's popularity in people's imagination, 163–4
Nasser's resignation speech, 187–96, 202, 211
neorealist film-makers, 183–5
Port Said (film), 165, 178
portraits, politics of, 177–87, 211
positive image of Nasser since the 1980s, 197, 212–13
Rudda Qalbi (film), 168–9
Sawwaq al-Utubis (film), 184
Shay' min al-Khawf (film), 175–7, 202, 212
Watani wa Hubbi (film), 179
Firqat Naji 'Atallah (drama), 162–3
Fischer, Michael, 98
formality, 51–2
Four Women of Egypt (documentary), 133–4
Free Officers Movement, 105, 166
freedom of expression *see* censorship
futuwwa, 168

Gamal Abdel Nasser (film), 195–6, 199
Gasiorowska, Xenia, 69–70
Genette, Gerard, 127
Ghazali, Zaynab al-, 146–51
Ghitani, Gamal al-, 73, 96–101, 213, 214–15, 217
Giovannucci, Perri, 143
God, 87
Goldberg, Ann, 23
Golia, Maria, 164–5
Gordon, Joel, 33, 165, 179, 182, 198, 199

grotesque, the, 89–90
Guevara, Che, 180

Habermas, Jürgen, 23, 24
Haddad, Fu'ad, 94–5
Hafez, Abdel Halim, 169, 200–1
Hagar, Khalid al-, 185, 193–4
hagiography, 99, 149
Hakim, Tawfiq al-, 72
Halim (film), 196, 200–1
Halim, Hala, 170
Hammuda, 'Abdil, 39
Haqqi, Yahya, 74–85, 89
Hassan, Waïl, 102
Haykal, Muhammad Hasanayn, 19, 32, 36, 41, 92, 187
Hisni, 'Afifa al-, 94
history, and fiction, 7–9
Honeyman, Susan, 119
Hosny, Soad, 177, 180, 181, 182
hubb (love), 36–7
Husayn, Imam al-, 98–9, 100–1
Hussein, Taha, 74, 76–7, 79–80
Huyssen, Andreas, 2

Ibrahim, Nabila, 169–70
Ibrahim, Sonallah, 37–8, 39, 40, 214–15, 217
identity, 102, 129–33, 143
Idris, Yusuf, 72, 73, 85–93
Ihna Btu' al-Utubis (film), 182–3, 192
illiteracy, 56
imagined communities, 118
Imam, 'Adil, 162–3
'In Times of Crisis, Fiction Has to Take a Back Seat' (Soueif), 213–14
Inkisar al-Ruh (Qandil), 121–5
Iser, Wolfgang, 8
Istishhad Gamal Abdel Nasser (Haddad), 94–5

Jahin, Salah, 201
journalists, letters to Nasser, 21–31

Kafka, Franz, 21
Kamal, Husayn, 175–7, 182–3, 192, 212
Kanafani, Ghassan, 44
Karbala, Battle of, 98–9, 146
Kashif, Radwan al-, 185
Kazem, Tahia (Nasser's wife), 136–41, 187
Kazim, Safinaz, 133–4
Khan, Muhammad, 183, 196, 199–200
Khishin, Hisham al-, 215–16
'Khitab Maftuh ila Gamal Abdel Nasser' (letter, Yusuf), 25–31
Khouri, Malek, 171
Kitab al-Tajalliyat (Ghitani), 96–101, 213
Kosygin, Aleksei, 181

Kulthum, Umm, 71, 200–1
kunya, 57
Kusturica, Emir, 122, 153n22

language, 51–2
　colloquialism, 56
letter writing, 13, 19–67
　Al-Fallah (Sharqawi), 45–9
　allegiance to Nasser, 37–43
　confidentiality, 21
　Faraj (Ashour), 54–8
　fictional letters, 31–7, 44–58
　journalists' letters, 23–31
　writing by proxy, 47, 50, 59
　Zeinat fi Janazat al-Ra'is (Bakr), 49–54
Lewis, Pauline, 149
Lih ya Banafsig? (film), 185
Litvin, Margarit, 70
Lukács, Georg, 68

Ma'at, 103
Magnusson, Lynne, 26
Mahfouz, Naguib, 71, 72, 101–7, 180, 184
Mahmud, Mustafa, 32
Makan li al-Hubb (film), 173, 180
Malti-Douglas, Fedwa, 147
Maqlid, Shahinda, 133–4
martyrdom, 93–101
Marzuq, Sa'id, 173, 180
masculinity, 134–6, 138, 142–3, 145, 147, 151–2
Massad, Joseph, 73
Mazhar, Ahmad, 171
Mehrez, Samia, 12, 71, 102, 104, 105, 195
Mercedes (film), 185
Mi'at Khatwa min al-Thawra (Shayti), 215
Milson, Menahem, 102, 103
Miramar (film), 33, 172, 179
mockery, 91–2
Mohieddin, Zakariya, 195–6
Morsi, Muhammad, 216
Mubarak, Hosni, 1, 2, 11, 54, 197, 201, 212, 214, 215, 216, 218
Mudhakkirati fi Sijn al-Nisa (El Saadawi), 141
Mulvey, Laura, 177
Muslim Brotherhood, 146–7, 150, 216, 218–19

Naguib Muhammad, 142
Nahhas, Mustafa al-, 105, 106
Naji al Ali (film), 192–3
Naji, Ibrahim, 70–1
Nasrallah, Yousry, 185
Nasser 56 (film), 164, 196, 197–9
Nasser, Gamal Abdel
　care for poor people, 106

character, 9, 70, 85
compared with Sisi, 216–19
contemporary presence in the Egyptian imaginary, 209–19
de-Nasserisation, 11, 15, 73, 166, 178, 202
death, 85–6, 93–4, 99
defeat, 1967, 15, 121, 125, 128, 141, 145, 174–5, 187, 189, 213
in film, cinema and television, 14–15, 162–208; *Abi Fawqa al-Shajara* (film), 169; *Abna' wa Qatala* (film), 192; *Ahlam Saghira* (film), 193–5; *Al-'Asifa* (film), 186; *Al-'Ayb* (film), 179; *Al-Ghira al-Qatila* (film), 183; *Al-Hubb Fawqa Hadabat al-Haram* (film), 184–5; *Al-Karnak* (film), 15, 177, 180–2, 191–2; *Al-Mukharribun* (film), 173; *Al-Mutamarridun* (film), 174–5; *Al-Nasir Salah al-Din* (film), 169, 170–2; *Al-Qadiyya 68* (film), 173–4, 202; *Al-Tajalliyat* (film), 213; *Al-'Usfur* (film), 190–1; *'Amaliqat al-Bihar* (film), 165; *'Amaliqat al-Bihar* (film), 178–9; army officers, image of, 168–9; *Ayyam al-Sadat* (film), 196, 199–200, 201; *Bahib al-Sima* (film), 194–5; biopictures, 196–201; censorship, 167–8, 174, 175–7; *Cinema al-Khawf*, 167; Cinema of Centers of Power movement, 179–83, 192; cinematic presence, lack of, 164–7, 168; *Dukkan Shihata* (film), 186; fear, concepts of, 167–77; *Firqat Naji 'Atallah* (drama), 162–3; *futuwwa*, 168; *Gamal Abdel Nasser* (film), 195–6, 199; 'green light' trend, 172–5; *Halim* (film), 196, 200–1; heroes as a metaphor for Nasser, 169–72; *Ihna Btu' al-Utubis* (film), 182–3, 192; leftist film-makers, 185–7; *Lih ya Banafsig?* (film), 185; *Maan li al-Hubb* (film), 173, 180; *Mercedes* (film), 185; *Miramar* (film), 172, 179; *Naji al Ali* (film), 192–3; *Nasser 56* (film), 164, 196, 197–9; Nasser's popularity in people's imagination, 163–4; neorealist film-makers, 183–5; *Port Said* (film), 165, 178; portraits, politics of, 177–87, 211; positive image of Nasser since the 1980s, 197; resignation speech, 187–96, 202, 211; *Rudda Qalbi* (film), 168–9; *Sawwaq al-Utubis* (film), 184; *Shay' min al-Khawf* (film), 175–7, 202, 212; *Watani wa Hubbi* (film), 179
first name, 87
funeral, 53–4
grave, 99

marriage, 138–41
monuments to, lack of, 166
and people as audiences, 19–20
physical attributes, 134, 139, 142–3, 144
presence in the 2011 revolution, 214–16
in public memory, 1–2, 4–5, 10, 11–12
relevance at the 2014 presidential election, 218
representation as fiction, 13–14, 68–116; *al-Khud'a* (Idris), 86–93; *Amam al-'Arsh* (Mahfouz), 101–7; fictional resurrection of Nasser, 99–101; fragmentation into multiple Nassers, 69–70, 117; *Istishhad Gamal Abdel Nasser* (Haddad), 94–5; *Kitab al-Tajalliyat* (Ghitani), 96–101; Nasser as a defendant, 101–7; Nasser as an intellectual, 74–85; portrayal of Nasser as a martyr, 93–101; as a protagonist of the text, 69, 70–4, 107–8; *Qindil Umm Hashim* (Haqqi), 74; representation of Nasser as an animal, 85–93; *Sah al-Nawm* (Haqqi), 75–85, 89; separation of Nasser from misdeeds, 82–3; *Shahid al-Tadhiyat* (Hisni), 94; *Tharthara Fawqa al-Nil* (Mahfouz), 71
representation in fiction, 14, 117–61; Arab identity issues, 129–33; *Ayyam min Hayati* (Ghazali), 146–51; *Border Passage, A* (Ahmed), 129–33; *Dhikrayat Ma'ahu* (Kazem), 136–41; 'Do You Remember, Nasser' (poem, Ya'qub), 135; as an embodiment of masculinity, 134–6, 138, 142–3, 145, 147, 151–2; *Faraj* (Ashour), 125–9; *Inkisar al-Ruh* (Qandil), 121–5; Nasser and children, 119–33; Nasser and women in fiction, 133–51; as a romantic hero, 133–4; *Tuyur al-'Anbar* (Abdel Meguid), 135–6; *Walking Through Fire* (El Saadawi), 141–6
separation of Nasser from his regime, 211–12
in social imaginary, 2–4
speeches, 19–20, 42, 128, 166–7, 187–96, 202, 211, 215–16
virtuous leader notion, 5–7
writing to Nasser, 13, 19–67; *Al-Fallah* (Sharqawi), 45–9; allegiance, 37–43; confidentiality, 21; *Faraj* (Ashour), 54–8; fictional letters, 31–7, 44–58; journalists' letters, 23–31; presence and absence duality, 21–2; relationship with Egyptians, personalisation of, 33; responses from Nasser, 29–31; writing by proxy, 47, 50, 59; *Zeinat fi Janazat al-Ra'is* (Bakr), 49–54
Nasser, Khalid Abdel, 1

'Nasser, the Dream' (exhibition), 215
nationalism, 38, 118, 129, 132–3, 134, 186, 191
Nietzsche, Friedrich, 83
Noorani, Yaseen, 5, 6
Nora, Pierre, 1–2

Odeh, Nadja, 149
Orientalism (Said), 132–3
Osiris, 102–3, 106–7
Otano, Alicia, 127

Peter the Great, 69–70
Petredes, Roxani, 40–1
pharonic literature, 102, 103–4
photography, 138, 177
Poetics of Islamic Legitimacy, The (Stetkevych), 6
poetry, 6, 70–1, 87, 94–5, 135
political memoirs, 137–8
Port Said (film), 165, 178
prison experiences, 141
    Ayyam min Hayati (Ghazali), 146–51
    Faraj (Ashour), 125–9
    Ihna Btu' al-Utubis (film), 192
    Inkisar al-Ruh (Qandil), 121–5

Qabbani, Nizar, 94, 95, 98
Qandil, Muhammad al-Mansi, 121–5
qaṣīda, 6
Qasim, Abdel Karim, 38
Qawadri, Anwar al-, 195–6, 199
Qindil Umm Hashim (Haqqi), 74
Quran, 87, 93

Rached, Tahani, 133
Radwan, Noha, 12
Ramzi, Kamal, 164
religion, 36
revolution of 1952, 12, 25, 39, 72, 75, 78–9, 82–3, 142
revolution of 2011, 213–16
Rooke, Tetz, 119–20
Rudda Qalbi (film), 168–9
Rushdie, Salman, 8
Ruz al-Yusuf (periodical), 25, 29, 33, 36

Sabahi, Hamdin, 216, 218
Sa'dani, Mahmud al-, 41
Sadat, Anwar, 54, 93, 99–101, 121, 141–2, 163, 166, 179–83, 186–7, 189, 196–7, 199–201, 203, 212–14
Sadat, Jehan (Sadat's wife), 136
Sah al-Nawm (Haqqi), 75–85, 89
    'Break, A,' 76–7
    'Meeting with the Professor, The,' 83–5

Sah al-Nawm (Haqqi) (*cont.*)
  'Today,' 77–9
  'Yesterday,' 75–6, 79
Said, Edward, 9, 118, 120, 132–3
Salih, Tawfiq, 174–5
Salih, Tayeb, 74
Samman, Ghada al-, 44
Sawwaq al-Utubis (film), 184
sexual relationships, 32, 35
Shafi'i, Shuhdi 'Atiyya al-, 37–43
Shafik, Viola, 165–6, 168, 191
shahid, 93–4, 96
Shahid al-Tadhiyat (Hisni), 94
Sharaf al-Din, Durriyya, 167, 172, 179–80
Sharqawi, Abdel Rahman al-, 45–9
Sharqawi, Galal al-, 179
Shay' min al-Khawf (film), 175–7, 202, 212
Shenkman, Rick, 138
Shi'ite community, 98
Shukri, Ghali, 10, 85
Siddiq, Muhammad, 12
Sisi, Abdel Fattah al-, 121, 216–19
social imaginary, 2–4
Sokoloff, Naomi, 117–18
songs, 10, 70–1, 123, 133, 178, 191, 197, 200–1
Soueif, Ahdaf, 213–14
Stephens, Robert, 128
Stetkevych, Suzanne, 6
Stock, Raymond, 102, 103
Sufism, 96, 97
Suleiman, Susan, 2
Supreme Council of the Armed Forces (SCAF), 1, 214
symbolism, 74–5, 173
  camels, use of, 86–92

Tahia (Nasser's wife) *see* Kazem, Tahia (Nasser's wife)
tajalli, 96, 97, 99
Tarabishi, Georges, 145, 189
Taylor, Charles, 3
Tayyib, 'Atif al-, 183–5, 192–3
television *see* film, cinema and television

Tharthara Fawqa al-Nil (Mahfouz), 71
theriomorphism, 87
Thirteen Days (film), 197–8
Todorov, Tzvetan, 87
torture, 148–50
trials, fictional trial of Nasser, 104–7
Turner, Joseph W., 69
Tuyur al-'Anbar (Abdel Meguid), 135–6

'Ukasha, Tharwat, 71
'Uways, Sayyid, 23–4

virtuous leader notion, 5–7

Wafd Party, 105, 106
Walking Through Fire (El Saadawi), 141–6
Warner, Michael, 4, 5
Watani wa Hubbi (film), 179
When Father Was Away on Business (film), 122, 153n22
White, Hayden, 8–9
women, 14
  autobiography, use of, 137
  Ayyam min Hayati (Ghazali), 146–51
  Dhikrayat Ma'ahu (Kazem), 136–41
  'Do You Remember, Nasser' (poem, Ya'qub), 135
  Four Women of Egypt (documentary), 133–4
  letters to Nasser, 24–31, 49–54, 54–8
  and Nasser in fiction, 75–6, 133–51
  Tuyur al-'Anbar (Abdel Meguid), 135–6
  Walking Through Fire (El Saadawi), 141–6

Ya'qub, Lusi, 135
Yunus, Sharif, 166, 188, 209
Yusuf, Khalid, 185–6, 199, 214
Yusuf, Ruz al-, 24–31, 83

Zaghlul, Saad, 105–6
Zakariyya, 'Isam, 167, 169, 173, 197
Zaki, Ahmad, 184, 196, 199
Zalman, Amy, 134
Zeinat fi Janazat al-Ra'is (Bakr), 49–54, 213

EU representative:
Easy Access System Europe
Mustamäe tee 50, 10621 Tallinn, Estonia
Gpsr.requests@easproject.com

www.ingramcontent.com/pod-product-compliance
Lightning Source LLC
Chambersburg PA
CBHW051114230426
43667CB00014B/2577